C0-AKU-268

SUBJECT SIAM

Family, Law, and Colonial Modernity in Thailand

TAMARA LOOS

Cornell University Press
Ithaca and London

This book has been published with the aid of a grant from the Hull Memorial Publication Fund of Cornell University.

First published 2006 by Cornell University Press

Printed in the United States of America

Library of Congress Cataloging-in-Publication Data

Loos, Tamara Lynn.
Subject Siam : family, law, and colonial modernity in Thailand / Tamara Loos.
p. cm.
Includes bibliographical references and index.
ISBN-13: 978-0-8014-4393-0 (cloth : alk. paper)
ISBN-10: 0-8014-4393-8 (cloth : alk. paper)
1. Domestic relations—Thailand—History—20th century. 2. Domestic relations (Islamic law)—Thailand, Southern—History—20th century. 3. Courts, Islamic—Thailand, Southern—History—20th century. 4. Law—Thailand—History—20th century. 5. Nationalism—Thailand—History—20th century. 6. Thailand—History—20th century. I. Title.
KPT540.L66 2005
346.59301′5—dc22 2005018414

Cornell University Press strives to use environmentally responsible suppliers and materials to the fullest extent possible in the publishing of its books. Such materials include vegetable-based, low-VOC inks and acid-free papers that are recycled, totally chlorine-free, or partly composed of nonwood fibers. For further information, visit our website at www.cornellpress.cornell.edu.

Cloth printing 10 9 8 7 6 5 4 3 2 1

With deep gratitude to my Grace family; my brother James;
and my partner, Sandy

Contents

List of Illustrations	viii
Acknowledgments	ix
One. Family, Law, and Colonial Modernity in Thailand	1
Two. Transnational Justice	29
Three. Colonial Law and Buddhist Modernity in the Malay Muslim South	72
Four. The Imperialism of Monogamy in Family Law	100
Five. Crisis of Wifedom	130
Six. Nationalism and Male Sexuality	155
Seven. Subjects of History	173
Glossary	189
Bibliography	191
Index	205

List of Illustrations

Figures

Figure 1. Unequal Treaties with Siam 43

Figure 2. Reformed Organization of Siam's Courts 46

Maps

Map 1. Early Twentieth-Century Siam xii

Map 2. The Seven Malay Principalities of Greater Patani in the Early Nineteenth Century 78

Photographs

1. Composite of Siam's Ministers of State in 1908 50
2. Jens Westengard, Prince Damrong, W. J. F. Williamson, and other officials, circa 1910 58
3. Siam's Foreign Legal Advisers in 1908 61
4. Pattani Central Mosque, built in 1963 in Pattani Province 73
5. Siamese woman (purportedly a servant of one of King Chulalongkorn's queens) in Western dress in the 1860s 112
6. Crown Prince Vajiravudh in 1908 156

Acknowledgments

The President's Council of Cornell Women and the Radcliffe Institute for Advanced Study at Harvard University generously funded my study leave, during which I wrote most of this book. Harvard Law School archivist David Ferris deserves special mention for his assistance with the Jens Iverson Westengard collection, as does Kari Smith in the Cornell University Kroch Library for her help. I am grateful to the staff at the National Archives and Supreme Appeals Court in Bangkok. Several judges in Thailand helped me understand the significance of this project: Judge Charunee Tantayakom, Dato Apirat Madsa-i, and Dato Haji Ismail Bin Haji Husain Che. In no way, however, can they be held responsible for the narrative I have written.

My endlessly energetic research assistant and friend Kallayanee Techapatikul contributed in multiple ways, making a significant difference to the quality of the book. Worrasit Tantinipankul, Jane Ferguson, and Chiranan Prasertkul also helped at various stages with the collection of court documents. My home bases at Cornell have been the Southeast Asia Program and history department for many years. In both places and elsewhere I have been blessed with generous colleagues and friends who have supported me intellectually and with encouragement throughout. They include Candace Akins, Ben Anderson, Coeli Barry, Sandy Bem, Judy Burkhard, Sherm Cochran, Ray Craib, Maria Cristina Garcia, Sandra Greene, Itsie Hull, Peter Jackson, Mary Beth Norton, Michael Peletz, Craig Reynolds, Sawaeng Bunchaloemwiphat, Megan Sinnott, Eric Tagliacozzo, Thak Chaloemtiarana, Thanet Aphornsuvan, Thongchai Winichakul, Rachel Weil, and Susan Wiser. Astute and generous suggestions made by the anonymous reviewers at Cornell University Press and Duke University Press (thanks to Ken Wissoker) vastly improved the quality of the manuscript. In this vein, I am grateful to my editor at Cornell University Press, Roger Haydon, for his reassuring advice as well as for being deeply funny. David Wyatt created two beautiful maps for the book, but I thank him for more than that. His support for me and my work, regardless of its trajectory, has never faltered.

At the core of my gratitude are my closest friends and family who teach me to stay in the here, in the now. My love and thanks go to my fellow Gracelings, my family, Teri Caraway, Gitanjali Gutierrez, Susie Gutierrez, Amy Lanou, James Loos, and most of all to my beloved partner, Sandy Crandall.

TAMARA LOOS

Ithaca, New York

SUBJECT SIAM

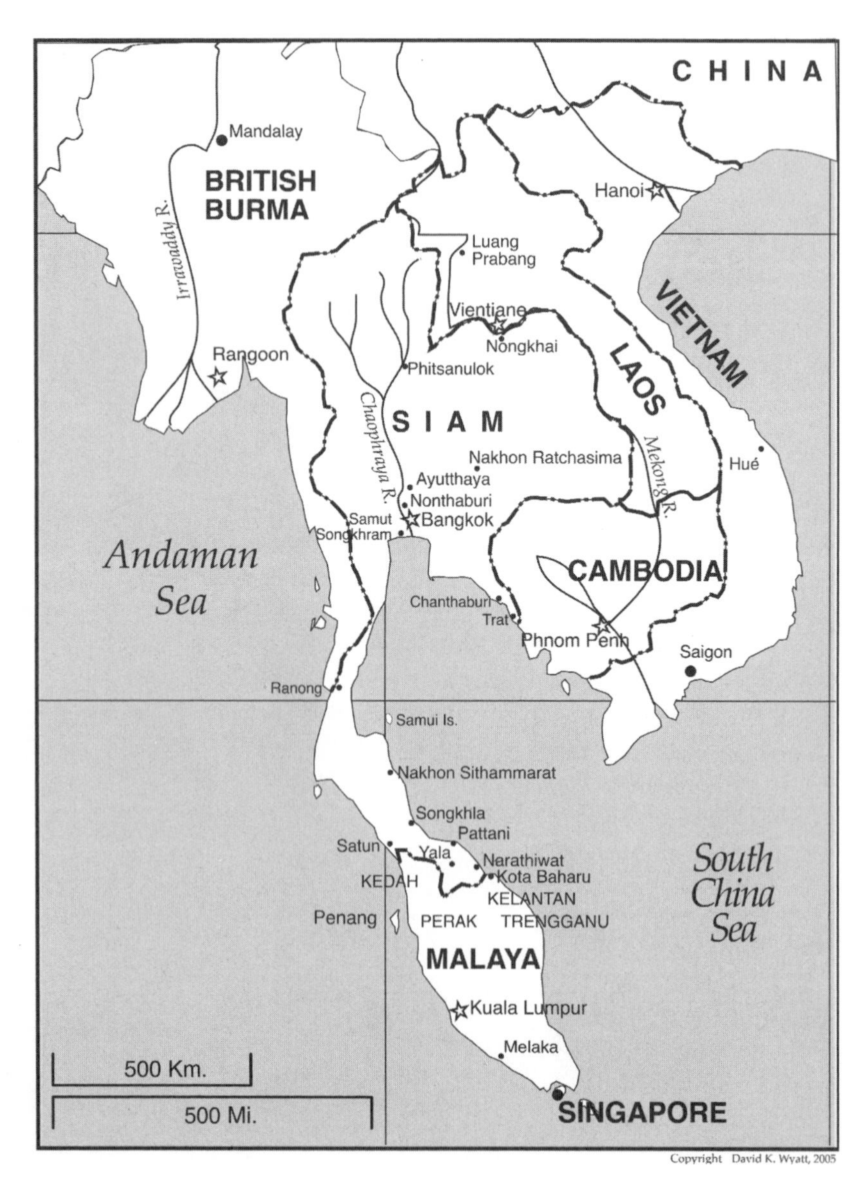

Map 1. Early Twentieth-Century Siam
David W. Wyatt, 2005.

ONE

Family, Law, and Colonial Modernity in Thailand

Two snapshots from Thailand's past blur in the photo album of global imperialism. In 1893 France sent gunboats to the mouth of the Chaophraya River, which leads to Bangkok, the capital of Siam, the former name of Thailand. There they established a blockade and held the king's palace at gunpoint. To the disappointment of Siam's leaders, France's imperial rival, Great Britain, failed to intervene on Siam's behalf. Siam's monarch reportedly suffered an emotional and physical breakdown as he forfeited substantial indemnities and territories to the French. France stationed troops in two Siamese towns, Chantaburi and Trat, until Siam fulfilled its extorted obligations. The confidence that Siam's leaders had in their ability to maintain Siam's territorial claims dwindled, even as they pursued modernizing reforms with renewed intensity.

Fewer than ten years later, in 1902, King Chulalongkorn (Rama V)[1] who reigned from 1868 to 1910, took a page from the French imperial handbook when he authorized the dispatch of a Siamese navy warship to the mouth of the Pattani River to end the local ruler's opposition to Siam's centralizing reforms. The river led to the seat of authority over territory on the Malay Peninsula populated by ethnic Malay Muslims. With naval and police muscle behind them, Bangkok's officials demanded that the formerly autonomous ruler, Raja Abdul Kadir, relinquish his authority and resources by instituting reforms that would incorporate Patani into Siam proper. The

[1] King Rama, or more frequently, Rama followed by the proper reign number is used to designate the kings of the Chakri dynasty.

British in Singapore, who previously had intervened diplomatically in negotiations between Bangkok officials and Raja Abdul Kadir, failed to do so—this time to the great disappointment of the raja. The Siamese government arrested Abdul Kadir, appointed a more amenable governor, and proceeded with centralizing reforms.[2]

These two incidents position Siam as a victim of European imperial aggression and as a colonizing power with imperial ambitions of its own, denying its easy categorization as either one. Siam was the sole country in Southeast Asia to have escaped colonization by an imperial power, yet it nonetheless suffered from many of the ignominies and asymmetries that directly colonized states endured. The French blockade offers one example of how imperial powers dictated Siam's territorial boundaries and the timing of its modernity. Unequal treaties between Siam and fifteen foreign powers offers another. The legal impositions on Siam's sovereignty began in the 1850s when King Mongkut (Rama IV, r. 1851–68) signed the first of a series of unequal treaties that opened Siam's economy to international trade and granted foreigners extraterritorial protection from Siam's legal system. Until Siam transformed its system of jurisprudence, the legal and economic asymmetries would remain intact.

These impositions locate Siam uncomfortably between a sovereign state and a colonized country, neither fully under the authority of a foreign power nor completely in control of its own population or territory. Its leaders consciously and carefully trod a tightrope over the hazardous chasm of direct colonization, mitigated by the knowledge that adopting European forms of institutional and legal modernity provided their only safety net. Perhaps because of this, Siam had much in common with imperial states, as indicated by Bangkok's aggression in Patani, a formerly autonomous territory that was eventually colonized by and incorporated into the Kingdom of Siam. Siam's leaders enacted a series of reforms in Muslim areas in and around Patani, including a colonial legal system modeled after that of the British on the Malay Peninsula. There the British created separate Islamic or customary courts for settling cases related to religion, marriage, and inheritance among Malays. Siam's leaders established Islamic courts with a similar jurisdiction in Patani and its environs. In this way, Siam resembled an imperial nation that instituted within its territory forms of colonial modernity that "preserved" indigenous traditions. Paradoxically, the notion that local traditions were in danger of disappearing was itself a product and consequence of colonial modernity.[3]

[2] Somchot Ongsakun, "Kan-patirup kanpok-khrong monthon pattani (p.s. 2449–2474)" (The Administrative Reform of Monthon Pattani [1906–1931]) (MA thesis, Sri Nakharinwirot University, Bangkok, 1978), 150–54, 189.

[3] For a thorough discussion of this process, see Eric Hobsbawm and Terence Ranger, eds., *The Invention of Tradition* (Cambridge: Cambridge University Press, 1983).

Siam sits at the nexus of colonialism and imperialism, where its sovereignty was qualified by imperial nations at the same time that its leaders enacted colonial measures domestically, sometimes in conscious competition with encroaching imperial powers. Rather than isolate Siam as exceptional, Siam's split identity as colonizer and colonized makes it eminently comparable to both and simultaneously capable of illuminating the limits of the categories. Connecting the halves of Siam's split identity is law—the institution of modernity par excellence in Siam. Law was the pivotal arena in which the leaders of Siam negotiated modernity, proved its "civilized" status to foreign powers, and legislated the meanings of modernity to its subjects. Moreover, the discourse of law was the language through which European imperial powers articulated and translated a "universal" modernity to Siam's leaders.[4] The project of colonial modernity engendered through Siam's encounters with imperialism first materialized in Siam in the form of unequal treaties, which initiated a cascade of multitiered transformations in the legal, economic, political, cultural, and social realms of Siamese society. For these reasons, law, more than any other domain, provided the overarching penumbra under which other negotiations—from international diplomacy and the legal empowerment of female debt slaves against their lords to determining new gender norms and fashions—about the meanings of modernity took place.

The transnational character of the legal reform process and the unique role of family law in Siam reveal the limits of the binary logic of cultural exchange between colonizer and colonized that dominates studies of the colonial encounter. Chapter 2, which provides the historical and contextual backdrop for understanding Siam's response to and appropriation of modernity, addresses the failure of binary logic to capture the "manically proliferating conditions of difference" at work in noncolonized Siam.[5] For example, legal reform in Siam was profoundly multinational, making it impossible to examine Siam's jurisprudence as a discrete, nationally bounded entity or to understand it as a dialectic between colonized and colonizer. Personnel, judicial concepts, and codes flowed through Siam as a part of a global circulation of colonial jurisprudence. Thousands of individuals from dozens of countries served throughout the administration from the 1850s to the mid-twentieth century, sometimes in posts second in importance to only the monarch and a handful of his most trusted relatives.[6] In the Ministry of Jus-

[4] Lydia Liu, "Legislating the Universal: The Circulation of International Law in the Nineteenth Century," in *Tokens of Exchange: The Problem of Translation in Global Circulations,* ed. Lydia Liu (Durham: Duke University Press, 1999), 127–64.

[5] Tani Barlow addresses this proliferation of difference in the context of "semicolonial" China in her "Introduction: On 'Colonial Modernity,'" in *Formations of Colonial Modernity in East Asia,* ed. Tani Barlow (Durham: Duke University Press, 1997), 5.

[6] Pasuk and Baker claim that in 1916 there were 208 foreign advisers in Siam. Batson notes that by 1927, just before the onset of the Depression, there were 124 foreign advisers, sixty-four of whom

tice alone, more than forty legal advisers from France, Britain, Japan, Ceylon, the United States, and Belgium served as officials. Many of these foreign legal reformers pledged their allegiance to Siam's monarch and devoted their lives to the project of Siam's modernity, indicating their fidelity to Siam over their national homelands to the point that some became naturalized as citizens of Siam. At the opposite extreme were those who regarded their employment in Siam as a substitute for experience in a colonized country.

In addition to the multiple nationalities, subjectivities, and experiences of foreign advisers in Siam, many Siamese men from royal, aristocratic, and nonelite backgrounds studied in England and other imperial metropoles in Europe and America. They returned, sometimes after having lived an impressionable decade of their youth abroad, to work in the highest posts in Siam's administration. Their cosmopolitan trajectories eventually led Siamese and foreign legal experts to Bangkok, where they reviewed numerous criminal and civil codes from across the colonized and imperial world to prepare drafts of Siam's new laws. They led the legal reform process, which they executed in the linguistic medium of English. With a few exceptions—family law being one—Siam's modern laws were first drafted in English and only later translated into Thai.

Chapter 2 explores the radical multiplicity of asymmetries in Siam not simply among Europeans, Americans, and Siamese but more important *within* this elite and cosmopolitan class that included both foreigners and Siamese. Allegiances did not follow straightforward ethnic or national lines but cut across them as often as not. Moreover, the existence of extraterritoriality in Siam introduced another level of legal complexity to national and racial hierarchies. Originally intended to "protect" white Europeans and Americans from Siam's system of justice, extraterritoriality eventually raised the legal status of Asian colonial subjects—Asiatic protégés—over that of Siamese. In other words, British Burmans, Dutch Javanese, French Indochinese, and Chinese and Siamese who worked for Europeans and Americans could and did deploy their status as foreign subjects to evade Siamese police and legal authorities.[7] Because these populations outnumbered that of white Europeans and Americans in Siam, it became an even higher priority for Siam's government to rid the country of the extraterritoriality clauses. The existence of Asian populations subject to European imperial control and outside the jurisdiction of Siamese authority exposes the contradictory position of Siam

---

were British. Pasuk Phongpaichit and Chris Baker, *Thailand: Economy and Politics,* 2nd ed. (Oxford: Oxford University Press, 2002), 259; Benjamin Batson, *The End of the Absolute Monarchy in Siam* (Singapore: Oxford University Press, 1984), 50.

[7] Hong Lysa, "Extraterritoriality in Bangkok in the Reign of Chulalongkorn, 1868–1910: The Cacophony of Semi-colonial Cosmopolitanism," *Itinerario: European Journal of Overseas History* 27, no. 2 (2003): 25–46; Hong Lysa, "'Stranger within the Gates': Knowing Semi-colonial Siam as Extraterritorials," *Modern Asian Studies* 38, no. 2 (2004): 327–54.

as simultaneously politically sovereign and yet subordinate legally and economically. Chapter 2 confounds the binary model of understanding colonial power relations by making room for a pluralized and heterogeneous vision of cultural transformation within the domain of law.

In this vein, no domain of jurisprudence better exposes Siam's compound experience of modernity as a colonized and imperial country than family law, as I argue in chapters 3 and 4. In nineteenth-century colonial India, Africa, and Southeast Asia, a plural legal system developed in which cases related to religion and family (marriage, divorce, adultery, and inheritance) were subject to indigenous "customary" laws rather than those of the purportedly secular colonial state, because practices related to family and religion were considered sources of local cultural authenticity.[8] Non-Christian religious beliefs such as animism, Islam, and Buddhism, and non-Christian marital practices (including sexual intercourse outside marriage and polygyny) were protected, in theory, from Westernized legal change for this reason. European and American colonials simultaneously deployed local beliefs and practices, however, to justify continued colonial domination over peoples who engaged in such "primitive" practices.[9]

In practice, of course, colonial administrations intervened in the religious, gender, and sexual practices of colonized populations even as they espoused the principle of noninterference in local traditions. Moreover, some Europeans and Americans indulged in the very practices they condemned, a discrepancy between espoused principles and comportment exposed most incisively in 2002 by Ann Stoler.[10] Although this hypocrisy pertains to European society in noncolonized Siam, where some European and American men obtained harems of their own, it is not the focus herein. Instead, my argument concentrates on the deployment of this model of managing cultural and legal hierarchies within Siam by Siamese authorities.

[8] For examples, see Richard Lariviere, "Justices and *Panditas:* Some Ironies in Contemporary Readings of the Hindu Legal Past," *Journal of Asian Studies* 48 (1989): 757–69; and Sally Engle Merry, *Colonizing Hawai'i: The Cultural Power of Law* (Princeton: Princeton University Press, 2000). The colonial ideology that located authenticity in family and religion is largely a product of the nineteenth century and applies to British and Dutch colonial projects. The Spanish colonial enterprise in the Philippines, which began in the sixteenth century when the Catholic Church was formally intertwined with the state, is an exception to this generalization.

[9] This legal duality is important today because in postcolonial nations the sites of family and religion continue to operate as sources of indigenous cultural authenticity that legitimate the postcolonial state, regardless of its politics. See, for example, Michael Peletz, "Judicial Process and Dilemmas of Legitimacy and Sovereignty: The Malaysian Case in Comparative Perspective," in *Sovereignty under Challenge: How Governments Respond,* ed. John Montgomery and Nathan Glazer (New Brunswick, N.J.: Transaction Publishers, 2002), 221–58; and Michael Peletz, *Islamic Modern: Religious Courts and Cultural Politics in Malaysia* (Princeton: Princeton University Press, 2002).

[10] Ann Stoler, *Carnal Knowledge and Imperial Power* (Berkeley: University of California Press, 2002); James F. Warren, *Ah Ku and Karayuki-san: Prostitution in Singapore, 1870–1940* (Singapore: Oxford University Press, 1993); Hanneke Ming, "Barracks-Concubinage in the Indies, 1887–1920," *Indonesia* 35 (April 1983): 65–93; Anne McClintock, *Imperial Leather: Race, Gender and Sexuality in the Colonial Conquest* (New York: Routledge, 1995).

The Siamese government in Bangkok applied this colonial theory of plural jurisdictions to its Muslim minority in the south at the same time that imperial geopolitics dictated its application to Siam as a whole. At the turn of the twentieth century, Siam's leaders applied colonial strategies of juridical conquest to its Muslim minority when they created separate "native" courts for the application of Islamic family law in southern Siam. This pluralistic legal system still exists today in Thailand, where national law applies throughout the country except in four Muslim provinces in the south. In these areas, where Muslims still comprise up to 80 percent of the population, Islamic family courts dispense Islamic marriage, divorce, and inheritance law in cases between Muslims. Chapter 3 traces the origins of these courts to the late nineteenth century, when Siam's ruling elite explicitly modeled the plural legal system in the south after colonial forms of jurisprudence found in British Malaya. It was part of a larger design to incorporate these hitherto autonomously ruled areas into Siam proper. Although most histories of Siam's incorporation of the south argue that Siam's leaders centralized Bangkok's control over the Patani region because they feared territorial losses to the British, Bangkok's efforts in Patani were not exclusively about claiming territory or maintaining sovereignty. Siamese leaders regarded Patani as a showcase for Siam's colonial modernity. In an effort to compete with British reforms in British Malaya, Siam's leaders imposed colonial-style measures of control such as the establishment of Islamic family courts where none existed before. The Islamic courts revealed the colonial sensibilities of Siam's leaders who sought to show that they too could protect "native" customs.

Paralleling reforms in the south was a kingdomwide effort, explicated in chapter 4, to overhaul all of Siam's laws except for its "native" Buddhist family law. These included laws on polygynous marriage, divorce, adultery, and inheritance. In this sense, Siam closely resembled a European colony where family law was "protected" from change because imperial ideology located a culture's authenticity in its familial structure. *Subject Siam* pivots on chapters 3 and 4 because they expose the dramatic parallels between Bangkok's creation of Islamic family law courts in Patani and attempts by both Siamese and foreign officials to protect Siam's "traditional" polygynous family law in the face of mounting domestic and foreign pressure. The structural similarities between Patani and Bangkok vis-à-vis imperialism require a revised history of Siam that brings gender relations and Siam's Malay Muslims centrally and integrally into the history of modern Siam. Despite this imperative to integrate the south into the history of Siam proper, little is known substantively about Patani's legal history beyond the creation of the family courts. Few sources from the nineteenth and early twentieth centuries appear to have been recorded, let alone to have survived. Documents about the Malay Muslim areas housed in Bangkok's National Archives are still classified, thus prohibiting researchers from accessing the few precious primary sources regarding the history of Bangkok's incorporation of the south.[11] For these reasons, the analysis of Islamic family law and court disputes is truncated in comparison with the rich archival sources available for the rest of Siam.

In Siam proper, the same imperial (and protoethnographic) ideology that linked family structure to cultural authenticity was used against Siam by foreign powers. A hierarchy embedded within the ideology of nineteenth-century colonial modernity associated modernity with a monogamous family structure that was, in turn, reflected in a legal standard of marriage that was monogamous and heterosexual. A society that did not at least formally abide by this standard of a civilized marriage was not considered fully modern by other powerful countries, most of which were Western, Christian, and imperialist. The continued existence of extraterritoriality protections even after Siam established a uniform court system and promulgated new penal and commercial codes, with the exception of family law, implicitly condemned Siamese family law because it condoned polygyny.[12]

Siam's officials, both Siamese and foreigners, split on the issue of polygyny, which had long been associated with political power and masculinity in Siam. In Siam's political culture, men in positions of power formed political alliances with one another through polygynous marriages and demonstrated masculine virility through their numerous wives and children. The frequency with which the sexual adventures of male officials arise in court cases, often incidental to the crimes of which they are accused, indicates that the association between male heterosexual virility and political power continued even after polygyny was denounced as a backward practice. For instance, police officer Nai (title for commoner men) Nim filed a complaint to the Ministry of the Capital in 1910 against his boss, the head constable, for numerous sexual exploits including adultery and unusually disturbing instances of rape.[13] The rapes and adultery committed by a powerful local police constable show up not as cases in their own right but because Nai Nim decided to submit a complaint after his boss began an affair with Nai Nim's wife.

Another petition serves as an example of the connection between male sexuality and official power. Nai Thep filed a petition in 1911 begging the monarch to provide a means to support him and his family, including six young children, who were destitute as a result of his dismissal from his gov-

[11] I was refused access to these documents at Bangkok's National Archives between 1994 and 1996, well before the recent upsurge of violence in southern Thailand.

[12] I prefer the term *polygyny* over *polygamy* because the former refers to the system in which a man could have two or more wives whereas the latter (polygamy) refers to a system in which a man could have two or more wives *and* a woman could have two or more husbands.

[13] Nai Nim mentioned his own stellar record for decreasing criminality on his beat and his dedication to his boss, whose venereal buboes received Nai Nim's salve. National Archives [hereafter NA], Ratchakan thi 5 [hereafter R5], Nakhonban 16 Special Patrol Division, 38/2, "Nai nim ha wa luang chan nakhon kratham chu kap phanraya nai nim" (Nai Nim Accuses Luang Channakhon of Committing Adultery with Nai Nim's Wife), 1910–1911; Loos, Archival Notebooks, vol. 6, 160–71.

ernment position in 1909.[14] The articulate Nai Thep created an undeniably sympathetic account of his life. Born to a poor family in Ranong on the Malay Peninsula, Nai Thep moved to British Malay territories in the 1890s for several years before deciding to return because, he declared, "I am a free son of the Siamese, servant of Your Majesty. I do not want to be the slave of foreigners any longer."[15] Although penniless and without any connections, he determinedly moved to Bangkok where he endeavored to become a government official. In 1900 he accepted a job as a servant and eventually as an apprentice to a judge in Nonthaburi, just outside Bangkok. By 1903 he had become a lawyer, and, by 1906, a judge.

Nai Thep's dreamlike rags-to-riches story came to a screeching halt when a defamation case he filed against a man named Nai Huan backfired at the appellate court. The ensuing investigation prompted the acting minister of justice to dismiss him from government office in 1909 for inappropriate behavior. The investigation discovered that Nai Thep, who was already a husband and father by the time he left Ranong, had an affair with Amdaeng (title for commoner women) Thim, the wife of Nai Huan. The Ministry of Justice further discovered that the people of Phumriang, where Nai Thep worked as a judge, had filed complaints against Nai Thep. These included attempted rape, alcohol abuse, opium consumption, indebtedness, the use of love potions on women he tried to bed, and an attempt to administer poison to his opponent's fighting cock in a match on which he gambled. For these reasons, the minister of justice dismissed Nai Thep from government service but did not charge him with any crimes.

Nai Thep appealed his dismissal through a narrative of patriotism and his responsibility as a loving father to provide for his six destitute children—"Little Thep, eleven years old; Little Thaen, five years old; Little Wii, four years old; Little Chalaem, three years old; Little Oeb, two years old; and Little Waat, one year old." In addition, he defended his relationship with Amdaeng Thim as legitimate. He argued that Nai Huan had already divorced Amdaeng Thim, who then had a relationship with Nai Thep's own clerk before Nai Thep began a relationship with her. He felt the investigation was prejudiced against him: "I am the little guy, the firefly competing against the moonlight, who of course will lose this competition."[16] In a sense he was right: the Ministry of Justice took no pity on him when he appealed to patriotism or to family responsibilities.

Nai Thep's case richly shows several key themes explored in *Subject Siam:*

[14] NA MR5, Yutitham 12 Dika rongthuk, 9. The case has no title and appears to have been wedged into case number 228. Loos, Archival Notebooks, vol. 10, 36–62.

[15] "Pen but thai[y-garan] chao sayam kha tai fa lo-ong thuli phrabat mai yak yu pen kha khon chao tang prathet to pai." Loos, Archival Notebooks, vol. 10, 42. Unless otherwise noted, all translations are my own.

[16] "Khaphraphuthachao phu noi hinghoi ru cha ma khaeng duai saeng phrachan yom cha phaiphae ratsmi kaekan." Loos, Archival Notebooks, vol. 10, 46.

the nationalist understanding of Siam as independent in juxtaposition to its colonized neighbors; the pilgrimage of ambitious commoner men from the far ends of the kingdom to Bangkok, where the government hired them to work at lower and middling levels of the bureaucracy; the link between official power and masculinity demonstrated through sexual exploits and the ability to provide for one's family; and the ambiguity of the meaning of "wife" and therefore the difficulty of adjudicating cases of adultery, divorce, and related legal issues. Each of these themes is explored in the following chapters, several of which feature court cases that highlight the significance of polygyny to Siam's status as sovereign yet not quite modern because of its official culture.

An examination of court cases such as Nai Thep's and of the creation of modern family law suggests that Siam's sovereignty was fundamentally a matter of gender and law as much as it was about politics and economics. *Subject Siam* centrally examines the deployment of family law in Patani, Siam proper, and in nineteenth-century imperial ideologies to demonstrate the operation of a multitiered colonial legal hierarchy in noncolonized Siam. Siam would not be free of burdensome extraterritoriality clauses until it "modernized" its legal system, which meant adopting a single standard of marriage rather than recognizing, as had been traditionally allowed, a broad range of relationships as "marriage." Chapters 4 and 5 discuss the construction and constriction of the definition of marriage, a process inextricably entangled with modernity in Siam. Until the early twentieth century, men and women were considered married in the eyes of the community if they, among other conditions, cohabited, had a child together, had undergone a formal ceremony, or engaged in intermittent sexual intercourse. The inclusive customary definitions of marriage came under increasingly intense legal scrutiny, however. Modern law began to be used as a means to distinguish legal marriage from other "promiscuous" sexual liaisons.

For example, in 1914 in Suphanburi, Nai Mat accused Nai Saeng of committing adultery with his wife, Amdaeng Ma, with the permission of Ma's mother. If convicted, the accused could be forced to pay as much as five hundred baht in marital property and fines.[17] Amdaeng Ma rebutted that Nai Mat was not legally her husband, which in effect freed her to become the wife of Nai Saeng. The lower court dismissed Nai Mat's case, but the Appeals Court fined Nai Saeng for "committing adultery with the estranged wife" (*phit mia rang*) of another man.[18] It appears that at one time Nai Mat and

[17] *Khamphiphaksa san dika* (Dika Court Verdicts [hereafter KSD]) 2457 Decision 36, June 1914; Loos, Archival Notebooks, vol. 13, 13. The Dika Court was the highest appeals court in the kingdom and has been translated as both the Royal Appeals Court and the Supreme Appeals Court. Hereafter the *Khamphiphaksa san dika* will be referred to as KSD.

[18] The Dika Court dismissed Nai Saeng's appeal for technical reasons, applying the Appeals Court decision by default.

Amdaeng Ma had been "married," but that they had later separated. When Amdaeng Ma began a relationship with another man, her former lover brought her to court in the hopes of obtaining financial recompense and perhaps of shoring up his reputation as a virile man who could control his wife's sexuality. Nai Mat ultimately won the case.

Because no single legal standard for marriage existed and because Siamese officials interpreted Buddhism as supporting a range of possible connubial unions, cases such as these frequently arose and created a crisis in the legal and social system over the definition of a legitimate wife. Theravada Buddhism, it should be noted, did not support any type of marriage over another despite later efforts on the part of some Siamese to argue that Buddhism supported polygyny over monogamy. Chapter 5 argues that the need for a legal standard stemmed from the changes in jurisprudence brought about by Siam's encounter with European imperialism. The new regime of law demanded the systemization of the legal definitions of family, wife, and legitimate children before it could require judges to apply these laws uniformly throughout the kingdom. The category of "husband," unlike that of "wife," never generated much legal dispute or confusion, except indirectly through debates in the early twentieth century about a man's (not a "husband's") female sexual partners. Moreover, a man's sexual past rarely came into question, since polygyny enabled him to obtain numerous wives, so long as they were not "married" to another man.

By contrast, determining the status of a woman as a wife or as a casual sexual partner was critical to applying the law and adjudicating cases about marriage, divorce, adultery, rape, and inheritance—cases that animate chapters 5 and 6. While men more frequently sued their former female lovers for adultery when the women attempted to remarry, women often fought to prove that a marriage existed so that they could then officially divorce their husbands before proceeding to collect marital property or alimony. Worse off were lower-class women who slept with men because they understood that the act of sexual intercourse would "marry" the couple. Instead of translating into connubial bliss, the sexual act instead became their first instance of commercial sex, with the carrot of marriage offered to dupe women into prostitution. Elite women, by contrast, might fight to prevent a legal divorce so they could continue to be financially supported by their husbands and maintain their reputations as honorable women. This was true for Mom (a title meaning consort of a prince) Saengmoni, a woman married to Mom Chao (child of a prince of the rank of *phra-ong chao)* Thongchua, grandson of King Mongkut and nephew to King Chulalongkorn.[19] As a part of their bitterly acrimonious divorce case in 1922, the notoriously philandering

[19] The case takes up an entire reel of microfilm and deserves a separate study. NA MR6 Yutitham 8 Khadikhwam 2, "Mom saengmoni kap mom chao thongchuathammachat," 1920–22.

Mom Chao Thongchua provided nearly three hundred pages of testimony that was used to show that the couple's enmity prevented them from reconciliation. However, Mom Saengmoni refused to allow the divorce unless she received a respectable separate residence and financial remuneration to support their four children.

The ambiguous legal definition of marriage gave rise to court cases that over time clogged Siam's new legal system, which required standardized legal definitions that judges could apply uniformly throughout the country. However, legal reformers could not resolve the situation until Siam's leaders could decide to make either monogamy or polygyny Siam's legal standard of marriage. That this law turned out to advocate monogamy is no coincidence given the international and domestic pressure brought to bear on the practice of polygyny. When lawmakers passed a monogamy law as Siam's standard of marriage in 1935, they exposed the power and efficacy of the associations among imperialism, monogamy, and modernity. The transformation of polygyny's meanings occurred at the nexus of imperial hegemonic discourses and subnational power struggles, neither of which can be analyzed in isolation.

The pressure on polygyny, however, played out in unanticipated ways in Siam, where leaders had the authority to adopt monogamy as the nation's marital standard as early as 1855, yet chose not to do so until 1935 despite court backlogs, imperial ideology, and even domestic advocacy for monogamy. Some Siamese supported monogamy because of its association with ideals of sexual equality and modernity. Others, however, relied on equally modern discourses of national and cultural authenticity to promote the continuation of polygyny as part of Siam's distinctive Buddhist heritage. They juxtaposed it explicitly with Christian monogamy, which they regarded as part of Europe's cultural heritage. Polygyny, in these ways, indexed the kingdom's ambiguous status as sovereign but not quite modern or equal to imperial powers in the minds of many Europeans and some Siamese. For others, polygyny offered an opportunity for Siamese to articulate their alternative modernity. Chapter 4 contends that the ideologically laden differences between monogamy and polygyny offered a space in which various groups within Siam could politicize transnational signs of modernity for their own purposes. Chapters 5 and 6 explore the politicization process in domestic debates about the definition of Siam's own culturally distinct form of modernity. Yet the terms of this debate were set for them by the marital, gender, and sexual hierarchies embedded in colonial discourse. The existence of this cross-border negotiation about the gendered and sexual meanings of modernity reveals the degree to which Siam's national history was also part of transnational history.

Because of the segregation of family law from the thoroughgoing reform of the rest of Siam's legal code, the definition of the family became a site of intense political contests within Siam. Chapters 5 and 6 reconstruct these contests. In chapter 5, the pressure placed on "civilizing" the family explains why Siamese intellectuals and statesmen engaged in raging debates over the "status of women," prostitution, and polygyny in Siam in the early twentieth century. Because polygyny still existed as a legitimate form of marriage, Siam's lawmakers had to distinguish among major wives and minor wives, who were recognized in the law and Buddhist canon, and other sexual partners such as mistresses, prostitutes, and "temporary wives," who had no legal standing as wives. All of these categories of women hinged on the meaning of a legitimate wife, whose identity was subject to a legal, social, and political war of definition. Wives—who could be one and how they functioned symbolically for their husbands and the nation—became the linchpin holding together the modern Siamese family.

The significance of the function of "family" as the space in which authentic Thai-ness originated had obvious political advantages for Siam's kings, who used laws on family to construct and stabilize a national identity that was founded on loyalty to the absolute monarch. Chapter 6 delineates how the state, for the first time, began in the early twentieth century to regulate the (hetero)sexuality of male officials by linking men's antiabsolutist political beliefs to their allegedly excessive sexual practices. King Vajiravudh (Rama VI, r. 1910–25) in particular targeted a specific demographic of male officials who sought to demote the absolute monarchy to a constitutional one. He accused them of engaging in depraved and hypocritically unprogressive sexual practices, thereby discrediting their modern political yearnings. The monarch harnessed the modern family and proper sexuality to a larger state-building project that aimed to ensure the continued centrality of the monarchy to Siam as a nation. His myriad cultural interventions, legal interdictions, and rulings in court cases undermined those who advocated anything less than an absolute monarchy. The writings of King Vajiravudh are particularly important because he was the most prolific contributor on this issue to the public press, which was more vocal in the 1910s and 1920s than anytime hitherto. No other political figure so intensely engaged the public, which is why King Vajiravudh's voice speaks the loudest and is contrasted with a range of voices in the public press.

His reign, unpopular with contemporaries and historians alike, initiated the demise of the absolutist system, which was eventually overthrown in 1932. In its place, the National Assembly promulgated a law on monogamy in 1935, which enabled the removal of the last remnants of the unequal treaty system. The timing of events gives the appearance that they are causally related. In other words, once a constitutional monarchy replaced the absolutist system, polygyny gave way to monogamy. However, chapter 7's closer look at the process, content, and parliamentary debates about monogamy and polygyny suggests otherwise. The endorsement of monogamy by Siam's last absolute monarchs and the promotion of polygyny by some members of the newly elected People's Representatives confound simple conclusions about the continuing significance of polygyny to politics and culture.

The following chapters expand on the themes of transnational jurisprudence, colonial family courts in the Malay Muslim south, polygyny, wifedom, male heterosexuality, and nationalism. These themes, which were integral to Siam's aspiration to gain global recognition as a modern sovereign nation, best exemplify the location of Siam as a country that shares a great deal with both colonized and imperial countries. Moreover, these themes were selected for their ability to interrogate the role of gender and the monarchy in Thai historiography, on the one hand, and the significance of Euro-American forms of modernity in non-Western areas of the globe, on the other. *Subject Siam*'s history of Siam's national family offers an alternative narrative for understanding politics and society in modern Thailand. Instead of recentering the monarch as the hero who saved Siam from colonization, it follows the trajectory of modern law, a transnational reform process that revamped the institution of the family and helped to colonize Muslim areas in the south. A focus on law provides an opportunity to bring Siam's history out of the narrow confines of Thai exceptionalism so that it can be compared to colonized, imperial, and other modern polities.

Thai Historiography

A single fact dominates the historiography of modern Thailand: unlike the majority of the globe and all of its Southeast Asian neighbors, Thailand was never colonized by an imperial power. All narratives about Siam, as Thailand was called until 1939, are fundamentally structured around its allegedly eternal national independence. Every serious historian of modern Siam must come to terms with this question by elucidating, assessing, and qualifying Siam's sovereignty in an era of global colonial domination. The master narrative credits Siam's monarchy for safeguarding the kingdom's sovereignty in the face of aggressive imperial expansion by modernizing the country along Western lines and opening it to "free trade," thereby obviating empire's rationale for colonization. Siam's kings, we are told, brilliantly and heroically navigated their country's path to independence. The ubiquity of this underlying emplotment of Siam's history points to its success within Thailand as well as to its conformity with conventional, Eurocentric accounts of the story of modernity. As a result, any account that lauds Siam's history as exceptional because it avoided colonization consequently venerates the monarch as the sole agent of history and modernity within Thailand. It simultaneously reaffirms the authoritative narrative of European modernity that maintains the Enlightenment ideals of freedom and equality without critically interrogating their historicist biases or paradoxical practice in situ.

When the field of Southeast Asian studies, of which Thai studies is one part, came into being in the United States after World War II, the ethos of postwar scholarship was motivated by anticolonial sentiment. Foreign scholars uncritically took the perspective of Siam's ruling elite as *the* indigenous perspective, despite the fact that an internal critique of that dynastic perspective had begun as early as 1950.[20] In 1950, Udom Srisuwan, then a leading member of the Communist Party of Thailand, published *Thailand, a Semicolony,* which contended that Siam's leaders empowered themselves and capitalist classes by joining forces with imperialists at the expense of Siam's farming class.[21] Despite the banning of the book by a succession of military governments after 1950, Udom's Maoist-inspired radical critique had an impact that persevered into the 1970s inside and outside Thailand. Within Thailand, Chit Phumisak's 1957 *The Real Face of Thai Feudalism Today* critiqued the class structure and thereby criticized the monarchy. It too was quickly suppressed, only to resurface as an ideological catalyst and foundational text for activist students in the 1970s.[22] At that time, Chatthip Nartsupha's political economy group continued to challenge dynastic narratives about Siam's eternal independence by producing scholarship that revealed the historical economic dependency of Siam on foreign powers.[23]

Outside Thailand, Benedict Anderson made this critique most incisively in 1978 when he let loose a specter that has haunted Thai studies ever since. He dared to ask whether the fact of Siam's noncolonization was an unqualified blessing, implying that Siam was unfortunate to have not been colonized.[24] Critical histories have started to chisel away at Siam's dominant dynastic version of history that was cracked open by Thai Marxist scholar-

[20] Benedict Anderson, "Studies of the Thai State: The State of Thai Studies," in *The Study of Thailand: Analyses of Knowledge, Approaches, and Prospects in Anthropology, Art History, Economics, History and Political Science,* ed. Eliezer B. Ayal, Papers in International Studies, Southeast Asia Series 54 (Athens: Ohio University, Center for International Studies, 1978), 196.

[21] Hong has provided the most sustained discussion of Udom's book in Hong Lysa, "'Stranger within the Gates,'" 327. Udom Srisuwan [Aran Phrommachomphu, pseud.], *Sen-thang sangkhom thai* (Bangkok: Akson, 1979), reprint of *Thai kung-muang-khun* (Bangkok: Mahachon, 1950).

[22] Chit Phumisak [Somsamai Sisuttharaphan], "Chomna khong sakdina thai nai patchuban" (The Real Face of Thai Sakdina Today), *Nitisat 2500 chabap rap sattawatmai* (The Faculty of Law Yearbook 2500 to Greet the New Century) (Bangkok: Thammasat University, Faculty of Law, 1957). For a contextualized analysis of Chit's impact, see Craig Reynolds, "Feudalism in the Thai Past," in *Thai Radical Discourse: The Real Face of Thai Feudalism Today,* ed. and trans. Craig Reynolds (Ithaca: Cornell University, Southeast Asia Program, 1987), 149–69.

[23] For a discussion of these and other critical discourses, see Chatthip Nartsupha and Suthy Prasartset, eds., *Socio-Economic Institutions and Cultural Change in Siam, 1851–1910* (Bangkok: Social Science Association of Thailand, 1981); Seksan Prasertkul, "The Transformation of the Thai State and Economic Change (1855–1945)," PhD diss., Cornell University, 1989; Craig Reynolds and Hong Lysa, "Marxism in Thai Historical Studies," *Journal of Asian Studies* 43, no. 1 (1983): 77–104; Thongchai Winichakul, "The Changing Landscape of the Past: New Histories in Thailand since 1973," *Journal of Southeast Asian Studies* 26, no. 1 (1995): 99–120; Maurizio Peleggi, *Lords of Things: The Fashioning of the Siamese Monarchy's Modern Image* (Honolulu: University of Hawai'i Press, 2002), 6.

[24] Anderson, "Studies of the Thai State," 198–99.

ship and Anderson's haunting question. Scholars have shown that while the dynastic version provides an inspiring nationalist narrative in which Thai national identity is routinely anchored, it also silences critical evaluation of the process by which the monarch used the reform process to centralize his power, suppress ethnic minorities, strengthen preexisting domestic class and gender hierarchies, and deploy the threat of colonial intervention to justify new territorial boundaries.[25] Thongchai Winichakul's work is especially important in this regard for exposing the capacity of Siam's rulers to justify, through recourse to the threat of foreign intervention, territorial aggrandizement and the consolidation of Bangkok's power at the expense of less powerful but nonetheless autonomous political entities.[26] Colonialism, in these ways, engendered rather than endangered modern Siam as a geopolitical entity.[27] These critiques have exposed the hegemonic narrative of Thai national history as the perspective if not the ideology of the ruling elite.

As a consequence, the heated historiographic debates smoldering in Thai studies revolve around evaluations of the monarchy, which helps explain why Siam has remained in a metaphorical isolation chamber of exceptionalism. Exceptionalism performs the vital political work of safeguarding the prestige of the monarchy in Thailand. By failing to compare Siam to colonized and imperial countries, scholarship on Siam's monarchy uncritically preserves its reputation as an agentic, nationalistic, altruistic institution. It resists exposing its underbelly for examples of collaboration with and dependency on foreign powers, unheroic moments of self-preservation, and acts of imperial aggression. The following chapters provide an alternative history of Siam at the turn of the century by acknowledging the undeniable significance of Siam's royal officials while simultaneously offering a critical interpretation of their role in Siam's modernity.

I focus on King Chulalongkorn's reign in particular because studies of it have established the terms of Thailand's relationship to modernity (or "globalization" in today's terminology); namely, that Thailand is independent because of its monarchs' ability to adopt foreign innovations and adapt them to Siam's distinctive culture. The royalist narrative, cemented in King Chulalongkorn's reign, is a crucial prop supporting the institution of the monarchy today, reinforcing the need to return to the history of that reign. The culture industry in Thailand has solidified the link between King Chulalongkorn and Thailand's regnant monarch, King Bhumibol Adulyadej (Rama IX, r. 1946–present), however, making it impossible to critique one without indirectly critiquing the other. In addition, lèse-majesté laws make it com-

[25] In the late nineteenth and early twentieth centuries, every major political and social policy enacted was justified on the grounds that it maintained Siam's freedom from foreign domination.

[26] Thongchai Winichakul, *Siam Mapped: A History of the Geo-Body of a Nation* (Honolulu: University of Hawai'i Press, 1994).

[27] The phrasing comes from Peleggi, *Lords of Things*, 6.

plicated if not dangerous to evaluate critically King Chulalongkorn's reign because the invocation of it automatically evokes comparisons with King Bhumibol, who is Thailand's longest reigning monarch. The longevity of his reign is associated with the transfer of his allegiances from right-wing U.S.-supported military dictators in the 1960s to his short-lived support for student radicals in 1973.[28]

Despite his inconsistent political loyalties, Thailand's monarch is not only unassailably popular among Thai Buddhists but also is a powerful unifying symbol of the nation that has been periodically deployed by Thai governments. A beloved but aging monarch, King Bhumibol possesses formidable cultural capital and informal political power because he represents political continuity and because of his association with the reign of King Chulalongkorn. This is despite that fact that no actual continuity between these two reigns exists—as indicated by the near demise of the monarchy between the 1930s and 1950s—outside the reconstructed historical memory of the nation. Like most nationalist narratives, this one privileges certain segments of the population as more authentic nationals over others. My study focuses on the privileging of ethnic Thai Buddhists over Malay Muslims and Siamese men over women, but studies of other social hierarchies are equally valid.

Cracks in the structure of this dominant narrative have widened of late, as the current monarch ages with an heir who does not match his popularity or authority. Symbolic attempts at patching the cracks through public articulations about the continuity of the monarchy are hard pressed to compete with the razing power of rumors about the demise of the institution. Despite this, it remains astoundingly difficult to question the master narrative—an act tantamount to treason for nationals—because of the symbolic patricide it commits, the lèse-majesté laws it potentially violates, and the cultural nationalism it offends.[29] Thailand may be on the brink of a major transformation in its national identity, historical plot, and political trajectory. During the first decade of the twenty-first century, an increase in lèse-majesté allegations, intensified government control over the media, refusal to allow independent investigations into violence in Malay Muslim areas of southern Thailand, and the rehabilitation of proroyalist figures all speak in part to fears of the demise of the dynasty, which might irreparably suffer under intense scrutiny.[30] This has also raised the stakes in challenging the received inter-

[28] Benedict Anderson, "Withdrawal Symptoms," *The Spectre of Comparisons: Nationalism, Southeast Asia and the World* (New York: Verso, 1998), 139–73.

[29] Peleggi, *Lords of Things,* 7.

[30] One of the best known cases involved two journalists working for the *Far Eastern Economic Review* who were accused in January 2002 of committing lèse-majesté for a report that mentioned tension between Prime Minister Thaksin Shinawatra and the king. Peter Jackson notes a less famous case that involved a Thai citizen, Piriya Krairirksh, who questioned the authenticity of the Ramkhamhaeng inscription and was consequently charged with lèse-majesté against King Ramkhamhaeng, a monarch who died seven centuries ago. Jackson also refers to the popular film *Suriyothai*

pretation of Siam's encounter with imperialism and colonialism, especially for Thai scholars.

In contradistinction to Thai nationalist historiography, the literature on colonialism, imperialism, and postcolonialism locates Siam as semicolonial, semi-imperial, semimodern—what I call the purgatory of in-betweens. Describing Siam's noncolonial yet not entirely sovereign status poses its own set of terminological problems. The use of the term *semi-*, used to modify *colonial, imperial,* or *modern,* risks interpreting Siam's historical situation as a failure to transition completely to a Eurocentric model of modernity. It positions Siam in between the very binaries—tradition/modernity, colony/empire—that critical scholarship seeks to dismantle. For these reasons, I do not refer to Siam as "semi," except when quoting other scholars, but instead attempt to expose the complex and multiple power hierarchies at work in their relevant contexts. Moreover, scholarship that qualifies Siam's sovereign status still tends to focus on the degree to which the kingdom approximates a colonized condition without emphasizing the equally important imperial aspects of Siam's position.

The studies most threatening to Siam's narrative of eternal independence are those that privilege empirical economic and legal facts. Scholars of the political economy of imperialism argue that Siam, far from being independent, suffered a form of indirect colonization. Accordingly, when Britain, France, and over a dozen other countries imposed unequal treaties in the 1850s, they limited Siam's sovereignty and forced its leaders to "Westernize" Siam's legal, economic, and administrative institutions. Siam qualifies as "semi-colonial" or as part of Britain's "informal," "excentric," or "peripheral" empire.[31] Seventy percent of Siam's export trade was under British control by the late nineteenth century,[32] and up to 95 percent of the export economy was in the hands of foreigners, if the ethnic Chinese are included among them.[33] In addition, British interests and advisers dominated Siam's Ministry

(2001) and the TV series *Kasatriya* (2003), both of which "reflect the dominance of monarchy-centred historiography in much contemporary popular culture." Peter Jackson, "Semicoloniality and Duality in Siam's Relations with the West," a paper presented at "The Ambiguous Allure of the West" conference held at Cornell University, Ithaca, New York, 5–7 Nov., 2004, 4. See also Hong Lysa, "Extraterritoriality in Bangkok," 25; Hong Lysa, "Of Consorts and Harlots in Thai Popular History," *Journal of Asian Studies* 57, no. 2 (May 1998): 333–53.

[31] Lenin is credited with popularizing the term "semi-colonial" in "The Highest Stage of Capitalism," from V. I. Lenin, *Imperialism: The Highest Stage of Capitalism* (New York: International Publishers, 1939), 76–84, 88–92, 123–27; Wolfgang Mommsen, "The End of Empire and the Continuity of Imperialism," in *Imperialism and After: Continuities and Discontinuities,* ed. Wolfgang J. Mommsen and Jurgen Osterhammel (London: German Historical Institute, Allen and Unwin, 1986), 339; John Gallagher and Ronald Robinson, "The Imperialism of Free Trade," *Economic History Review* 6, no. 1 (1953), 11; P. J. Cain and A. G. Hopkins, *British Imperialism: Innovation and Expansion: 1688–1914* (London: Longman, 1993), 8, n. 10.

[32] James C. Ingram, *Economic Change in Thailand, 1850–1970* (Stanford: Stanford University Press, 1971), 2.

[33] Anderson, "Studies of the Thai State," 209.

of Finance, the construction of the southern railway, and other key economic sectors in the late nineteenth and early twentieth centuries. Finally, extraterritoriality provided most foreign nationals, even those who were "Asiatics," with legal protections similar to those enjoyed by foreign nationals generally in colonized areas.[34]

According to these studies, Siam was locked into an asymmetrical set of relations with various world powers that had enormous economic, political, and legal repercussions domestically. It was not a sovereign country, except in the most formal political sense, but suffered a kind of surrogate colonization overseen by its own rulers, who collaborated with imperial countries in order to maintain their positions at the helm of an "independent" Siam.[35] Within Thailand and in Thai studies more generally, however, the term *semicolony* has gained no authoritative purchase.[36] Instead of ushering in a flood of criticism of Siam's leaders for collaborating with foreign enemies to undermine Siam's economic independence, local traditions, and legal autonomy, the economic "facts" of subjugation have been effortlessly appropriated by the dynastic narrative. The greater the threat to Siam's independence, economic or otherwise, the more heroic were Siam's monarchs who ingeniously adapted foreign law, administrative techniques, and economic measures to rescue the nation from unequal treaties and from the imminent threat of colonization. In this way, Thailand's nationalist narrative hegemonically interprets events of the colonial period.

Alternative Modernities

Is it possible to study Siam's history since the nineteenth century without condemning it to "semicolonial" status or, quite the opposite, is it possible to evaluate its political sovereignty without venerating the monarchy? Despite their different interpretations of historical agency and crucial implications for Thai national identity, both narratives presume that Siam replicated European patterns of modernity. This raises two related and equally important questions. How can one study Siam's modern history without condemning it as an imitation of European modernity? How can a study emphasize Siam's *unique* trajectory toward modernity without glorifying the monarchy? These seemingly intractable dilemmas stem from the intimate links forged between

[34] Tamara Loos, "Gender Adjudicated: Translating Modern Legal Subjects in Siam," PhD diss., Cornell University, 1999.

[35] This notion of "collaborating regimes" homogenizes them regardless of their cultural and historical differences or degree of agency—a view of indigenous rule available only from the perch of empire. Robinson and Gallagher, "Imperialism of Free Trade," 4; Mommsen, "End of Empire," 334.

[36] Craig J. Reynolds, "On the Gendering of Nationalist and Postnationalist Selves in Twentieth Century Thailand," in *Genders and Sexualities in Modern Thailand,* ed. Peter Jackson and Nerida Cook (Chiang Mai: Silkworm Books, 1999), 263.

national identity and modernity not only in the discourse of Thai studies but in colonial discourse more broadly.

Elusive yet omnipresent, modernity is notoriously difficult to define. Allusions to European modernity herein refer to an archetype of modernity—one that never existed, even in Europe, except as an ideal.[37] This paradigm of modernity was transported throughout the world by colonialism as a conceptual model that nonetheless exerted power as a yardstick against which nonmodern societies and individuals were judged. By *modular modernity,* I refer both to an ideal type of what it means to be modern and to the transportability of the concept beyond Europe. I do not, however, mean to imply that all instantiations of modernity are purely imitative. Instead, this study remains attuned to the specificities of cultural practices in Siam as they became entangled with imperialism, colonialism, and definitions of modernity.

Modernity refers to inseparable political, economic, social, and cultural processes—all of which evolved in relation to colonial conquest—that developed in eighteenth-century Western Europe. Its philosophical rationale included the doctrine of progress, rationality, secularity, individualistic understandings of the self, mastery over the forces of nature by human knowledge, and the abolition of "superstition." These discourses and institutions found their way to Siam, albeit in modified forms and as they were subjectively interpreted by the individuals who brought them there. The discourses associated with modernity include the Enlightenment ideal of inherent individual equality, which dominated European understandings of social relationships despite the paradoxical coexistence of slavery and coverture. Through this lens, both Siamese slavery and polygyny were regarded as backward practices. Although few philosophers of modernity include as central a monogamous nuclear family structure, it too formed a cornerstone of European modernity undergirding critiques of polygyny, especially in the colonial era.[38]

Economically, modernity refers to the global expansion of trade, capitalist development, and the institutionalization of market-driven economies, products, material wealth, and consumption. Politically, modernity's transformations include the shifts from absolutism, religious rule, and feudalism to secularity, bureaucratically administered states, popular forms of government, rule of law, and territorial sovereignty that are characteristic of the nation-state.

[37] My delineation of modernity is amalgamated from several sources including Bill Ashcroft, Gareth Griffiths, and Helen Tiffen, *Key Concepts in Post-Colonial Studies* (London: Routledge, 1998), 144–45; Dipesh Chakrabarty, *Provincializing Europe* (Princeton: Princeton University Press, 2000); Dipesh Chakrabarty, *Habitations of Modernity: Essays in the Wake of Subaltern Studies* (Chicago: University of Chicago Press, 2002), xix–xxiv; Dilip Parameshwar Gaonkar, "On Alternative Modernities," *Public Culture* 11, no. 1 (1999), 2; and Stuart Hall et al., eds., *Modernity: An Introduction to Modern Societies* (London: Blackwell, 1996), 4.

[38] Nilufer Göle, *The Forbidden Modern* (Ann Arbor: University of Michigan Press, 1996).

Postcolonial and postmodern critiques of the neat dichotomies of modernity have exposed its underlying hypocrisies, ironies, greed, and violence. Ann Stoler and others have demonstrated the racial and class-based ideologies undergirding Dutch discriminatory policies regarding modern marriage as opposed to informal mixed-race unions in the Netherlands East Indies. Peter van der Veer has critiqued British colonial secularity as a product of Christianity, while others argue more strongly that secularity is nothing more than the ideological mystification of Protestant Christianity.[39] Dipesh Chakrabarty has best articulated a critique of modernity for its historicist attitude toward time. Modernity imagines not only the present as superior to the past but also sees colonial peoples as historically locatable at an earlier stage of modern development that Europe had previously experienced. Colonial subjects were not yet educated, civilized, or developed enough to rule themselves.[40] In addition, Foucault's work has made it imperative to deconstruct the privileged concept of the individual subject and the two most cherished philosophic ideals of modernity—freedom and equality, especially for individuals. These ideals, he argues, paradoxically ushered in a more thorough form of domination through technologies of biopower, individuation, and self-discipline.[41]

The chapters that follow reveal the particular relationship of Siam to modernity that resulted from its noncolonization. I focus on Siam's historically contingent and contextually specific formulation of modernity—an alternative modernity in current discourse. Alternative modernity is a phrase coined "to conceptualize the Asian, African, and Latin modern"[42] that were modeled after, yet formulated against, European modular modernity. While the notion of alternative modernity acknowledges the indispensability of European political thought to representations of non-European political modernity, it refutes the value-ridden historicism embedded in defining people, practices, and concepts as non- or premodern that serve to delimit the term *modernity.*[43]

The ideals of modernity and their imperfect implementation inform my use of the term *modernity.* Colonial modernity builds upon this definition of modernity but underscores the fact that most countries around the globe ex-

[39] Peter van der Veer, *Imperial Encounters: Religion and Modernity in India and Britain* (Princeton: Princeton University Press, 2001).

[40] Chakrabarty, *Provincializing Europe,* 7.

[41] Biopower refers to a technology of political power that allows states to control entire populations. Michel Foucault, *Discipline and Punish: The Birth of the Prison* (New York: Vintage, 1979). For a discussion of Foucault's contribution to theories of modernity, see Lisa Rofel, *Other Modernities: Gendered Yearnings in China after Socialism* (Berkeley: University of California Press, 1999), 10–11.

[42] "Editor's Comment on Querying Alternativity," *Public Culture* (1999): viii.

[43] Dipesh Chakrabarty, *Habitations of Modernity,* xix. See also Chakrabarty, *Provincializing Europe;* Gaonkar, "On Alternative Modernities"; and van der Veer, *Imperial Encounters,* for analyses of European modernity and historicism.

perienced modernity under the radically asymmetrical global conditions of imperialism. The pervasive and persuasive ideologies associated with modernity came to Siam during the era of high imperialism, which skipped over Siam but nonetheless exerted undeniable authority. Despite this, like those in formal colonies, the Siamese challenged, often consciously, the hegemony of colonial modernity by refusing to transform key aspects of their local cultural and institutional landscape.

By highlighting Siam's alternative modernity, I decenter the model of modernity based on the historically specific case of Europe. However, it is in Siam's relationship to European forms of modernity that Siam's noncolonization makes a crucial difference. The scholarship on alternative modernities that focuses on political modernity in directly colonized states, such as India, is courageously rebellious, invigorating, and comfortably anticolonial.[44] In Siam, by contrast, indigenous rulers rather than colonial overlords directed Siam's modernity. Revealing Siam's trajectory to modernity as uniquely modern runs the risk of revitalizing and authorizing the dominant dynastic narrative, which would serve a conventional rather than a critical agenda.

In this book I offer an analysis of Siam's history that disrupts the self-legitimizing narrative of the monarchy as the sole agent of history, ends the isolation engendered by the scholarship invoking Siamese exceptionalism, and elucidates the conscious approach of Siam's leaders to European modernity. I situate Siam at the crossroads of colonized countries and sovereign, imperial powers, sharing some of the traits of both but reducible to neither. All cultural appropriations of modernity are unique to that culture, in which case Siam's distinctiveness refers to its own cultural and historical specificity rather than a radical and incomparable uniqueness that has so far characterized Siam's historiography. In addition, this systematic critique of the dynastic narrative does not exclude or render contradictory recognition of the astute decisions made by Siam's leadership. It is meant instead to make room for other protagonists and for equally powerful alternative narratives of Siam's history that do not incessantly reaffirm the centrality of the monarchy.

Although Siam's form of modernity is indebted to Europe, Siam did not adopt modern European forms of rule and institutions in their entirety. Siam's leaders resolutely refused some forms and consciously adopted others, all of which were transformed in the process. Siam's type of modernity was characterized by the following "alternative" forms over the course of the nineteenth and early twentieth centuries. Politically, a functionally divided, national bureaucratic administration developed in Siam after the 1890s, but

[44] Chakrabarty is aware that advocating an "alternative" modernity distinct from that of Europe might play into the hands of cultural nationalists, but he argues that this polarization is a result of "the pathologies of modernity itself." Chakrabarty, *Habitations of Modernity,* xvi.

personal patronage networks continued to dominate it. For example, Prince Ratburi received a thoroughly British education at the heart of empire—a law degree from Oxford—before he returned to Siam to serve as one of its first ministers of justice from 1897 to 1910. Under his fourteen-year direction, the system of justice in Siam was transformed into a uniform system of courts and codes that were thoroughly rationalized in the modern sense. When he resigned in 1910, out of anger, exhaustion, and resentment, Prince Ratburi's loyal entourage of nearly thirty senior judges retired with him.[45] The (temporary) mass exodus of a group of subordinate officials devoted to a senior official reflects the coexistence of "traditional" forms of political loyalty within the modern, impersonal bureaucracy.[46]

Another paradox of Siam's alternative political modernity is that its rationalized administrative apparatus did not lead to the creation of a representative form of government but, paradoxically, centralized absolute power in the monarchy, at least during the long reign of the modernizing monarch, King Chulalongkorn. Only after the conclusion of all major modernizing reforms was the absolute monarchy overthrown by a coup in 1932. In fact, some argue that King Chulalongkorn's reforms ultimately caused the demise of absolutism because the reforms led to the creation of a class of educated, nonroyal rivals.

Secularism is often considered a hallmark of modernity, which contends that governments must be religiously neutral in order to be inclusive of the entire population, regardless of their religious differences. However, in Siam modernity wedded reformed Theravada Buddhism to national identity and official praxis. Reformed Buddhism was a key feature of Siam's alternative modernity, as the annexation of Muslim Patani best exemplifies. Unlike European rulers of colonial states, Siam's leaders did not base their policy of noninterference in "native" religious practices on the ideology of rational secularism. Instead, a rationalized Theravada Buddhism accompanied Siam's reforms and imbued official spaces.[47] In the south (and elsewhere), Buddhist temples served as government training centers that, as such, unsurprisingly failed to attract the local Muslim population. Moreover, the same year that the government incorporated the southern Malay provinces into Siam proper it promulgated the 1902 Sangha Law, which elevated the Thammayut Buddhist sect as the royally patronized religion and standardized Thammayut practices across throughout the kingdom. The law required the appointment

[45] NA MR5 Yutitham 1 Miscellaneous Documents 67, "Kromaluang ratburi lae kharatchakan krasuang yutitham la-ok nuang duai ruang kromamun nara taeng bot lakhon wa priap-prei" (Prince Ratburi and Ministry of Justice officials resign on account of a slanderous play written by Prince Nara), 1908–11.

[46] All but one of the senior justices was required to resume his position.

[47] On reforms in the Buddhist tradition and the ascendancy of the Thammayut tradition, see Craig Reynolds, "The Buddhist Monkhood in Nineteenth Century Thailand," PhD diss., Cornell University, 1972.

of ecclesiastical officials to posts that corresponded to the civilian administrative hierarchy. The precise parallels between Buddhist ecclesiastical and state bureaucratic hierarchies reveal the degree to which Buddhism and state power were conflated.[48]

Buddhism, however, was itself "rationalized" in the sense that Theravada Buddhism after 1902 eschewed all practices deemed superstitious by Bangkok authorities. The *phumibun* or "holy man" rebellions, led by so-called millenarian Buddhist figures, which occurred in Siam's north and northeastern provinces in 1902, suggest the conflation of unorthodox Buddhist practices with political treason. A classified, "confidential" court case from 1896 also associates treason with unorthodox spiritual practices.[49] In that year, King Chulalongkorn personally recorded the verdict for a couple that hired a practitioner of magic to perform a ritual that would not only bind the king to their daughter but also harm a queen and a princess. The couple, Phraya (civil administration rank below Chao Phraya and above Phra) Nakhonchaisri, governor of Nakhonchaisri, and his wife, Talap, were one of more than 150 couples who had offered their daughter as a consort to King Chulalongkorn. When they discovered that their daughter was pregnant but that she would not receive the expected bequest of a larger residence within the royal compound, the parents hired a renowned practitioner of love spells (*mo fang rup roi*). He performed a ritual to magically bind King Chulalongkorn to their daughter. The ritual involved, among other sacred ingredients, cemetery dirt, incantations, the spirit of a harnessed soul (*phi phrai*), and transcriptions of the names of the monarch, the consort, a queen, and a princess.

A nursemaid in the household of Phraya Nakhonchaisri informed the government by petition of the suspicious activity because she feared harm would come to the royal family—in other words, she believed in the efficacy of the ritual. The governor, his wife, the practitioner of love spells, and all others involved were interrogated and found guilty of treason. King Chulalongkorn justified the verdict because the three defendants performed the ritual with malicious premeditation to cause destructive harm. They were guilty because they *believed* the ritual would work, not simply because they performed the ritual. While the king emphatically rejected the notion that these kinds of rituals had a genuine efficacy, he argued that the practitioners must be punished to deter others from imitating and following them. Phraya Nakhonchaisri and his wife received sixty lashes and life imprisonment, while the ritual specialist received ninety lashes, had his face tattooed to indicate his crime, and was sentenced to life imprisonment in the equivalent of soli-

[48] Ibid.

[49] NA R5 Ratchalekanukan [RL] 99 Bet talet 1/210 mai het 64/5, "Nangsu ratchakan ruang tham sa-ne lae tham wethamon tang tang" (Government Documents about Making Various Charms and Incantations), 1896. Loos, Archival Notebooks, vol. 6, 172–89. Officials at the National Archives allowed me to read and take notes on the case but would not allow me to make a photocopy of it.

tary confinement.[50] Siam integrated Buddhism with state practices but heavily penalized "superstitious" rituals that fell outside the bounds of rationalized Theravada Buddhism. Despite attempts to clamp down on unorthodox spiritual practices, they continued and have resurfaced in a reinvigorated form in the late twentieth century.

Economically, Siam's modernity also developed along its own trajectory. Siam was not transformed from a "feudal" agricultural system to an industrial economy or one based on the control of land. Aristocrats were not transformed into powerful (absentee) landlords in control of massive agricultural tracts. Instead, land holdings remained subdivided into small plots owned by individual peasant farmers well into the 1960s.[51]

Finally, socially Siam's leaders adopted European institutions of modernity such as a monogamous nuclear family structure, but only after nearly a century of agonizing debate. While this was legally endorsed, it was never socially or culturally enforced. Instead Siamese (and some foreign) officials advocated polygyny as an authentic Siamese practice, legitimated by their selective interpretation of Buddhism in contradistinction to Christian monogamy. Even after Siamese ceased to deploy Buddhism in defense of polygyny, they defended polygyny as a positive sign of their national distinction and uniqueness from Europe and America. The enduring practice of polygyny throughout the era of high imperialism and toleration of it after the promulgation of a law that allowed the registration of only one wife evidences a form of Siam's alternative modernity.

In sum, over this period in Siam, monarchical power was strengthened, Buddhism and state power were explicitly conflated, domestic agricultural assets remained fragmented, and the state and culture continued to endorse polygyny. Siam's statehood did not replicate European forms of modernity, yet it was nonetheless a modern state.

Methods and Sources

Siam's unequal status vis-à-vis imperial powers and its power to subjugate its own populations, especially Malay Muslims, through colonial models of law provide the framework for analyzing court disputes and national debates about polygyny, marriage, adultery, and divorce, which constantly index Siam's unique place in the global arena. *Subject Siam* brings social history to life through a study of these conflicts as they occurred between the 1850s and 1930s. Because Siam's modernity was initiated and shaped by law, legal watersheds mark the parameters of this study, which begins in 1855, when

[50] The king wrote, "Do not allow any opportunity for others to pay him respect or give him a chance to deceive others under any circumstances for the rest of his life."

[51] Pasuk and Baker, *Thailand,* 454–55.

King Mongkut signed the first of a series of unequal treaties with foreign powers, and ends in 1935, when the Siamese government promulgated the family law code. It was the last of the "modern" codes that Siam was bound, by treaty, to pass before foreign powers rescinded the unequal treaties. By 1939, overt forms of Siam's national subordination to foreign powers had been eliminated and Siam could claim full sovereignty. As if to mark this moment of independence, in 1939 Siam's prime minister, Field Marshall Phibun Songkhram, changed the name of Siam to Thailand—an appellation that means "land of the free."[52]

The following is the first book-length study that integrates court cases, as well as legal codes, into Siam's history, and among the first to analyze gender and family as categories with a history. As such the book is informed by, even when it cannot detail, thousands of archived trial records documenting the conflicts and concerns of lower class and elite women and men.[53] These cases reveal the social impact of institutional and codified legal transformations. They also demonstrate concretely how the legal system provided an opportunity for both the intensification of elite power and for new forms of agency by nonelites.

The study is linguistically dependent on central Thai and English, and on the accumulation of law codes and court documentation by Siamese courts. Disputes adjudicated in consular and international courts are not considered here, nor can the study incorporate Islamic court cases from the south because these records no longer exist. All case records from courts of the first instance, including those decided in the Islamic courts, are burned after ten years unless they have been appealed to higher-level courts. Although the surviving court cases come from all over the kingdom, they are apprehended and transcribed through the eyes of officials trained in the capital. Attention to this dynamic certainly helps avoid taking the official interpretation at its face value, yet it cannot compensate for the fact that access to the illiterate rural population is many steps removed. Relatedly, this is not a study of legal subjectivity. An examination of how litigants understood laws and engaged the legal system, if it were possible at all, would require a different approach to the sources. Finally, I deliberately selected court cases that privilege gender issues over other topics, including most blatantly Chinese ethnicity, because cases involving gender speak most directly to the importance of family law in constructing Siam as a modern, imperial, and colonized nation. Chinese subjects are overrepresented as litigants in Siam's court system and as such deserve to form the basis of a study in their own right.

[52] The term *Thai* is an ethnic marker and also refers to a language thus giving Siam's leaders the additional advantage of "monopolizing the nation semantically for Thai speakers." Craig Reynolds, ed., *National Identity and Its Defenders: Thailand, 1939–1989,* Monash Papers on Southeast Asia 25 (Clayton, Victoria: Monash University, Centre of Southeast Asian Studies, 1991), 4–5.

[53] For a more detailed study based on these court cases, see Loos, "Gender Adjudicated."

I rely on court cases that reached the Dika (Supreme Appeals) Court, which was the court of final appeal in Siam. Because litigants were successful in appealing their lawsuits to the highest court, they are in some sense unique cases. Given their potential atypicality, it is doubly difficult to argue that conclusions drawn from them apply broadly to Siamese society. Still, they are underutilized sources for their ability to access the lives, loves, and concerns of those—criminals, the lower classes, women, and others—who have not otherwise merited mention in Siam's histories that are concerned with elites and the normative political trajectories of the state. Admittedly, this study is also concerned with elites and key events in Siam's political history. However, unlike many histories of Siam, my analysis is not performed to the exclusion of nonelites. Instead, their stories percolate and surface throughout the book, which is the result of more than two years of research in Bangkok's archives and the Dika Court library where I read court documentation of the conflicts and concerns of Siam's subalterns. As such, this history begins to tap into those rich legal sources.

Finally, although I would enjoy providing an extensive review of the literature on gender, family, and law in Thai history, I cannot because that literature is in its infancy.[54] While no critical book-length examinations of family law and legal history exist, there are a number of studies on women's rights in Thai legal history. These typically explain the substantive and normative content of traditional laws on polygyny, modern laws on the family, and a narrative of political rights granted to women over time. Although informative, they do not critically assess the historical context or process by which the categories of "family," "wife," "man," and "woman" were transformed.[55]

[54] Two articles that critically assess the construction of family in Siam's legal history are Junko Koizumi, "From a Water Buffalo to a Human Being: Women and the Family in Siamese History," in *Other Pasts: Women, Gender, and History in Early Modern Southeast Asia,* ed. Barbara Watson Andaya (Honolulu: University of Hawai'i at Manoa, Center for Southeast Asian Studies, 2000), and Tamara Loos, "Issaraphap: The Limits of Individual Liberty in Thai Jurisprudence," *Crossroads* 12, no. 1 (1998): 35–75. Dararat Mettarikanond has written a superb but unpublished master's thesis on the prostitution tax in Siam's history and how it was used to build the modern infrastructure of the state. See her "Sopheni kap naiyobai rathaban thai pho so 2411–2503" (Prostitution in Thai Government Policy, 1868–1960), MA thesis, Chulalongkorn University, 1983.

[55] Chali Iamkrasin, "Sao phu su phua sithi satri samai ro si" (A Young Woman Who Fought for Women's Rights during the Reign of Rama 4), *Muang thai samai kon* (Thailand in the Past) (Bangkok: 1991), 31–37; Suphatra Singloka, ed., *Khruangmai haeng khwamrunkruang khu saphap haeng satri* (A Symbol of Civilization: The Status of Women) (Bangkok: Samakhom banthit satri thang kotmai haeng prathet thai, 1992); Siriphon Skrobanek, "Kan riakrong sithi satri khong ying thai (2398–2475)," (Thai Women's Feminist Movement [1855–1932]), *Satrithat* (Friends of Women magazine) 1, no. 3 (Aug.–Oct. 1983): 28–35; Sumalee Bumroongsook, *Love and Marriage: Mate Selection in Twentieth-Century Central Thailand* (Bangkok: Chulalongkorn University Press, 1995); Chittima Pornarun, "Kanriakrong sithi satri nai sangkhom thai pho so 2489–2519" (Demands for Women's Rights in Thai Society, 1946–1976), MA thesis, Chulalongkorn University, 1995; and Lamphan Nuambunlu, "Sithi lae nathi khong satri tam kotmai thai nai samai krung ratanokosin" (The Rights and Duties of Women according to Thai Laws during the Bangkok Period), MA thesis, Chulalongkorn University, 1976.

By contrast, there are a plethora of critical studies of law, family, and gender in most colonial settings, where the primary sources exist to support the writing of such histories. Christian missionaries and officious bureaucrats kept track of marriages, births, and wills. Christian missionaries kept baptismal records, to the great relief of historians. Colonial states, concerned with managing the social boundaries between ruler and ruled, often kept extensive marriage records. Both types of records were necessary pieces of evidence when individuals contested wills, since church- and state-sanctioned marriage determined the legitimacy of offspring and their right to inheritance.

None of these documents exist in Siam. In this Buddhist country where converts to Christianity came almost exclusively from among the immigrant Chinese population, baptismal or birth records for the vast majority of Siamese were not kept. Marriage, inheritance, and even land ownership fell outside the purview of the state and Buddhist Sangha, despite state attempts to regulate marriage and register land by the early twentieth century. Even today, after the state has implemented laws requiring the registration of marriage, only a small portion of the population does so. The dearth of source materials makes a study of family in praxis next to impossible and has resulted in a focus on prescriptive family law. Given these limitations, the court cases themselves become crucial documents of social history. I include them here to the extent that they exemplify the contradictory and ambiguous position of Siam in relationship to imperial powers and its own subject populations.

In the following pages I attempt to respond to the questions that dominate studies of Thailand without recentering European modernity or the monarchy. By focusing on law as the subject of Siam's history, I seek in the following chapters to end Siam's isolation as a "unique" case, to demote the role of the monarchy as the sole agent of history, and to show that Siam's modernity stubbornly retained features that distinguished it from Europe. The book comes to terms with this construction of Siam as eternally Thai/free by considering its lack of a comfortable "fit" within the dominant categories in colonial historiography: colonizer and colonized. Siam is both and neither, a position best exemplified through a study of family law as it was applied to Siam as a whole by imperial hierarchies, and as it applied to the Muslim provinces of the Malay Peninsula by Bangkok.

In this vein, the multiple meanings implied by the term *subject* in the title of *Subject Siam* are intended. Epistemologically, *subject* is a noun that refers to the active or agentic subject that observes, acts on, and imposes its will upon objects. Siam, as a political entity, constitutes this sense of a subject that relates in various asymmetrical ways to its objects, which include here Malay Muslims, Siam's lower classes, and European forms of modernity. Siam itself also became an object of knowledge, power, and Orientalist discourse, which brings up a second meaning of *subject*. Siam, as a polity and an object of knowledge, is *subjected* to European norms of civility, economic dependency, and legal penalties that discipline and reconstitute Siam in the process of creating knowledge about it. Indebted to Foucault's theories about knowledge as a form of power, this dual conception of *subject* allows this study to conceive of Siam as simultaneously an agent and object of knowledge.[56]

[56] Although Siam's leaders may have coalesced provisionally into a unified representation of Siam when negotiations with foreign powers demanded it, "Siam" was not a stable, unified, or monolithic subject. In other words, the precise constitution of Siam (and its subjects) is heterogeneous and continually being transformed as it interacts with ideologies, discourses, and institutions.

TWO

Transnational Justice

In 2003, Islamic judges (*dato yutitham*) in southern Thailand referred to an English language version of the *Minhaj et Talibin,* a thick manual of Islamic law written by Mahiudin Abu Zakaria Yahya ibn Sharif en Nawawi, as one reference source to use when settling Islamic family law disputes. The translation of *Minhaj et Talibin* is an astounding artifact of colonial history. Nawawi's Arabic text, a cornerstone of the legal literature of the Shafii school of Islamic law, was compiled sometime before the sixteenth century. This text was translated by a Dutchman named L. W. C. van den Berg into French but not literally, which according to the preface of the English-language version would have rendered the text "unintelligible." Instead it was paraphrased from several principal Islamic commentaries, two of which were originally written in the sixteenth century.[1] In 1882, van den Berg published the text in Batavia, the capital of the Netherlands East Indies, to enable European colonial officials and magistrates unfamiliar with Arabic to gain access to the legal literature of the Shafii school of Islam, which was practiced by most Southeast Asian Muslims. A Briton and former district judge in Singapore, E. C. Howard, then translated the French text into English in 1914 for the same reason.

This version found its way in 2003 into the hands of some of Thailand's Islamic judges, who also use Arabic, Malay, and Thai language texts in the

[1] E. C. Howard, "Prefatory Note," in Mahiudin Abu Zakaria Yahya ibn Sharif en Nawawi, *Minhaj et Talibin: A Manual of Muhammadan Law According to the School of Shafii,* trans. E. C. Howard (London: W. Thacker and Co., 1914).

course of their duties. It is profoundly ironic that dato yutitham in Thailand today might utilize Islamic law through the English translation of a French translation of an amalgamation of sixteenth-century Arabic commentaries on an Islamic law text compiled by a Dutchman for application in nineteenth-century Netherlands East Indies (Indonesia). More importantly, it indicates the lack of Thai language reference material that these judges can access as they decide cases that come before the Islamic family courts in southern Thailand. For example, a Thai language translation of Shafii law on marriage, inheritance, and related issues, compiled from dozens of Arabic and Malay language *kitab* (commentaries on the Quran and hadith) was not completed until 1941, nearly half a century after the establishment of Islamic family courts in the south.[2]

According to postcolonial theories about knowledge production, the translation into European languages of Islamic law helped colonial officials better contain and control Muslim populations. These theories seem inapplicable to Siam's system of rule in the south. There is no comparable "colonial" scholarship produced in Thai about the Muslim south. The translation efforts of Siam's officialdom pale in comparison to those of European colonials. Siamese officials, some of whom worked in the southern Malay Muslim areas for a decade or more, did not produce memoirs or handbooks about their experience, unlike their colonial counterparts next door in British Malaya. The distinction between Siamese imperial methods and those of the British is cast in high relief by a book by W. A. Graham published in 1908.[3] Graham wrote a "handbook of information" based on his experience as the resident commissioner and adviser for Siam's government in Kelantan, one of the areas on the Malay Peninsula loosely under the authority of Siam that eventually became part of British Malaya. Graham, a British citizen, had worked for the British government in India before his employment in Siam. His assistant in Kelantan was also a British citizen who had recently been "borrowed" by Bangkok from the British government of the Federated Malay States. Graham was the only "Siamese" official who published a classically colonial text on one of Siam's Malay states. The silence in the written record about the south limits its full integration into the following discussion of Siam's legal and transnational reform process.

The incongruities and global migrations of colonial translations and knowledge production abound. In chapter 2 I explore the ironies and transnational trajectories that accompanied the creation of Siam's modern laws

[2] Hadith refers to a secondary body of Islamic scripture attributed to the Prophet Muhammad that provides religious guidance and describes law and customs. Narong Siripachana, *Khwampenma khong kotmai itsalam lae dato yutitham* (The Origins of Islamic Law and Judges) (Bangkok: Khana kamakan klang itsalam haeng prathet thai, 1975), 21–37.

[3] W. A. Graham, *Kelantan, A State of the Malay Peninsula: A Handbook of Information* (Glasgow: James Maclehose and Sons, 1908).

and court system between 1892 and 1935. As a part of that long process, hundreds of foreigners such as Graham found employment with Siam's government, an experience about which many of them wrote. Their memoirs, handbooks, letters, and remaining archival records allow for a relatively rich account of their efforts in Siam compared to the lack of documentation of the experience of Siamese officials. This chapter appears, as a result, imbalanced because it details more biographical information about foreign legal experts than their more numerous Siamese counterparts. However, biographical details about the foreigners involved in legal reforms convey information about their attitudes regarding Siam's sovereignty because many of them also had experience working as officials in directly colonized countries. Including their accounts helps to qualify Siam's status as an independent kingdom.

The few Siamese about whom information has survived are members of the royal family, such as Prince Ratburi, who receive perhaps undue credit at the expense of their nonroyal Siamese counterparts. Unlike nonroyal Siamese reformers, about whom little information remains, Siamese royal figures participated often only indirectly in the legal reforms because of the intensive demands on their time in other areas of administration. The inclusion of stories about Siamese royal officials and foreign officials is not meant to reinforce the cultlike status of some royal figures or to replace Siamese royal heroes with Europeans and Americans. Their inclusion instead aims to underscore the deeply international and collaborative nature of the legal reform process.

Studies of legal transplantation or pluralism in colonized polities by Martin Chanock, Jean and John Comaroff, Dan Lev, Sally Merry, Michael Peletz, and others have demonstrated conclusively the centrality of law to the process of colonization and modern meaning making.[4] In Siam, law was no less central to its transformation into a colonial modern state. The most vibrant way to reveal this is by viewing the transculturation of Siam's law through an examination of legal experts. Siam's legal personnel, both Siamese and foreign, pursued careers that moved them to and from Siam, Europe, and colonized territories throughout the world. They drove the legal reform process in Siam

[4] Martin Chanock, *The Making of South African Legal Culture, 1902–1936: Fear, Favour and Prejudice* (Cambridge: Cambridge University Press, 2001), and *Law, Custom and Social Order: The Colonial Experience of Malawi and Zambia* (Portsmouth, N.H.: Heinemann, 1998); Jean and John L. Comaroff, *Of Revelation and Revolution,* vol. 1, *Christianity, Colonialism, and Consciousness in South Africa* (Chicago: University of Chicago Press, 1991), and *Of Revelation and Revolution,* vol. 2, *The Dialectics of Modernity on a South African Frontier* (Chicago: University of Chicago Press, 1997); Daniel Lev, "Judicial Institutions and Legal Culture in Indonesia," in *Culture and Politics in Indonesia,* ed. Claire Holt (Ithaca: Cornell University Press, 1972), and "Colonial Law and the Genesis of the Indonesian State," *Indonesia* 40 (Oct. 1985): 57–74; Merry, *Colonizing Hawai'i;* Sally Merry, "From Law and Colonialism to Law and Globalization: A Review Essay on Martin Chanock, *Law, Custom, and Social Order: The Colonial Experience in Malawi and Zambia,*" *Law and Social Inquiry* 28, no. 2 (2003): 269–90; and Peletz, *Islamic Modern.*

as well as the revisions of international treaties between Siam and foreign powers. Their legal expertise varied. Some were more familiar with colonial jurisprudence and others with law as it operated in Europe proper. They propelled the process by which Enlightenment-based juridical concepts were translated into Siamese. They also constructed Siam's new legal order, replete with a centralized national court system and uniform procedural and substantive codes between the 1890s and 1930s.

Siam's prereform legal traditions and social hierarchies form the necessary background to the transformations that transpired over this forty-year period. The first section explicates prereform conceptions of the function of law and methods of administering justice. Siam's courts of law had been highly decentralized, much like the political and administrative systems in Siam prior to reforms. The systematization of law codes and courts transformed the meanings and value of law, which lost their sacral power through their administrative institutionalization. Siam's prereform jurisprudence was founded on a social and moral hierarchy that appears diametrically opposed to the Enlightenment ideals of the new system, yet nonetheless continued to inform Siam's modern laws. The second section addresses the history and historiography leading up to the 1855 Bowring Treaty, which inaugurated the "modern" era in Siam and Siam's entrance into the international family of nations on asymmetrical terms. The revolutionary transformations in Siam compelled by the Bowring and similar treaties set in motion domestic legal reforms, including the employment of foreigners and foreign-educated Siamese in the Ministry of Justice. These transnational figures and the colonial jurisprudence in which they traded form the subject matter of the third and forth sections of the chapter. The partial adoption of foreign legal concepts, institutions, and personnel by Siam's government constituted part of a larger effort to engage imperial powers on their own terms—an engagement that propelled Siam toward imperialism on its own borders.

The Sacred and Social Value of Law

In perhaps no other arena of Siamese society was the transformation in values and practices more all-encompassing or extreme than in law. The nineteenth century ushered in a new kind of treaty that pried open Siam's capital and markets to European entrepreneurs who, unlike Chinese, South Asian, and other local traders, carried with them the threat of military intervention if trade conditions were unfavorable. Treaties, justified on the basis of European condemnation of Siam's existing law and backed by the threat of imperial force, initiated Siam's leaders into the so-called family of nations by coercing Siam to relate to imperial powers on European legal and commercial terms. In the nineteenth century, Britain most notoriously used brute force to coerce foreign countries to sign unequal treaties that ironically required these subject countries to obey the very set of international laws that Britain had broken by using extralegal military power.[5] Britain's violation of international law during the Opium War (1839–42) was a case in point, and one that Siam's leaders keenly observed. Unsurprisingly, concepts of law and justice functioned differently in Siam before the introduction of European regimes of law in the nineteenth century.

The received narrative of "traditional" Siamese jurisprudence was created at the moment of its modernity, so the terms and texts in which it is described often invoke the colonial discourse of the traditional and modern.[6] In fact, the scholarship on Siam's legal history falls into two major categories that parallel the division between the traditional and modern: studies of Siam's sacred legal text, the *Three Seals Laws,* said to have originated in the fourteenth century; and studies of law as it was "Westernized" during the reign of King Chulalongkorn (r. 1868–1910). Legal genealogies of the *Kotmai Tra Sam Duang* or *Three Seals Laws* (hereafter KTSD), Siam's single most important legal text, trace its origins to the Kingdom of Ayutthaya, which existed from the fourteenth to the eighteenth centuries. Similar to other sacred religious texts, the KTSD is a collection of religious and legal scriptures based in the Theravada Buddhist tradition, written in Thai and Pali during the Ayutthayan period by numerous individuals and supplemented with additional royal decrees over time.[7] While the majority of the text was purportedly written at different points prior to 1805, the earliest extant version comes from that year when the first monarch of the now-reigning Chakri dynasty had the KTSD rewritten or "cleansed" (*chamra*) of impurities and inconsistencies. The resulting recension of the KTSD arguably better reflects the legal philosophy of Rama I (r. 1782–1809) and successive Chakri kings than that of Ayutthayan monarchs or society. For this reason, most scholars rely on the KTSD to understand the system of justice prior to the massive reforms and codification process that began in the 1890s.

After Rama I purified the codes, royal scribes made three official copies, placing one in the royal bedchamber for the king's use, one in the court of justice for use by judges (*lukkhun*), and one in the royal library where the royal scribes would maintain it. In determining sentences, legal officials had to cite an official copy of the KTSD. Even if secondary copies had been transcribed, as some have proposed, there is no evidence that these copies were

[5] Liu, "Legislating the Universal," 127–64.

[6] But in Siam, as a result of its noncolonization, *tradition* is less often a disparaging term implying backwardness and more often one suggesting authenticity. This may seem a negligible difference in theories about colonial discourse, but it remains important nonetheless in Thai nationalism.

[7] Robert Lingat, *Prawatisat kotmai thai* (The History of Thai Law), vol. 2, ed. Charnvit Kasetsiri and Wikal Phongphanitanon (Bangkok: 1983), 58. For a discussion of the historiography of the KTSD, see Yoneo Ishii, "The Thai Thammasat (with a Note on the Lao Thammasat)," in *Laws of South-East Asia,* vol. 1, *The Pre-Modern Texts,* ed. M. B. Hooker (Singapore: Butterworth and Co.), 154–57.

disseminated to areas outside the royal capital. Implementation of the letter of the law, a foreign concept in any event, was also nearly impossible in practice. That is not to say that Siam was lawless, but that the regime of law did not operate primarily as an institution or set of codes emanating from Bangkok. The authority and jurisdiction of Bangkok's courts and codes likely decreased with distance, measured both in terms of geography and kinship ties, from the capital and its major ministries. In the Malay Muslim regions on the peninsula, Bangkok's laws did not apply until the twentieth century. Even in regions inhabited by populations that adhered to local varieties of Buddhism, local rulers resolved disputes and meted out punishment without reference to Bangkok. As late as 1904 in Battambang, a region contested by the Siamese and the French in Cambodia, the Battambang governor exercised complete legal authority over his population. Jens Westengard, an American working for Bangkok's government as assistant legal adviser in 1904, described the situation in Battambang in a letter to his wife as follows: "I see a province, which is in reality a little kingdom. At its head is a man who is certainly the Lord of his people. His rule has been almost absolute. Law? Yes, there is law—his word. But as for the law of the printed page, you can hardly find a line of it."[8] Although over thirty judicial courts existed, with largely overlapping functions, in Siam's various government ministries, their jurisdiction was limited geographically and otherwise.

Gauging the "implementation" of law and courts according to a uniform system of national law, however, misconstrues the point of Siam's KTSD. The existence of only three copies of the KTSD evidences the law's inaccessibility and suggests that the text served a sacred function as part of the royal regalia. From the 1780s until the 1880s, Siam's Buddhist kings dispensed justice, or *thamma,* as a function of their position as monarch. In theory, the king embodied morality as did the judges and legal magistrates throughout the kingdom. Justice, accordingly, sprang from the laws of a universal, moral truth to which the king, judges, and other representatives of the king had access by virtue of their position rather than by virtue of their application of legal codes to case "facts." As a result, all appeals of decisions necessarily impugned the judge of the original suit, who would be personally penalized if the next court overturned his decision.[9]

The KTSD also served a symbolic and moral purpose in nineteenth-century Siamese society. It is in the KTSD that scholars have located the template for a social hierarchy of enormous complexity known as the *sakdina*

[8] Jens Westengard to Rebecca Westengard, 16 Sept. 1904, Papers of Jens Iverson Westengard, Harvard Law School Library, Box 1, Folder 4.

[9] From Prince Phichit Prichakon's article on justice, as translated and paraphrased by David Engel, *Law and Kingship in Thailand during the Reign of King Chulalongkorn,* Michigan Papers on South and Southeast Asia No. 9 (Ann Arbor: University of Michigan, Center for South and Southeast Asian Studies, 1975), 82.

system, which structured a subject's relationship to the state and powerful individuals. The relative social position of every individual was specified in numerical units, called *sakdina,* which translates as "field power" or control over the rice field.[10] The sakdina units, which the king allotted to each of his subjects according to rank and position, may have corresponded to the units of land and number of people to which the subject was entitled.[11] Theoretically, the higher an individual's sakdina, the larger the individual's retinue of subordinate individuals and the more land possessed by that individual.

Scholars concur that the sakdina system recognized, and thereby perpetually reproduced, four main categories of people: royalty (*chao*), aristocrats (*khunnang*), commoners (*phrai*) and slaves (*that*).[12] Each category carried with it privileges that increased commensurably with an individual's standing. For instance, royalty possessed sakdina ranks ranging from eight hundred to one hundred thousand, and were subject to courts and laws specifically created for them. Aristocrats, or khunnang, are defined as those born into a family that has high and mid-ranking non-royal officials who obtain four hundred to thirty thousand sakdina marks. They never had to perform corvée labor and male members of these families were usually assigned prestigious and lucrative positions in the government bureaucracy. Phrai or commoners, who were subject to corvée labor and military conscription, formed the majority of the population and made their living as farmers. They never possessed a sakdina ranking over three hundred or under five. *That,* glossed as *slaves,* occupied the lowest rungs on the sakdina ladder, had little recourse to the law, and held a sakdina rank of no more than five.[13] Everyone from slave to princess could be compared and evaluated by the state based on their relative sakdina ranking.

In a polity where authority was rooted in a Buddhist conception of kingship, Siam's justice was (and is) saturated with Buddhism, though the precise meanings of Buddhism shifted according to context. In the nineteenth century, a Buddhist cosmography justified the sakdina hierarchy, so it follows that the nominally ethnically, religiously, and gender-neutral social status cate-

[10] David K. Wyatt, *Thailand: A Short History* (New Haven: Yale University Press, 1984), 73; Thanh-dam Truong, *Sex, Money and Morality: Prostitution and Tourism in South-East Asia* (London: Zed Press, 1990), 143.

[11] H. Q. Quaritch Wales, *Ancient Siamese Government and Administration* (New York: Paragon Book Reprint, 1965), 49–50; Akin Rabibhadana, *The Organization of Thai Society in the Early Bangkok Period, 1782–1873,* Data Paper 74 (Ithaca: Cornell University, Southeast Asia Program, 1969), 28–29.

[12] The translation of these categories into English is misleading because of their grounding in the European feudal system. They cannot be applied transparently to the Siamese context without eradicating the many differences that existed between the two systems (see Reynolds, "Feudalism as a Trope"). For an interesting take on the European feudal system from a leading Thai writer, see Khukhrit Pramoj's *Farang sakdina* (European Feudalism) (Bangkok: Kao-na Publishers, 1973).

[13] The applicability of the translation of *that* as "slave" has been treated by Andrew Turton, "Thai Institutions of Slavery," in *Asian and African Systems of Slavery,* ed. James L. Watson (Berkeley: University of California Press, 1980), 251–292.

gories of chao, khunnang, phrai, and that, were also subtly but profoundly constituted by religious and other social hierarchies.[14] Religious difference, within which was often embedded ethnic difference, may ultimately have functioned as the most basic form of othering in the KTSD, as suggested by a royal proclamation issued in the 1660s and reissued in the 1770s. In it, reigning monarchs attempted to delimit, by controlling women's sexuality, those who fell under royal protection to include Buddhists but not religious others. The decree states:

> These days, *khaek* [here, it could mean Muslims, Middle Easterners, and/or South Asians], French, British, *khula* [Thai Yai or Shan], Malays, [and others from] foreign countries, have come under royal protection in large numbers. However, from now on it is prohibited for Thai, Mon, or Lao to engage in clandestine sexual intercourse with *khaek,* French, British, *khula,* or Malays who adhere to a misguided faith.[15]

One characteristic linking Thai, Mon, and Lao populations was their shared faith in Buddhism, suggesting that the primary division between "us" and "them" in early modern Ayutthaya was religious, which often mapped onto ethnic differences.[16] This helps explain why the decree did not single out the Chinese as a potential threat, even though they likely comprised the largest ethnically non-Thai sojourner group in the kingdom. The Chinese typically adopted local religious practices.

The decree operated along gendered lines as well because it prohibited Thai, Mon, and Lao women, not men, from engaging in sexual relations with men who adhered to other religions.[17] Siam's port cities, like others in early modern Southeast Asia, served as temporary residences for foreign trading populations, which were almost exclusively male.[18] Intimate relationships that developed in this context produced children whose loyalties were suspect in the king's estimation.[19] This decree may have been an aberration in

[14] Reynolds's article substantiates the link between Buddhist cosmography and the social hierarchy. Craig Reynolds, "Buddhist Cosmography in Thai History, with Special Reference to Nineteenth-Century Culture Change." *Journal of Asian Studies* 35, no. 2 (Feb. 1976): 203–19.

[15] *Kotmai tra sam duang* (*Three Seals Laws;* hereafter KTSD), vol. 5, matra 55 (Bangkok: Thammasat University Press, 1938), 298.

[16] See also Yoneo Ishii, "Thai Muslims and the Royal Patronage of Religion," *Law & Society Review* 28, no. 3 (1994): 455.

[17] That it operated along gendered lines is indicated by the clause that pledged the execution of individuals who engaged in these illicit unions if authorities "are able to investigate and apprehend the *woman.*" The Thai reads "phicharana sup sao chap dai." KTSD, vol. 5, matra 55: 298. In addition, her relatives were held culpable for not preventing the union. It is unclear whether the male (foreign) partner was also subject to this law.

[18] Barbara Andaya, "From Temporary Wife to Prostitute," *Journal of Women's History* 9, no. 4 (Winter 1998): 11–34; Dhiravat na Pombejra, "Ayutthaya at the End of the Seventeenth Century," in *Southeast Asia in the Early Modern Era,* ed. Anthony Reid (Ithaca: Cornell University Press, 1993), 250–72.

[19] The king feared that children produced by such a union would side with the father's religious

a kingdom that has been described as comparatively inclusive of ethnic others, or it may indicate that inclusiveness was defined on the basis of religious and customary practices.

Gender-based distinctions are relatively easy to discern compared to religious and ethnic ones. The sociolegal system as a whole pivoted primarily on gender and status; within each status category, a second hierarchy based on the gender of the individual clearly operated. It privileged the power of fathers and husbands over that of mothers and wives.[20] Distinctions between social groups—whether religious, ethnic, or status based—were maintained by laws that policed the boundaries of elite female sexuality and, to a lesser extent, the sexuality of lower class men.[21] Because social rank or sakdina status operated patrifilially—a father's rank passed to his children—a woman was pressured to marry her social equal or better. The legal system reflected this principle by regulating the sexuality of women as a way to preserve her social rank, which was in turn important for the prestige of her entire family. In fact, until the creation of the Penal Code in 1908, marrying below one's status was explicitly criminalized for chao and khunnang women. One of the most reprehensible sex crimes entailed the sexual union between an elite woman and a lower status man, an act that stripped her and their children of rank since she married down, as it were.[22] The act of transgressing social status lines by marrying down for women was considered a form of adultery (*chu*), which might be better translated here as familial infidelity or treason, because the crime of adultery applied even if she were single. By contrast, the laws encouraged relationships between elite men and lower ranking women.

Although scholars argue over whether the sakdina number represented land, people, or both, they agree that it nevertheless served as a technique to evaluate the relative legal privilege and political power of individuals.[23] The KTSD defined crime and apportioned penalties according to the sakdina ranking and gender of the perpetrator relative to that of the injured party, re-

---

loyalties during a war. Since at least the 1660s, loyalty to the Buddhist monarch had been traced through one's father, which suggests that women could relate to the state only indirectly through their male relatives.

[20] This is explained in detail in Loos, "Gender Adjudicated," 26–34.

[21] For a superb and hard-hitting critique of studies about the role of women in maintaining social hierarchies, see Sherry Ortner, "The Virgin and the State," in her *Making Gender: The Politics and Erotics of Culture* (Boston: Beacon Press, 1996), 43–58.

[22] Loos, "Issaraphap"; Hong Lysa, "Of Consorts and Harlots"; Hong Lysa, "Palace Women at the Margins of Social Change: An Aspect of the Politics of Social History in the Reign of King Chulalongkorn," *Journal of Southeast Asian Studies* 30, no. 20 (Sept. 1999): 310–24.

[23] Akin Rabibhadana argues that "manpower," not land, was the most valuable resource and indicator of wealth, prestige, and political power before 1873. Akin Rabibhadana, *Organization of Thai Society in the Early Bangkok Period*. Akin's study of the operation of the sakdina system and its implications for benign power relations contrasts the work of another scholar, Chit Phumisak, who drew negative conclusions about power relations from the sakdina system. On Chit's hypothesis, see Reynolds, "Feudalism in the Thai Past," 149–69.

flecting the tendency of the law to perpetuate status distinctions rather than to criminalize categorically types of offenses. For example, the KTSD did not categorically define physical assault as an offense, but alternately penalized or legitimized assault depending on the relative social positions of the perpetrator and victim.[24] The same act could be encouraged in one social circumstance and penalized by death in another, depending on the status and gender of the individuals involved.[25] Criminal acts in Siam prior to the late nineteenth-century legal reforms were a complex mix of the social location of the individuals involved and the degree to which the act upset the status quo. This fluid definition of crime illustrates that Siam's social system stressed hierarchy and group-based subjects rather than equality, uniformity, and individuals, in contrast to the European Enlightenment *ideal* of inherent individual equality.

The KTSD, despite its comprehensive delineation of social rankings that were used in court disputes among elites, could not systematically control the behavior of the general population. Rather, the social hierarchy was likely implicitly based on the explicit sakdina hierarchy delineated in the KTSD, and it probably applied more intensely the closer one was to Bangkok. The thirty-odd courts that existed in the kingdom prior to the overhaul of the legal system in the nineteenth century accepted cases on the basis of the sakdina status of the individuals involved and the official ministry to which they were attached through their patronage networks. One early twentieth-century observer who wrote a legal history of Siam, Briton P. W. Thornely, painted a Furnivallian portrait of plural societies in seventeenth-century Ayutthaya in which foreigners lived in small communities settled in particular locations. He suggested, without much evidence, that these groups maintained their own laws and customs inside their respective boundaries.[26] However, this kind of plural legal system, in which the king allowed separate communities to police themselves, hardly amounts to the institutionalized and systematic apparatus of extraterritoriality. Instead, it blends smoothly into the political system extant in the kingdom until the nineteenth century. The

[24] For instance, law and social custom authorized class and gender superiors, including slave owners, parents, husbands, and teachers, to beat slaves, children, wives, and students, respectively. However, the law considered a beating between two individuals whose relationship fell outside these established hierarchical bonds as assault, which meant it could form the basis of a legal claim.

[25] For example, in the KTSD, the same act of sexual intercourse between a man and woman incurred a gamut of penalties depending on rank and relationships. Sexual intercourse between a royal concubine and any male other than the king resulted in the execution of the two individuals; between an unmarried woman in the royal family and a man of lower rank could result in the life imprisonment and flogging of both parties; between a monk and a single woman resulted in three to seven years in prison; between a commoner man and an unmarried commoner woman without the permission of her parents resulted in a fine, unless the man formally apologized to them, in which case the couple would be considered married; and between any male slave owner and his female slave resulted in an improvement in her status and eventual freedom if she bore him children.

[26] P. W. Thornely, *The History of a Transition* (Bangkok: Siam Observer Press, 1923), 38–39.

closer a settlement was to the royal capital the more likely the monarch's courts operated and his decrees were enforced. In areas that ruled themselves semiautonomously, a combination of the local lord's "word" and customary law applied. This was true in the Malay states on the peninsula where rajas (*chao muang* in Thai) resolved disputes either alone, without the assistance of written codes, or in consultation with *to-kali,* experts in relevant Islamic scriptures.[27] Most individuals, regardless of where they resided, likely resolved their differences outside the official space of the courts, which were notoriously expensive and "corrupt" by the logic of modern law.

The conception of law as sacred and its consequent sequestering in the bedchambers of monarchs and hall of justice gradually changed as a result of encounters with technologies and ideologies propagated by American missionaries, who brought the first printing press that used Siamese type to Siam in the 1830s. Attempts to print the first copies of the KTSD by American Presbyterian missionary Dan Beach Bradley and a young Siamese noble, Nai Mot Amatayakul, failed. Rama III (r. 1824–1851), apparently operating on the notion that the KTSD was a sacred text legitimizing the monarchy, ordered all copies confiscated and allegedly burned. Rama III's successor, King Mongkut, or Rama IV (r. 1851–68), allowed Dr. Bradley to publish the KTSD in two volumes in 1862 and 1863. The volumes became popularly known as the two-volume laws (*kotmai song lem*) and enjoyed ten reprints, the last of which was published in 1896.[28] When provincial judges mentioned codes at all, they referred to Bradley's law books in their decisions, indicating ironically that his was the authoritative version, enjoying greater currency than the royal edition of the KTSD. Even the *Government Gazette* (*Ratchakitchanubeksa*), established in 1858 as the vehicle through which the government circulated laws, decrees, announcements, and domestic news to a growing reading public, published various laws from the Bradley edition between 1875 and 1879.[29] According to legal scholar Yoneo Ishii, the Bradley version was "widely circulated and eventually became an indispensable reference book for every Siamese jurist, especially during the transitional period prior to the total overhaul of the Siamese codes in the twentieth century."[30]

It is significant that an American, Bradley, succeeded in printing the KTSD under King Mongkut, while a Siamese noble had been punished for the same act decades earlier under the previous king. Much had changed between the two reigns regarding the concept of law, including most importantly the signing of the Bowring Treaty in 1855. In the wake of this and similar treaties,

[27] Somchot, *Kan-patirup,* 75–77.

[28] Ishii, "Thai Thammasat," 151–52.

[29] Mattani Mojdara Rutnin, *Modern Thai Literature* (Bangkok: Thammasat University Press, 1988), 9; Ishii, "Thai Thammasat," 152.

[30] Ishii, "Thai Thammasat," 152.

the KTSD was no longer a source of legitimacy and sacral power that had to be secluded, but was transformed into a source of applicable and practical law. For the first time in history, any literate individual who had enough money to purchase a copy of the *Government Gazette* could read portions of the KTSD, or have it read to them.[31] The publication of laws in the newspapers placed law in the public domain, distributing a uniform code more widely than ever before.[32] At the same time, however, the new laws promulgated by the monarch increasingly forced the KTSD into the background as an obsolete tool by the late nineteenth century. Ironically, at the very moment the KTSD enjoyed its widest dissemination it was transformed from a powerful and sacred text into a passive object of historical study.[33]

Imperialism and the Regime of Modern Law

The KTSD's obsolescence was a direct consequence of the legal treaties signed with European and American powers. Siam's first commercial treaty with a European power since it had banished Europeans from the country in the late 1600s was signed with Great Britain in 1826. Prior to the 1826 Burney Treaty, restrictive trading practices employed by Siam's kings purposefully discouraged European merchants from trading in Siam because Siam's leaders saw what trade had led to in India.[34] They conceded to signing a treaty with Britain, which received little more than the gift of opening diplomatic relations with Siam. Historian Walter Vella notes that the Burney Treaty was remarkable for its "absolute reciprocality on every point."[35] It

[31] Reading aloud in public spaces was a common method of disseminating information to an illiterate public. To the extent that the population was informed of changes in government policy, laws, court verdicts, and so on, it occurred by reading these missives aloud to a gathering.

[32] Prince Damrong, brother to King Chulalongkorn and the force behind the massive administrative overhaul, wrote that all officials and judges "depended on reading the *ratchakitchanubeksa* newspaper" to administrate the country. Prince Damrong Rajanubhap, *Laksana kanpokkhrong prathet siam tae boran* (The Administration of Siam from Ancient Times) (Bangkok, 1933), 116.

[33] A study of this process would necessarily have to examine the work of European "Orientalist" legal scholars, such as G. E. Gerini and Robert Lingat, to take two extremes. Gerini's 1895 article on Siam's trials by ordeal was no doubt calculated to produce and justify feelings of repugnance toward Siamese jurisprudence in the European and American population in Siam just as Siam was reforming its legal system to get rid of extraterritoriality. Lingat's scrupulous historical work on Siamese jurisprudence and especially the KTSD, by contrast, is lauded by Thai scholars today for documenting aspects of Siam's legal past that may not have otherwise been preserved. Charnvit Kasetsiri and Wikal Phongphanitan, "Khamnam" (introduction) to *Prawatisat kotmai thai* (Thai Legal History), by Robert Lingat (Bangkok: Foundation for Sociological and Anthropological Texts, 1983). G. E. Gerini, "Trial by Ordeal in Siam and the Siamese Law of Ordeals," *Asiatic Quarterly* (1895); Robert Lingat, *L'influence Indoue dans l'ancien droit siamois* (Paris: Domat-Monchretien, 1937), and *The Classical Law of India* (Berkeley: University of California Press, 1973).

[34] Walter Vella, *Siam under Rama III* (Locust Valley, N.Y.: J. J. Augustin, 1957), 115–17.

[35] Vella, *Siam under Rama III,* 120. Burney, an envoy for the British in India, remained in Siam long enough to learn Thai and to use it in the negotiations, which may well have set the stage for a more reciprocal treaty.

promised mutual respect for each country's boundaries, denial of the right to import opium, denial of extraterritoriality, restriction of royal monopolies, establishment of a single duty on ships in place of myriad fees, and a vague definition of British and Siamese spheres of influence on the Malay Peninsula.[36] The Siamese spheres of influence included Kedah, Kelantan, Patani, and Trengganu, but the definition of Siam's rights within those spheres was more complicated. For example, Siam could not occupy Kelantan or Trengganu and pledged not to interfere in British commercial enterprises there. The fledgling competition between the British and the Siamese governments over these contested territories was complicated from the beginning by the ambiguity of the Burney Treaty.

By the 1840s, Siam's leaders had reimposed trade restrictions and had introduced tax farms, which operated indirectly like the royal monopolies that the Burney Treaty had banned. For a number of reasons, the restrictive attitude in Bangkok changed in the early 1850s, which led to the Bowring Treaty. Siam's trade with China experienced an irreparable slump as a result of the Opium War and Taiping Rebellion. Private European traders were intent on opening Siam as a market for Indian opium, and a new king in Siam, supported by a group of Siamese who desired expanded trade with European powers, had ascended the throne.[37] King Mongkut, backed by the powerful Bunnag family, signed the Bowring Treaty with Britain in 1855.

The Bowring Treaty typically marks the beginning of "modern" Siam in most histories. Normative accounts of Siam's history suggest that King Mongkut was forced to open Siam to international trade by Great Britain, which sent Sir John Bowring to negotiate the protection of British merchants and trading interests. Far from being forced to open Siam in 1855, however, Siam's elites had voluntarily initiated many of the changes *before* they invited Bowring to Bangkok, where Bowring simply ratified these changes and required some new reforms.[38] The Bowring Treaty restricted import duties to 3 percent and export taxes to 5 percent on all items except opium and bullion, allowed British subjects to reside and own land in restricted areas around

[36] Ibid. For more on the negotiations, see *The Burney Papers,* 4 vols. (Bangkok: Committee of the Vajiranana National Library, 1910), esp. vol. 2, 257–87.

[37] Pasuk and Baker, *Thailand,* 101–2.

[38] James Ingram notes that Mongkut was open-minded about the West: "He seems to have been convinced that Siam would benefit from closer relations with the Western nations, and he deliberately and voluntarily sought to develop such relations." King Mongkut voluntarily reduced certain duties on ships calling at Bangkok, removed the ban on rice exports, and abolished some government monopolies *before* the Bowring Treaty and without request of anything in return. James Ingram, *Economic Change in Thailand 1850–1970* (Stanford: Stanford University Press, 1971), 33 and n. 73. Pasuk Phongpaichit and Chris Baker have also upended the normative understandings of King Mongkut and Siam as victimized by the imposition of unequal treaties. They make clear that a segment of Siam's elite (the economically and politically powerful Bunnag family) had political and economic motivations to invite Bowring to Siam in 1855 to sign a treaty that merely endorsed changes they had already initiated. King Mongkut was merely one player among royal and aristocratic factions. Pasuk and Baker, *Thailand,* 102–3.

Bangkok, allowed British subjects freedom of religion, reduced tariffs on British vessels to match the tariffs on Chinese and Siamese ships in order to place all ships on an equal commercial footing, and granted extraterritoriality to British subjects.[39] Unlike the Burney Treaty, it did not mention the border issues between Siam and the British on the Malay Peninsula.

The second treaty clause delineated extraterritoriality protections. Extraterritoriality divided jurisdiction over the population residing in Siam between subjects of Siam, who were under the authority of Siam's law and courts, and the subjects of foreign powers that had extraterritorial privileges, in which case the laws of that foreign power applied. Individual subjects of treaty powers received this protection in all civil and penal cases in which they were defendants, and in all cases in which both parties to the suit were foreign subjects of countries with exterritorial rights.

Treaties similar to that signed with Britain were soon repeated with fourteen nations between 1856 and 1899 (figure 1).[40] Because the treaties ended all state monopolies except for the collection of taxes, the sale of opium, and the operation of gambling establishments, it catalyzed a revolutionary change in state finances in Siam. The country moved from a nearly self-sufficient economy to one that saw marked growth in the volume and value of exports and imports, the gradual and geographically uneven monetization of the economy, and rice rapidly becoming Siam's dominant export commodity.[41]

Major but gradual shifts occurred over the next century in the basis of Siam's economy, and little immediate change occurred in administrative, political, or judicial arenas in large part because King Mongkut was beholden to other elites for his position as monarch.[42] The "revolutionary" changes in law and administration aimed at ridding Siam of the Bowring Treaty impositions began in the 1890s, nearly forty years after Siam's leaders "invited" Bowring to Siam. Despite the agency with which Siam's leaders may have acted in this regard, many scholars have interpreted the Bowring and similar treaties as initiating a period of indirect colonization in Siam.

Siam's sovereignty was qualified economically and legally. Plural legal systems, including consular and international courts that existed as the insti-

[39] The Thai and English language versions of the Bowring Treaty can be found in *Anuson nganphraratchathan phloengsop nai somsak chanthanasiri* (Cremation Volume for Nai Samsak Chanthanasiri) (Bangkok: 2000), 121–70. For a detailed explanation of the treaty provisions, see Ingram, *Economic Change,* 33–35.

[40] The data comes from Ingram, *Economic Change,* 35.

[41] Rice cultivation was the chief occupation of 80 to 90 percent of the population, and rice exports represented 60 to 70 percent of total exports between 1850 and 1950. The century saw a twenty-five-fold increase in rice production and a two-fold population increase. Cultivated rice land grew from about 5.8 million *rai* (2.25 *rai* = 1 acre) of land in an 1850 estimate to 34.6 million *rai* in 1950. Most of the rice cultivation was done by individual Thai smallholders, not by the large plantations characteristic of colonial economies. See Ingram, *Economic Change,* 36–43.

[42] See David Wyatt, *The Politics of Reform in Thailand: Education in the Reign of King Chulalongkorn* (New Haven: Yale University Press, 1969).

United Kingdom	1855	Norway	1868
United States	1856	Belgium	1868
France	1856	Italy	1868
Denmark	1858	Austria-Hungary	1869
Portugal	1859	Spain	1870
Netherlands	1860	Japan	1898
Germany	1862	Russia	1899
Sweden	1868		

Figure 1. Unequal Treaties with Siam

tutional manifestation of extraterritoriality, operated in directly colonized countries as well as in noncolonized countries such as Japan, China, and Siam. Yet the exercise of these rights varied. As noted by Hong Lysa, extraterritoriality rights were exercised in a virtually unrestricted fashion in China (and in directly colonized countries), whereas foreigners in Siam had to take the local government into account.[43] Compared to native rulers of other colonized and "indirectly colonized" countries, Siam's leaders maintained a high degree of agency over domestic transformations but less agency over international negotiations. How this agency is defined and who receives credit for it—Siam's kings, Franco-British rivalry, foreign legal advisers, historical contingency—remain subjects of intense historiographic debate.[44]

The significance of legal reform as the arena in which Siam's leaders had to prove the country's modernity was not immediately apparent because the European community in Bangkok was quite small. Few foreign legal subjects invoked extraterritoriality clauses, which were originally intended to protect white Europeans and Japanese nationals. However, by the turn of the century, Chinese, Cambodian, Burman, Javanese, Laotian, and even Siamese were able to claim extraterritorial status with foreign powers either because they worked for foreign employers, were subjects of foreign powers with treaty protections, or had illegally purchased their extraterritorial status on the black market.[45] Moreover, with each increase in British or French territory along

[43] Hong Lysa, "'Stranger within the Gates,'" 336, 351.

[44] Agency presumes a unified subject, which was far from the case in Siam after the signing of the Bowring Treaty. Nearly all historians of Siam (myself included), regardless of their stance on the dynastic narrative, discuss the conscious agency of Siamese in "selectively borrowing," adapting, or localizing foreign concepts, material objects, technologies, and institutions. It remains nearly impossible to qualify the degree to which Siamese leaders exercised choice—whether it was strategic, compelled, consciously enthusiastic, or hegemonically dictated by the configurations of modernity—because it suggests the possibility that Siam's elites were "'colonized in consciousness.'" Reynolds, "On the Gendering," 263. Hegemony as a concept has not gained purchase in Thai historiography because admitting it would deny agency, power, and control to Siamese royal leadership and hence rob them of their legitimacy past and present.

[45] Hong Lysa, "Extraterritoriality in Bangkok," 133; Thornely, *History of a Transition,* 100–101.

Siam's borders, the number of their Asian subjects similarly increased, quickly outnumbering the white European and Japanese populations. The Siamese government renegotiated treaties several times with the British (1874, 1883, 1909) and the French (1904, 1907) to establish greater Siamese control over the Asian subjects claiming extraterritorial protections. With each negotiation, Siam typically had to concede territories in the east and northeast to the French and in the south to the British.[46]

In addition to treaty revisions, the Siamese government set about the task of ridding the country of all remaining vestiges of extraterritoriality by radically reforming the government in the 1890s. In 1892, King Chulalongkorn initiated comprehensive reforms in governmental institutions that he had introduced in 1888 in his now classic "Speech Explaining the Governmental Reforms."[47] His speech invoked a vision of Siam's governmental "tradition" against which his own rule would be measured.[48] Its telos was the production of an independent, modern kingdom modeled on a rational bureaucratic state. Though he used a multiplicity of terms to describe the past rather than simply invoking the term *traditional,* the monarch, in effect, created a sense of the traditional as an accumulation of negative administrative characteristics from which Siam had to distance itself. King Chulalongkorn purposefully characterized the existing Siamese administration as muddled, inefficient, overlapping, chaotic, hopelessly confused, corrupt, disorderly, and altogether untidy. The import of his speech was not its accurate description of judicial and administrative practices but its creation of an image of Siam's existing government as backward, unwieldy, and disorderly in the context of regional imperialism. He did so in order to accentuate positively his own massive reform effort in Siam in the eyes of both foreigners and Siam's elite classes, on whose support he depended to pass his reforms. By marking the existing administration as traditional and backward, King Chulalongkorn effectively distinguished himself from this outdated system, justified to other elites the dire need to institute revolutionary reforms, and positioned the reformers on the side of modernity.

King Chulalongkorn's construction of a dichotomous, ideological divide between traditional and modern Siam also resonated with imperial conceptions of the kingdom. In fact, the monarch's historic speech sounds suspiciously similar to imperialistic rhetoric about progress and civilization. Foreign powers justified their insistence on the continuing need for extraterritoriality "protections" because Siam's system of justice was barbarous in their eyes. He targeted the system of justice in particular because it was

[46] For a thorough description of this process, see Thornely, *History of a Transition.*

[47] King Chulalongkorn, Phraratchadamrat nai phrabatsomdet phrachulachomklao chaoyuhua, *Songthalaeng phraboromaratchathibai kaekhai kanpokkhrong phaendin* (Speech Explaining the Governmental Reforms) (Bangkok: Sophonphiphanthanakon, 1927) [hereafter *Songthalaeng*].

[48] King Prajadhipok, "Khamnam" (introduction) to *Songthalaeng,* 1.

administered by profit seekers "exploiting the fear and nervousness [of litigants]" rather than by people of integrity.[49] The state of justice had irreparably deteriorated like a rotting ship, with plugs continually inserted in newly formed holes. Now, the king emphasized, was the right time to replace the rotting timbers in Siam's ship of justice. These sweeping reforms reorganized Siam's administration into twelve functionally differentiated ministries, including the Ministry of Justice.

Siam's leaders reformed the indigenous legal system in order to establish sovereign authority within Siam's territorial boundaries over its inhabitants. The legal reforms offered a domestic strategy of control that helped Siam's leaders claim Siam's status internationally as fully sovereign. The extraterritoriality protections granted to foreign subjects in Siam required the creation of consular and international courts in addition to domestic courts. Foreign powers would, Siam's leaders came to believe, abolish extraterritoriality once Siam reformed the court system by promulgating a modern penal code, a civil code, criminal and civil procedural codes, and a law on the organization of the courts. Beginning in 1892, Siam's courts were eliminated, reorganized, or created anew. Although King Chulalongkorn initiated these reforms, he did not dictate how the juridical system and substantive codes would be reformed.

Siam's restructured court system had jurisdiction over all individuals living within the borders of Siam who could not claim foreign subject status with one of the many treaty powers that had extraterritorial privileges in Siam. In Bangkok and the provinces, the reforms established three basic levels of courts for the adjudication of disputes between individuals under Siamese (not foreign) jurisdiction: a court of first instance, the Appeals Court, and the Dika (Supreme Appeals) Court (figure 2). Reforms reduced the thirty-odd courts spread throughout various ministries to seven new courts and several misdemeanor or magistrate (*borisapha*) courts in the capital to handle minor cases.[50] Provincial courts in the provincial capitals, cities, and districts were established gradually as need arose and budget allowed.

Cases typically moved from a court of first instance to the Appeals Court and then to the Dika Court, although there were exceptions to this general rule.[51] In Bangkok, the courts of first instance included a civil court, a criminal court, and several misdemeanor courts. After the promulgation of the 1896 Law on Provincial Courts, several types of courts were gradually es-

[49] King Chulalongkorn, *Songthalaeng,* 32.

[50] David Engel, a scholar of Thai legal history, presents a lucid account of the transformation in Siam's legal structure in his *Law and Kingship,* 59–90.

[51] For instance, if the defendant involved was a subject of a foreign power, the case was remanded to a consular or international court. If a royal family member or someone connected to the Ministry of the Royal Household was involved in a case, the case was adjudicated by the Ministry of the Royal Household Court.

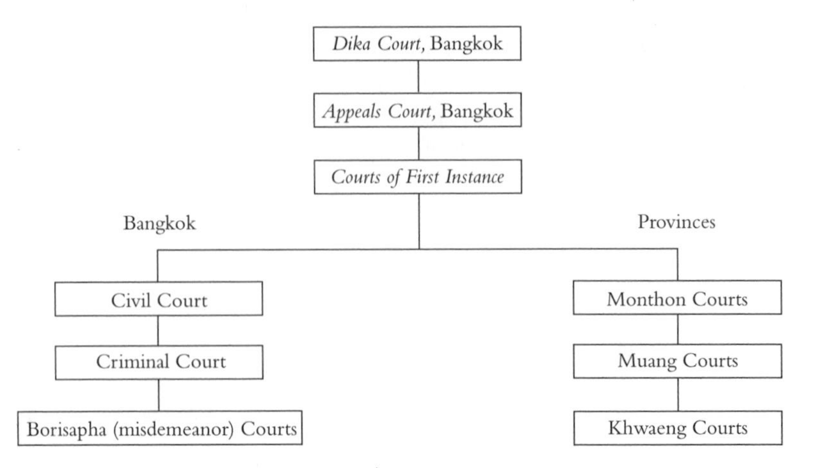

Figure 2. Reformed Organization of Siam's Courts
Source: This figure is adapted from David Engel, *Code and Custom in a Thai Provincial Court,* Association for Asian Studies Monograph No. 34 (Tucson: University of Arizona Press, 1978), 19.

tablished in the provinces. Their jurisdiction depended on the gravity of the offense in a criminal suit or on the amount of money at stake in a civil suit. The highest level of provincial justice was the *monthon* court, which corresponded to the regional unit combining several provinces. *Muang* courts were the highest level of courts in a given province, and *khwaeng* or district courts corresponded to the administrative subunits of the muang.[52] The king also appointed (temporarily) special commissioners (*kha luang phiset*), some of whom were Europeans. They constituted their own mobile court with the authority to reorganize the provincial courts and try cases in accordance with the reforms.[53] The commissioners acted as intermediaries, relaying orders from Bangkok and gathering local information such as the amount of judicial fees collected and the number of cases pending in local courts. Once they established a working relationship with local officials, the commissioners maintained order in the provinces by creating their own police force (*phontrawen*) to enforce the law.[54]

[52] The provincial courts were under the jurisdiction of the Ministry of the Interior, headed by Prince Damrong, until 1912, when all courts were placed under the authority of the Ministry of Justice.

[53] The special commissioner courts were established in 1896 and usually had a foreign legal adviser, two other legal advisers from the Ministry of Justice, a member from the locality under inspection who was chosen by the Ministry of the Interior, and the chief administrator of the monthon. Engel, *Law and Kingship,* 71, citing *Prachum kotmai prachamsok* [hereafter PKPS], vol. 13, *Nai Roi Tamruat Tho,* comp. Sathian Laiyalak et al. (Bangkok: June 1935), 144.

[54] Tej Bunnag, *The Provincial Administration of Siam, 1892–1915* (Kuala Lumpur: Oxford University Press, 1977), 104–5.

Transnational Justices

A lack of personnel experienced in modern bureaucratic techniques to run Siam's newly forming administration affected all ministries, not just the Ministry of Justice. The government adopted a policy of hiring foreigners as a temporary measure to help it rapidly modernize the administration until sufficient numbers of Siamese received appropriate training.[55] The system had begun during the reign of King Mongkut, who hired more than eighty foreigners to advise on military, shipping, and taxation issues, and police infrastructure.[56] King Chulalongkorn followed in his father's footsteps. He hired British nationals to work with the treasury, police, and education system; Germans to work on the post office and railways; Danes to act as advisers to the navy and provincial gendarmerie department; and Americans, Belgians and Frenchmen, mostly, to assist with legal reform. It was believed that hiring different nationals to advise different ministries would balance their relative power and ensure that no single country could assert, through its advisers, undue authority over Siam.

In the preamble to the 1908 Penal Code, King Chulalongkorn stated that Siam heeded the example set by Japan, which employed foreign legal advisers in order to

> order and arrange them [indigenous laws] in the same style as laws used in most European countries, and to organize the courts of justice, updating them as appropriate for modern times throughout Japan. When all the countries saw Japan's laws and courts were in perfect, systematic order, they then consented to change the treaties, abolishing the power of consular courts and allowing foreigners to be placed under the power of Japanese laws and courts from then on. (King Chulalongkorn, preamble, "Kotmai laksana aya" [Penal Code], 22 PKPS 4–5)

In Siam's judicial administration, foreign legal advisers served in three main capacities. First, they worked with Siam's minister of foreign affairs to revise the unequal treaty system. Second, foreign advisers worked alongside Siamese lawyers to codify and translate modern penal, civil, and procedural codes, most of which were informed by the codes of foreign countries rather than taken from Siam's KTSD. Third, they helped Siamese judges implement newly codified laws in court cases. The minister of justice and minister of the interior sent foreign legal advisers to assist Siamese judges in provincial, Bangkok, and international courts during the first decades of legal reform when Siam suffered an acute shortage of qualified personnel.

[55] Walter Vella, *Chaiyo! King Vajiravudh and the Development of Thai Nationalism* (Honolulu: University of Hawai'i Press, 1978), 82.

[56] Charnvit Kasetsiri and Wikal Phongphanitan, *Khamnam*.

Foreign legal advisers worked at all levels of justice; legal reform was an international process. The legal advisers came from Belgium, Britain, France, Japan, the United States, Ceylon, and other countries. They embodied the transnationality of Siam's modern jurisprudence. All reformers, Siamese and foreigners alike, moved easily in international circles abroad and in Bangkok. Their educational backgrounds, linguistic fluency, and experiences in Europe and colonial settings exemplify this. Legal experts brought with them culturally specific concepts of justice, legal codes, and institutions that circulated throughout Siam, Europe, and colonized countries. The transformations wrought in Siam as a result defy analysis within an exclusively national or dyadic colonial framework.

The Siamese involved most intensely in reforms include King Chulalongkorn; his half-brother Prince Damrong Rajanubhab, who was minister of the interior for twenty-three years (1894–1915); another brother, Minister of Foreign Affairs Prince Devawongse (1885–1923), who occupied that post for thirty-seven years; and the king's son Prince Ratburi, who was minister of justice for fourteen years (1897–1910) (photograph 1). Although only Prince Ratburi was educated abroad, the other three men obtained an English-language education in Siam from foreigners resident in Bangkok alongside a traditional Siamese one.[57] All three men were proficient, if not fluent, in English and could converse with English-speaking foreigners without translators. The milieu of Bangkok from the mid-nineteenth century on provided numerous opportunities for members of the ruling classes to interact with foreign diplomats, merchants, educators, and missionaries, something Bangkok shared with port cities throughout Asia.

King Chulalongkorn's education is representative of the reformers of his generation and mind-set.[58] Born in 1853 and the eldest surviving son of King Mongkut, Chulalongkorn received a traditional education in the affairs of state by working intimately with his father. King Chulalongkorn was the last monarch educated wholly within Siam. Yet, this education was far from narrowly domestic in focus. He obtained an education in English, a language he appears, based on his missives, to have mastered. The renowned Anna Leonowens, an American missionary named Dr. Chandler, and another Briton, Mr. Patterson, taught the young prince.[59] King Mongkut's untimely death in 1868 placed the fifteen-year-old prince on the throne, where he ruled under the aegis of a powerful regent, Chao Phraya (the second highest civil government rank after Somdet Chao Phraya) Sri Suriyawong. The re-

[57] Wyatt, *Politics of Reform,* 71.

[58] This summary of King Chulalongkorn's educational path is taken from Wyatt, *Politics of Reform,* 36–42.

[59] Anna Leonowens taught English in the Inner Palace from 1862 to 1867 and wrote two books based on her experience. She is best known through the books, plays, and films based on her life, which include *The King and I* and *Anna and the King of Siam.*

gent sent King Chulalongkorn on his first educational trips abroad in March and December of 1871, at age nineteen, to study the British colonial governments of Singapore, India, and Burma (part of British India), and the Dutch administration of Java.[60] In Java and Singapore he observed the details of colonial administration by visiting prisons, military forts, law courts, railways, factories, commercial centers, schools, and other institutions.[61] The king's hands-on education continued as he traveled within Siam extensively, to Java at least three times, to Europe twice—for nine months in 1897 and for eight months in 1907. Prince Damrong and Prince Devawongse also journeyed abroad, but Prince Devawongse in particular, as minister of foreign affairs, traveled frequently.

All nineteen of King Chulalongkorn's surviving sons studied in England, and some of them continued their education in St. Petersburg, Berlin, and other European and American metropoles. One of the brightest among them, Prince Ratburi, studied law at Oxford so he could assume the post of minister of justice, which he did, serving between 1897 and 1910.[62] Like so many of his fellow princes, the future minister spent the formative years of his life in a European metropole, living there from age eleven to twenty-two. He spoke English fluently and had to have a Siamese official tutor him in the Thai language while he resided abroad so that he would not forget how to speak his mother tongue. Despite his experiences in Protestant monogamous England, Prince Ratburi remained a Buddhist, and appears to have engaged in polygyny rather than monogamy.

On his return from London in 1896, the prince was whisked away by his father, King Chulalongkorn, and his uncle, Prince Damrong, who took him on a trip to Singapore and Java. There the young prince visited and studied prisons, police organization, irrigation systems, and administrative techniques.

[60] Krom Silpakon, *Chotmaihet sadet praphat tang prathet nai ratchakan thi 5 sadet muang singkhapo lae muang betawia khrang raek lae sadet praphat india kap chotmaihet khong mo brad-le* (Documents concerning Rama V's First Trips Abroad to Singapore, Batavia, and His Trip to India with Documents by Dr. Bradley) (Bangkok: Krom Silpakorn, 1969 [1917]).

[61] According to Kannika Sattraprung's study of newspaper articles published in the Netherlands East Indies and Singapore, King Chulalongkorn's trip offered those governments an opportunity to show off their power and progress as much as it offered the king a chance to place Siam on the map of civilized countries. Kannika Sattraprung, *A True Hero: King Chulalongkorn of Siam's Visit to Singapore and Java in 1871* (Bangkok: Tana Press and Graphic Co., 2004).

[62] Prince Ratburi was born in 1874 to King Chulalongkorn and Chaochommanda Talap. He studied in England from 1885 to 1896 when he graduated with a law degree from Christchurch College, Oxford University. Rungsaeng Kittayapong, "The Origins of Thailand's Modern Ministry of Justice and Its Early Development," PhD diss., University of Bristol, 202–4. Before he returned, the king appointed his own brother, Prince Svasti Sobhon, as Siam's first minister of justice from its establishment on 25 March 1892 until he left for Europe and was replaced (after an interim period) by Prince Phichit Prichakon in October 1894. On 3 March 1897 Prince Ratburi replaced Prince Phichit Prichakon, who diplomatically resigned because of "poor health," only to later take up a position as a Dika Court judge.

Photograph 1. Composite of Siam's ministers of state in 1908. 1. Prince Ratburi (minister of justice), 2. Prince Devawongse (minister of foreign affairs), 3. Prince Damrong Rajanubhab (minister of interior), 4. Chao Phraya Yomarat (minister for local government).
Arnold Wright, *Twentieth Century Impressions of Siam* (London: Lloyd's Greater Britain Pub. Co., 1908), 93.

He traveled widely in Europe and Southeast Asia before his return to Siam, after which devoted his life to official service in the administration.[63] His contributions to legal education are legion. Known today—somewhat ironically, given his foreign experience and education—as the "Father of Thai Law," Prince Ratburi established Siam's first law school in 1897 and taught there for more than a decade. He obtained a wealth of experience both as a member of every commission that codified Siam's penal and civil codes and as the minister of justice for over a decade of the ministry's most dynamic years. Prince Ratburi is the key source of knowledge about turn-of-the-century conceptions of Siamese traditional law and modern codes, in part because he could bridge the gap between the two.[64]

His impressive contributions to Siam's reform process must, however, be tempered. Siam's social hierarchy, patronage networks, and sponsorship of royal scions enabled princes to receive educations abroad and the highest positions in Siam's bureaucracy, despite their often tender ages and lack of relevant experience. Prince Ratburi, for example, became the minister of justice, a position selected for him before he returned from his schooling in London, when he was only twenty-two. With the exception of visits home, he had not lived in Siam since he was eleven and had little experience with Siam's legal system. Once back in Bangkok, Prince Ratburi learned about Siamese law and its practice from two prominent but nonroyal Siamese judicial figures, even as he assumed the position of minister of justice in 1897.[65] In addition, the same political economy of scholarship that promotes the dynastic narrative also produces scholarship about royal protagonists in Siam's history. Less effort is directed at recuperating the contributions by other, nonroyal individuals. For example, the court verdicts published between 1899 and 1936 from Siam's highest and final appeals court, the Dika Court, were issued by at least sixty-two judges.[66] The number of judges increases many

[63] He died of tuberculosis at age forty-six. Marcel Barang, preface to Akatdamkung Rabibhadana, *The Circus of Life* (Bangkok: Thai Modern Classics, 1995), 17.

[64] Even after his death on 7 August 1920, at the age of forty-six (born 21 October 1874), Prince Ratburi's explanations of these concepts persisted through future lecturers at the law school who cited him. See, for instance, Phra Nitisat Phaisan [Wan Chamaraman], *Thammasat Lectures* (Bangkok: Daily Mail, 1923–24), 23–24. He taught from 1919 until at least 1923 and cited some of Prince Ratburi's lectures verbatim. Woraphong Chirawuti, *Raphiphatonsak ramluk* (Recalling Prince Ratburi) (1973). "Phraprawat yo krom luang Ratburi direkrit" (An abridged history of Prince Ratburi Direkrut), *Wan raphi* 33 (7 Aug. 1973); NA MR5 Yutitham 23 Pramuan kotmai aya (1–3), "History [of the Ministry of Justice)," 1.

[65] When he returned to Siam, he studied Siam's law under Khun Luang Phraya Kraisi [Pleng Wephara] and worked closely with Chao Phraya Mahithon [La-o Krairoet], two prominent judicial figures. Woraphong Chirawuti, *Raphiphatonsak ramluk* (Recalling Prince Ratburi) (Bangkok: 1973).

[66] Three judges form a quorum for each case and must sign their decisions. I collected these signatures from Dika records, called *Khamphiphaksa san dika* (Dika Court Verdicts), to tally these results. The Siamese titles are tricky for two reasons. First, they are titles, not necessarily the given names of the judges, so if a judge's title changed, he might be listed twice. Second, infrequently a foreigner is given a Siamese title, in which case he would be counted as Siamese rather than as a foreigner.

times over once the judges of the appeals, monthon, muang, khwaeng, and borisapha courts are included. Very little is known about most of the Siamese judges sitting on these courts. Of the sixty-two judges who sat on the Dika Court, which decided all final appeals cases that fell within Siam's jurisdiction, between 1899 and 1936, forty-two names were Siamese and twenty were foreign (only eleven of whom were active for more than one year).

Most of the Siamese judges graduated from Siam's law school, which began immediately to produce legal experts to fill the judicial bureaucracy. Of the one hundred students in the first class that entered Siam's law school in 1897, only nine passed the exam that allowed them to work in the judicial administration. Several of the nine eventually became judges.[67] This small but inspired group could not hope to fill all the posts opened as a result of the centralization and standardization of the court system.[68] Until sufficient numbers received a legal education, either abroad or in Siam's law school, the positions were filled by foreigners without substantial knowledge of Siam's legal apparatus or by Siamese untrained in the new legal system.

The most important foreign-held post in the kingdom was that of the general adviser, a position created in late 1891. Its title changed after 1915 to adviser of foreign affairs, but the continuity between the two positions is clear. Until 1949, lawyers who specialized in international law filled the posts. The general adviser advised the monarch on legal matters regarding foreign relations as well as domestic reforms generally, whereas the adviser of foreign affairs focused on legal and treaty issues between Siam and other powers rather than on domestic reforms. In addition, Siam's government hired at least forty foreigners to assist with juridical reforms in Siam's various courts, where they served as judges, lawyers, attorneys, and legislative advisers who drafted new laws between the 1890s and 1930s. They all performed slightly differ-

[67] Chao Phraya Mahithon, Khun Luang Phraya Kraisi, Phraya Phicharana Pruchamat, and Phraphiphaksa Satayathipatai were among them. Pakdi Phakakrong, "Kanchatrang pramuan kotmai phaeng lae phanit haeng sayam: p.s. 2451–2478 (The Drafting of the Siamese Civil and Commercial Code, 1908–1935 A.D.)," MA thesis, Silpakorn University, 1994, 139. For the first two decades, between 1897 and 1918, the law school offered a one-year program. Its instruction increased to two years in about 1919, and to three years in 1924. Pakdi, "Kanchatrang pramuan kotmai," 140.

[68] Between 1897 and 1933, 1,077 individuals graduated from Siam's law school to become judges, attorneys, and public prosecutors. Pakdi, "Kanchatrang pramuan kotmai," 142. The law school combined with Chulalongkorn University's Faculty of Law and Public Administration in 1933, while the new government established Thammasat University's law school. *Thailand Official Yearbook 1968* (Bangkok: Government Printing Office, 1968), 311. The professionalization of law continued in 1914, when Rama VI established the Bar Association (Netibanthitsapha), which had supervisory control over the conduct of legal advocates. Pakdi, "Kanchatrang pramuan kotmai," 144. Two of the 1,077 graduates were women, the first of whom graduated in 1931–32. Women, however, were not allowed to work as judicial officials until years later. Women could not serve as judges or public prosecutors but only as private lawyers (*thanai khwam*). Chittima Pornarun, "Kanriakrong sithi satri nai sangkhom thai pho so 2489–2519" (Demands for Women's Rights in Thai Society, 1946–1976), MA thesis, Chulalongkorn University, 1995, 50–51. In addition to a formal education in the law school, several legal journals and the daily papers, which printed information about law and current court decisions, furthered the state of legal knowledge in Siam. Pakdi, "Kanchatrang pramuan kotmai," 146–47.

ent functions, had varying degrees of authority, and remained in Siam for different lengths of time. While it has proven impossible to account for them all statistically, it is important nonetheless to review the lives of a few to demonstrate the circuits of exchange within which they and their ideas traveled.[69]

During the nineteenth and early twentieth centuries, imperialism still operated hegemonically for most people. For example, foreign advisers in Siam believed they were (sometimes selflessly) working for Siam's best interests, rather than participating in its subordination. They were simultaneously defensive of Siam's monarchs—whom they described as benevolent and enlightened—and colonialist in seeing Siam's population as passive, uneducated, and unprepared for democratic institutions that would render an absolute monarchy obsolete. These men worked in the service of colonial ideals alongside Siam's leaders, many of whom shared similar beliefs. Their lives and decisions demonstrate the porousness of Siam's legal domain, which was sovereign yet employed dozens of foreigners, many of whom understood their experience in Siam as a stint in a colonized country. Their attitudes, experience, and employment in Siam qualify Siam's independence in subtle but profound ways.

Although it is tempting to dismiss them all as part of the homogenizing machinery of European capitalist modernity, the foreign advisers made enormous sacrifices that cannot be captured by evaluating them as purely self-interested imperialists. Gustave Rolin-Jaequemyns and Edward Strobel, Siam's first two general advisors, died as a result of their service in Siam. The third, Jens Westengard, forfeited twelve years of his family life, including the entirety of his son's childhood. The sacrifices were great, and the egos were often larger. The foreign advisers who worked for Siam, who owed their positions to racialized colonial power politics, participated in it to different degrees. The analysis below evaluates and individuates their levels of complicity, rather than homogenizing and dismissing them uniformly.

The general advisers exercised the greatest amount of authority, indirectly, of all foreign officers in Siam. Of the ten general advisers to His Majesty of Siam's Government between 1892 and 1949, nine were American.[70] Of these

[69] No one has been able to calculate their total number because documents regarding their service are scattered throughout archives in Europe, the United States, and Bangkok. In addition to nine major legal advisers, there were at least twelve Belgians hired in various capacities, at least eleven Frenchmen, one Japanese, several Britons, and a handful of Americans. Walter Tips, *Gustave Rolin-Jaequemyns (Chao Phraya Aphai Raja) and the Belgian Advisers in Siam (1892–1902)* (Bangkok: White Lotus, 1992); and Walter Tips, *Gustave Rolin-Jaequemyns and the Making of Modern Siam* (Bangkok: White Lotus, 1996).

[70] They included Henry Strobel (1903–08); Jens Westengard (1909–15); Wolcott Pitkin (1915–17); Eldon James (1917–23); Francis B. Sayre (1923–25); Courtney Crocker (1925); Raymond Stevens (roughly 1926–35); Frederick Dolbeare (roughly 1936–46); and Kenneth Patton (1946–49). The dates of service for Pitkin, James, Sayre, Crocker, Stevens, Dolbeare, and Patton are approximate. Kenneth T. Young, "The Special Role of American Advisers in Thailand, 1902–1949," *Asia* (New York: Asia Society, 1969), 6–11, in Jens Iverson Westengard Papers, Harvard Law School Library, Box 1, Folder 9.

nine, all but the last two graduated from Harvard University Law School. A mix of historical contingency and realpolitik determined the selection of one Belgian and nine Americans to the highest post held by a foreigner in Siam's government. Americans, like the Belgian general adviser who was Siam's first appointee, were not from countries with serious economic, military, or political interests in Siam, unlike French and British candidates. Many had extensive international legal experience, and several were professors of international law at Harvard Law School.

I describe, in brief, the four most accomplished general advisers (Rolin-Jaequemyns, Strobel, Westengard, and Francis B. Sayre) to locate them in a global network of exchange in colonial-era legal reforms and practices. King Chulalongkorn created the position as part of his administrative reform program. The monarch sent Prince Damrong to Europe in 1891 to search for a general adviser. Having failed to find an appropriate individual in Europe, Prince Damrong stopped in Cairo on his way to India, where presumably he planned to continue his search. In Cairo, he met Gustave Rolin-Jaequemyns, a Belgian lawyer, born in 1835 and in need of a well-paid position fitting his social stature but located outside his native state.[71] Damrong considered Rolin-Jaequemyns ideal because he was well mannered, had six years of experience as a minister of state in Belgium's capital, spoke English and French fluently, came from a neutral government vis-à-vis Siam, and needed a high-paying position due to a younger brother's financial difficulties. The perception that he "was an Anglophile and a Franco-phobe," as a later general adviser described Rolin-Jaequemyns, may have been a factor in Prince Damrong's decision to recruit him.[72] The Egyptian government was in the process of hiring Rolin-Jaequemyns as attorney general of Egypt's Mixed Courts when Prince Damrong negotiated a position for him in Siam.[73] The circuits within which Rolin-Jaequemyns searched for intellectual stimulation and financial recompense were colonial. They included not just the prospective foray into Egypt but also service as a councilor and later vice president of the Belgian monarch's High Council for the Congo Free State in 1889–90.[74]

Rolin-Jaequemyns served in Siam for nine years, between 1891 and his

[71] There are now several sources available about Gustave Rolin-Jaequemyns. S. Phlai-noi, *Chao tang chat nai prawatisat thai* (Foreigners in Thai History) (Bangkok: Ruamsan Co., 1995 [1963]), 130–36; Sawaeng Bunchaloemwiphat, *Prawatisat kotmai thai (Thai Legal History)* (Bangkok: Winyuchon Publication House, 2000), 157–61; Tips, *Gustave Rolin-Jaequemyns (Chao Phraya Aphai Raja)* and *Gustave Rolin-Jaequemyns and the Making of Modern Siam.*

[72] Jens Westengard to Rebecca Westengard, 28 Dec. 1911, Papers of Jens Iverson Westengard, Harvard Law School Library, Box 1, Folder 9.

[73] NA R5 Tang prathet 2/1, "Chang mr yakmin khao ma rap ratchakan nai muang thai" (Employment of M. R. Jaequemyns in Siam's Government Service), cited in Sawaeng, *Prawatisat kotmai thai,* 157–58.

[74] The council served as the last court of appeal in the Belgian colony. Tips, *Gustave Rolin-Jaequemyns and the Making of Modern Siam,* 16. One of the sons of Rolin-Jaequemyns was also a "veteran of the Congo." Tips, *Gustave Rolin-Jaequemyns and the Making of Modern Siam,* 200.

death in 1902. He was paid the highest salary permitted at the time in the Siamese government, £3,000 per year, a rate future general advisers received until 1910, when it began to inflate.[75] According to his biographers, Rolin-Jaequemyns played a vital role in Siam with his daily advice on foreign affairs and domestic judicial reforms as well as in conciliating with the French during the Paknam crisis of 1893, when the French dispatched gunboats up the Chaophraya River.[76] He is alleged to have said in 1892: "I will in one word be as faithful and loyal a counselor to His Majesty the King of Siam as I was to His Majesty the King of the Belgians."[77] Poor health, brought on by living in Siam, caught up with him in January 1902. No replacement could immediately be found.

How Harvard Law School became the recruiting grounds for all future general advisers is disputed.[78] Edward Strobel eventually came up as a potential replacement for Rolin-Jacquemyns because he was an authority on international law. A Harvard man through and through, Strobel received his bachelor's degree from Harvard College in 1877 and his law degree from Harvard Law School in 1882, and he returned to teach international law at Harvard Law School in 1898.[79] Strobel, like his predecessor, also possessed international legal contacts and had extensive experience abroad as an American diplomat, chargé d'affaires, and special arbiter, among other positions in Spain, Morocco, and Chile.[80] He took a leave of absence from Harvard to serve as Siam's general adviser from 1903 until his premature death in 1908. After he was hired, Strobel and the assistant general adviser, Jens Westengard, traveled to Paris to renegotiate an 1893 treaty with the French. They sought

[75] Westengard's salary increased to £3,500 in 1910 and to £4,000 in 1912. Westengard to Prince Devawongse, 12 Apr. 1909, Papers of Jens Iverson Westengard, Harvard Law School Library, Box 2, Folder 10. He asked for this salary increase over time, and it was granted.

[76] Sawaeng, *Prawatisat kotmai thai,* 160; Tips, *Gustave Rolin-Jaequemyns and the Making of Modern Siam,* 42, 49–71.

[77] Statement attributed to Gustave Rolin-Jaequemyns on 31 Jan. 1892, relayed in Tips, *Gustave Rolin-Jaequemyns (Chao Phraya Aphai Raja),* copyright page. When King Leopold of Belgium requested that Rolin-Jaequemyns use his position in Siam to grant Belgium various concessions and landholdings in a manner suggestive of the way the Belgian Congo was administered, the adviser did not respond, suggesting his integrity. Tips, *Gustave Rolin-Jaequemyns and the Making of Modern Siam,* 200.

[78] According to one version, it had to do with an encounter between Crown Prince Vajiravudh, touring in the United States after having completed his education in Britain, and Mr. Potter, a former ambassador, in Philadelphia in 1902. According to another source, the Siamese minister in Washington contacted Secretary of State John Hay for names after Rolin-Jaequemyns failed to recruit a European before his death. For the first version, see Papers of Jens Iverson Westengard, Harvard Law School Library, Box 3, Folder 1. For the second version, see Young, "Special Role of American Advisers in Thailand, 1902–1949, in Jens Iverson Westengard Papers, Harvard Law School Library, Box 1, Folder 9.

[79] "Explanatory Notes," Papers of Harold Hazeltine, Harvard Law School Library, Box 4, Folder 25.

[80] *Harvard Graduates' Magazine* 16, no. 63 (Mar. 1908): 395–406, in the Biographical Folder for Edward Henry Strobel, HUG 300, Harvard University Archives.

the removal of French troops from Chantaburi, where they had been stationed since the Paknam crisis to ensure that Siam paid its indemnities. Their first trip to Siam occurred after these negotiations ended in 1904.

Strobel, a bachelor without a family to whom he might send letters, left little documentation so it is difficult to get a sense of his personality. A Southerner from South Carolina, his students at Harvard found him informal and generous. Strobel worked hard, and he did not shun high praise. Several English-language articles suggested that Strobel, not King Chulalongkorn, ruled Siam in fact, and there is little to suggest that he refuted this tribute. One article from the *Herald* (16 Jan. 1908) written the day after Strobel's ignoble death by insect bite (received while he was in Egypt), echoes this theme: "As a general adviser he was the virtual ruler of Siam, one in whom the *titular* monarch had the greatest confidence."[81]

Jens Westengard, unlike Strobel, had a more modest understanding of his role, if his letters to his wife and Harvard associates are any indication (photograph 2). He distanced himself from any claim in the English-language press that he was the "power behind the throne."[82] Westengard served as assistant general adviser to Strobel from 1903 to 1908 and as general adviser from 1909 to 1915.[83] He traveled extensively in areas such as Battambang, Siemreap, and the Malay Peninsula, which were contested by France and Britain. He helped Strobel negotiate the removal of French troops stationed in Chantaburi in January 1905. His crowning achievement, in his own assessment but not necessarily that of Siam's leaders, was the Anglo-Siamese Treaty of 1909, which finalized Siam's border with British territories on the Malay Peninsula.

Westengard is a particularly sympathetic figure, described by others as charming, warm, and sweet.[84] Born in Chicago in 1871 to Danish immigrants, Westengard came from more modest means than Strobel and put himself through Harvard Law School by working as a stenographer. When he graduated in 1898, Harvard Law School hired him as an instructor, which is the post from which Strobel plucked him in 1903. Throughout his twelve years in Siam, he was separated nearly the entire time from his wife, Rebecca,

[81] Emphasis added. Biographical Folder for Edward Henry Strobel, HUG 300, Harvard University Archives.

[82] He explained this to a reporter of the *Boston Transcript* who wrote an article about Siam and Westengard on 23 Oct. 1923. He said it was important to correct the impression that "he or any other outsider is any power behind the Siamese throne," which was run by the king and his ministers. He reiterated that the Europeans in Siam are in fact and name simply advisers. Biographical Folder for Jens Westengard, HUG 300, Harvard University Archives.

[83] Westengard has received far less attention than Rolin-Jaequemyns even though he served the longest, if one counts the five years he spent as assistant general adviser. For a relatively uninformative review that no doubt reflects the lack of information available, see S. Phlai-noi, *Chao tang chat,* 165–68. Harvard Law School Special Collections has an excellent collection of Westengard's personal correspondence, largely with his wife and son, and related documents.

[84] Papers of Harold Hazeltine, Harvard Law School, Box 4, Folder 25.

and son, Aubrey. As a result, there is rich documentation of his personal life through his letters to his family and colleagues in the United States. These letters contextualize his ambitions as a man who wanted to make his mark on history by improving the disadvantageous international position occupied by Siam. In one letter to Harvard President Charles Eliot, Westengard describes the position of the general adviser: "He has behind him nothing whatever except the moral force which he may be able to exert when he has won the confidence of the Government by convincing them, through a series of years, that his advice is good."[85]

From the temper of the correspondence between Westengard and various Siamese leaders, including Kings Chulalongkorn and Vajiravudh, Prince Devawongse, and others, Westengard had warm relations with the officials for whom he worked.[86] This fondness developed over time. When he arrived he suspected the Siamese government of reading his letters home, and he occasionally wrote segments in stenographic code.[87] However, he is quoted as feeling a deep personal loss at the death of King Chulalongkorn in 1910: "I loved him much and he liked me. I doubt if he has ever felt for any other European as I think he felt towards me."[88] While still assistant general adviser, he traveled with King Chulalongkorn's entourage to Europe in 1907 and was affectionately portrayed in *Klai ban* (Far from Home), the king's memoirs of that trip.[89]

Westengard had a less intimate relationship with King Vajiravudh (Rama VI). Rama VI did not send for his adviser for a full year after the new monarch ascended the throne. About this meeting, Westengard observed that King Vajiravudh "speaks very sensibly. But one feels the absence of the personal bond which united me to his father. His problems are many and difficult, and I hope he may be granted the wisdom to deal with them."[90] Even before the

[85] Letter from Jens Westengard to President Eliot, 30 Jan. 1912, Papers of Jens Iverson Westengard, Box 2, Folder 4.

[86] Thirty-page draft biography, Papers of Jens Iverson Westengard, Harvard Law School Library, Box 3, Folder 1.

[87] For example, in one letter to his wife he mentions a painful (to King Chulalongkorn) political incident that caused the downfall of one of the king's sons and cabinet member, Prince Ratburi, the minister of justice. Much of the letter is written in shorthand sprinkled tantalizingly with "independent . . . a radical . . . main . . . hurt . . . another prince . . . together." Jens Westengard to Rebecca Westengard, 20 Sept. 1910, Papers of Jens Iverson Westengard, Harvard Law School Library, Box 1, Folder 5.

[88] Jens Westengard to Rebecca Westengard, 23 Oct. 1910, Papers of Jens Iverson Westengard, Harvard Law School Library, Box 1, Folder 6.

[89] King Chulalongkorn wrote with affectionate humor about one incident involving Westengard, suggesting that he rated highly among the king's men. S. Phlai-noi, *Chao tang-chat,* 165–66. There is an English rendering of this section of *Klai ban* in Papers of Jens Iverson Westengard, Harvard Law School Library, Box 2, Folder 10.

[90] Jens Westengard to Rebecca Westengard, 28 Sept. 1911. Papers of Jens Iverson Westengard, Harvard Law School Library, Box 1, Folder 10. Westengard's letters also confirm that King Vajiravudh brought to power a different group of men, younger and from different backgrounds. He writes in March 1911, just a few months after King Vajiravudh replaced his father: "I am a little uneasy at the way things have been going. The late King's strong hand is no longer at the helm. The younger men

Photograph 2. Foreign advisers and other officials with Prince Damrong, circa 1910. Second from left, Jens Iverson Westengard (general adviser); middle (seated), Prince Damrong Rajanubhab (minister of the interior); and second from right, W. J. F. Williamson (financial adviser). Detail of a photo in the Papers of Jens Iverson Westengard. Courtesy of Special Collections Department, Harvard Law School Library.

death of King Chulalongkorn, Westengard noted in a letter to his wife, "I feel as if, with the signing of the British treaty [of 1909], the 'heroic age' closed. . . . However, there is no denying the need for my services is not so great any more."[91]

Little is known about the remaining advisers in foreign affairs, with the exception of Francis B. Sayre, in part because he published extensively on Siam and served in high posts in U.S. administrations after he returned from Siam. Sayre wrote prolifically. Like Strobel, he had a robust understanding of the significance of his role in Siam. He claimed credit for ending extraterritoriality in Siam. In 1923, Sayre left his post as a professor at Harvard Law School to work in Siam. He and Prince Traidos, the son of former Foreign

are more inclined to deal with little things. The heroic days are past." Jens Westengard to Rebecca Westengard, 28 Mar. 1911, Papers of Jens Iverson Westengard, Harvard Law School Library, Box 1, Folder 8. And one month later, "Conditions have changed, especially since the King died . . . for the men who apparently are rising to power are of a different class from Prince Damrong." Jens Westengard to Rebecca Westengard, 20 Apr. 1911, Papers of Jens Iverson Westengard, Harvard Law School Library, Box 1, Folder 8.

[91] Jens Westengard to Rebecca Westengard, 29 Sept. 1910, Papers of Jens Iverson Westengard, Harvard Law School Library, Box 1, Folder 5.

Minister Devawongse, campaigned to convince leaders of every major European country to renegotiate their unequal treaties with Siam. The new treaties established firm guidelines by which extraterritoriality and import-export duty restrictions would be abolished.[92] More important from the perspective of judicial autonomy, the new treaty promised to end extraterritoriality after the promulgation of the last of Siam's modern law codes, except to maintain the right of evocation of court cases involving U.S. subjects for up to five years.[93] The United States and Japan had already agreed to this on their own accord in 1920 and 1924, while Sayre and Traidos signed up every remaining power by 1926.[94] Sayre left Siam in 1926 to rejoin his family, who found Bangkok's climate unbearable. He returned to teach at Harvard and served, among many other positions, as a high commissioner to the Philippines in 1939.[95] After his departure, Sayre noted that the real work of international treaty revision had been accomplished and that it remained now in the hands of Siam's judicial officials to finalize the remaining legal codes, the laws on marriage and inheritance.[96]

Siam had hired dozens of legal advisers to draft these codes (photograph 3). Having observed Siam's judicial affairs for about ten years, William Alfred Tilleke (Khuna-dilok in Thai), a Ceylonese man who headed Siam's office of attorney general for two decades, was well placed to understand the role of foreign legal advisers beyond drafting Siam's penal and civil and commercial codes:[97]

> In many of the courts there sits a foreign legal adviser whose duty is to advise the judges in any matter of difficulty. These advisers have the full status of judges and draft and sign judgments. The appointment of such advisers, however, is not a matter which is obligatory by any treaty, but is entirely voluntary on the part of the Government, the desire being simply to make the judiciary as efficient as possible. The first duty of the advisers is to learn the language,

[92] They followed the model set by the 1920 treaty between Siam and the United States, in which Sayre's father-in-law President Woodrow Wilson abrogated the 1856 treaty with Siam.

[93] Francis Sayre, "Siam's Fight for Sovereignty," *Atlantic Monthly* (Nov. 1927): 674–89.

[94] Francis Sayre, "The Passing of Extraterritoriality in Siam," *American Journal of International Law* 22 (Jan. 1928), reprinted by the American Council of the Institute of Pacific Relations, 19–37.

[95] *Boston Globe* (30 Mar. 1972), obituary, Biographical Folder for Francis B. Sayre, HUG 300, Harvard University Archives. His role in Siam provided the United States with a certain leverage in Siam during the Pacific War, when the Allied powers dropped leaflets with images of Sayre and important leaders from the Allied powers. S. Phlai-noi, *Chao tang-chat,* 169–75, 169.

[96] According to Sayre, "The Royal Code Commission, charged with the formulation of a Siamese code of law, cannot proceed with the new law of inheritance and of the family until a decision has been reached upon the fundamental question of monogamy or polygamy." Francis Sayre, "Siam," *Atlantic Monthly* (June 1926), 845.

[97] He worked in the office of the attorney general from 1897 to his death in 1917 and eventually adopted Siamese citizenship. S. Phlai-noi, *Chao tang-chat,* 141–47; W. A. G. Tilleke, "Administration of Justice," in *Twentieth Century Impressions of Siam,* ed. Arnold Wright (London: Lloyd's Greater Britain Pub. Co., 1908), 95.

> and they have to pass an examination in Siamese before being attached as adviser to any particular court. (W.A. G.Tilleke, "The Administration of Justice," 95)

Tilleke and Tokichi Masao were the only ethnically non-European legal advisers hired in Siam. Tilleke decided to forsake Ceylon and relinquish his British subject status when he moved to Siam in 1888, adopting Siamese citizenship after 1910.[98] He put his legal degree from Colombo to use when he and a Siamese lawyer, Luang Damrong Thammasan, defended Phra Yot in a famous trial in 1893 in which the French accused Phra Yot of shooting a French officer.[99] He began his government service in the Attorney General's office of Siam in 1897 and became increasingly involved with Siam's capitalist development by investing privately in railway, rubber, and manufacturing companies.[100] His Bagan Rubber Company was active in Kelantan. A man named "Tilleke" (which could be W. A. G. or his brother, A. F. G.) was one of the "lessees" of the Bagan Rubber Estate, which covered four thousand acres in Kelantan, the second largest estate there.[101]

Tokichi Masao wrote a thesis on "Studies in Ancient Siamese Laws" at the Imperial University of Tokyo,[102] studied law at West Virginia University in 1895, and received a doctorate from Yale University in 1897. He served in the Ministry of Justice from 1897 until 1913, when he left to pursue a political career in the Japanese Diet. He worked alongside Rolin-Jaequemyns as his secretary, helped draft Siam's criminal code, and served as a Dika Court of Appeals (San Dika) judge.[103] Tokichi Masao, unlike other foreign legal advisers, opposed legalizing polygyny as "immoral," perhaps because his own country had recently purged itself of the practice under similar accusations of barbarity. Thoroughly imbued with a sense of the challenges faced by Siam, he spent sixteen years there deploying his fluency in English and legalese to Siam's advantage.

[98] Information about Tilleke comes from S. Phlai-noi, *Chao tang-chat,* 141–47, and W. A. G. Tilleke, "Administration of Justice," 96.

[99] Prince Damrong Rajanubhab, *Prawat bukkhon samkhan* (Histories of Important People) (Bangkok: Bannakit, 1988), 330–32. The French accused Phra Yot of shooting a French officer in a border skirmish along the Siamese-Lao border, thereby "provoking" the French to retaliate. He was tried in a mixed Siamese-French court. Today Phra Yot is memorialized in a military fort with his namesake located in Nakhon Phanom Province along the Thai-Lao border.

[100] By his own admission he was involved in commercial life of Bangkok as chairman of the Bagan Rubber Company and a director of the Bangkok Manufacturing Company Ltd., the Bangkok Dock Co., Ltd., the Siamese Tramways Company Ltd., the Prabad Railway Co., the Transport Motor Co., and the Paknam Railway Company. Tilleke, "Administration of Justice," 96.

[101] "Appendix," W. A. Graham, *Kelantan: A State of the Malay Peninsula* (Glasgow: James Maclehose and Sons, 1908), 138.

[102] Tokichi Masao, "The Sources of Ancient Siamese Law," *Yale Law Journal* (Nov. 1905): 28.

[103] Rungsaeng Kittayapong, "Origins of Thailand's Modern Ministry of Justice," 258–61; Tokichi Masao, "The New Penal Code of Siam," *Yale Law Journal* (Dec. 1908): 85–100.

Photograph 3. Siam's foreign legal advisers in 1908. Top row from left: René Sheridan, Tokichi Masao. Bottom row from left: Lawrence Tooth, C. L. Watson, C. R. A. Niel, and W. A. G. Tilleke.

Arnold Wright, *Twentieth Century Impressions of Siam* (London: Lloyd's Greater Britain Pub. Co., 1908), 95.

Between the mid-1890s and the early 1900s, Belgians comprised the vast majority of assistant legal advisers, no doubt because of Rolin-Jaequemyns's recruiting networks.[104] The Belgians who assisted as legislative and judicial advisers included Corneille Schlesser, Pierre Orts, Auguste Dauge, Charles Symon, R. Tilmont, F. Cattier, A. Henvaux, Charles Robijns, L. De Busscher, A. Baudour, René Sheridan, and Émile Jottrand.[105] They worked in various courts in Bangkok and in international and provincial courts outside the city. For example, Schlesser, Robert Kirkpatrick, and Sheridan sat occasionally on the highest court, the Dika Court. Schlesser served on the multinational

[104] Rolin-Jaequemyns's assistant general adviser, Kirkpatrick (1894–1900), was Belgian. He died from an illness contracted in Siam.

[105] René Sheridan, another Belgian known also by his Siamese name Phraya Vides Dharmamontri, served for twenty-five years until he died in Bangkok in 1927. See Christian de Saint-Hubert, "Rolin-Jaequemyns (Chao Phya Aphay Raja) and the Belgian Legal Advisers in Siam at the Turn of the Century," *Journal of the Siam Society* 53, no. 2 (July 1965): 188–90.

committee that drafted Siam's penal code in 1905.[106] Émile Jottrand, another Belgian, served on the International Court in Korat, and on the borisapha and Appeals Court in Bangkok.

The influence of the Belgians on Siam's legal practices declined soon after Rolin-Jaequemyns died. In 1904, when the terms of the new treaty between France and Siam compelled the Siamese government to appoint French advisers to high positions, Georges Padoux was hired.[107] From that point on, French legal advisers were employed in larger numbers than other nationals to help draft Siam's penal and civil codes. These included Riviere, René Guyon, Moncharville, Charles L'Evesque, Louis Duplatre, C. R.A. Niel, Delesday, Buzzard, and others.

Padoux quickly became a key figure in the creation of Siam's penal and civil codes, most of which were drafted by committees under his oversight between 1905 and 1913, when he left Siam.[108] Although the penal code, once drafted in English and correctly translated into Thai, was adopted without a problem, snags slowed the process of promulgating the civil codes, the drafting of which Padoux supervised. In a letter to Westengard in early 1910, King Chulalongkorn wrote that, while relations with France had improved, "there is only one thing that will give trouble and that is M. Padoux's draft of the Code. The Minister of Justice [Prince Ratburi], Judge Skinner-Turner and Masao think that it will not do at all. Not only will it have to be altered but it will be necessary to re-draft it altogether because Padoux and his five assistants are quite incapable of making a civil code."[109]

The problem appears to have been in part their lack of proficiency in English. Despite the entirely French and Siamese membership of the drafting commission, the civil code was initially drafted in English by the French members, three of whom were sent to improve their English in London in 1908 before coming to Siam.[110] They drafted the codes without input by bilingual Siamese, not because of imperial tendencies on the part of the French legal advisers or inabilities of Siamese officials, but because of the limited availability of and great demand for Siamese officials with bilingual flu-

[106] Georges Padoux, "Report on the Proposed Penal Code for the Kingdom of Siam," (Bangkok: American Presbyterian Mission Press, 1906). Reprinted in *Laws of South-East Asia,* vol. 2, *European Laws in South-East Asia,* ed. M. B. Hooker, 582–83 (Singapore: Butterworth and Co., 1986).

[107] In the 1904 treaty, the French specifically instructed the Siamese government to appoint French advisers to high positions and threatened Siam if it failed to do so. France had followed through on its threats before, humiliating Siam with gunboats in 1893. The French, feeling outdone by the British who had placed a national as Siam's financial adviser, regularly used treaties to maintain influence in Siam on par with Britain.

[108] For a detailed history of the drafting of Siam's codes, see Loos, "Gender Adjudicated."

[109] King Chulalongkorn to Jens Westengard, 24 Feb. 1910, Papers of Jens Iverson Westengard, Harvard Law School Library, Box 2, Folder 9.

[110] The French members of the civil code drafting committee were Georges Padoux, Mr. Riviere, René Guyon, Mr. Moncharville, and Mr. Charles L'Evesque. Riviere, Guyon, and Moncharville were sent to London to improve their English in 1908. Pakdi, "Kanchatrang pramuan kotmai," 41–42.

ency in English and Thai. When Padoux returned to Paris in 1912 for reasons of ill health, he also was disappointed in his work.[111] By 1913, poor health or not, Padoux resigned his post in Siam and signed on to work as an adviser in China.[112]

René Guyon deserves mention because of the longevity of his service (1908 to 1963), his decision to naturalize as a Siamese citizen (with the name of Phichan Bunyong) in 1942, and his arresting French-language publications.[113] Guyon served as a judge on the Dika Court and was Siam's last foreign legal adviser to help draft portions of the Civil and Commercial Code. Guyon's life, worthy of its own study, reveals the reciprocal nature of the exchange between colonial powers and Siam. Typically, the exchange is understood as one of mimicry, in which non-Western countries adopt Euro-American economic, technological, cultural, and political principles and practices. It is far more difficult, given the asymmetrical power relations between European and American imperial powers and Asia, to delineate the ways in which countries like Siam influenced imperial powers. The examination of René Guyon enables this kind of a study. He agreed with Siamese members of the codification committee that Siam should follow "Siamese legal principles"—that is, maintain polygyny as the marital standard rather than adopt monogamy—in its family and marriage code. This makes sense in the context of the books he wrote on sexual ethics, which use his long experience in Siam as a largely unacknowledged springboard for his views on *La Liberté Sexuelle* (the title of his second book). These texts, written in the early 1930s from an explicitly comparative (East-West) framework, advocated sexual emancipation including the promotion of polygyny (but not polyandry).[114]

Circulation and Translation of Colonial Jurisprudence

Many foreign advisers wrote for international law journals or published personal accounts of their experiences in Siam in English and French. Gustave

[111] Jens Westengard to Rebecca Westengard, 13 Feb. 1911, Papers of Jens Iverson Westengard, Harvard Law School Library, Box 1, Folder 7.

[112] Jens Westengard to Rebecca Westengard, 1 May 1913 and 4 June 1913, Papers of Jens Iverson Westengard, Harvard Law School Library, Box 1, Folder 11.

[113] His decision to naturalize might have been due to pressures placed on French citizens during the Pacific War to naturalize or to leave Siam. Sarit Thanarat, "Khamnam" (introduction) to *Phichan anuson* (Cremation Volume for Phichan Bunyong [René Guyon]) (Bangkok, 1963); Pakdi, "Kanchatrang pramuan kotmai," 104.

[114] His books were published in France and translated into English, enjoying no small amount of publicity. Thailand's most sexually notorious dictator, Sarit Thanarat, sponsored and wrote the introduction to the funerary volume, *Phichan anuson,* published to mark Guyon's death in Thailand in 1963.

Rolin-Jaequemyns helped found and served as chief editor of *Revue de Droit International et de Législation Comparée* in which he (via his son, Eduoard) and Pierre Orts published articles about Siam.[115] Émile Jottrand, another Belgian legal adviser, and his wife published their personal journal, *Au Siam,* in 1905.[116] Sayre disseminated his tale about his brief but intense time as adviser of foreign affairs in *Glad Adventure.*[117] Louis Duplatre, a Frenchman, wrote his PhD dissertation on the status of women in Siam at the University of Grenoble in 1922 before King Vajiravudh employed him as director of Siam's Legal Studies Association in 1924, and later as director and professor of legal studies at Chulalongkorn University.[118] Tokichi Masao also wrote his thesis on Siam's ancient laws and published on modern legal reforms in the *Yale Law Journal.*

At issue here is not the fact that they produced orientalist discourse about Siam but that they engaged in an international circulation of ideas about colonial-era jurisprudence and customary law. Their audience was not primarily Siamese but international. The cosmopolitan milieu of Siam's juridical reform was founded ultimately on an international hierarchy, which motivated the reforms in the first place. The colonial career trajectories of foreign legal advisers demonstrate this. While some of Siam's foreign advisers pledged loyalty to Siam's monarchy and devoted their lives to securing Siam's sovereignty, others regarded their experience in Siam as a stepping stone to loftier careers in directly colonized territories. Several of the Belgian advisers worked in the Belgian Congo before or after their employment in Siam. Félicien Cattier surveyed the customary laws of tribes in the Congo before he worked in Siam in 1895 and was later "instrumental in dealing with the excesses going on in the Congo Free State and helped to force its annexation by Belgium so that proper and just administration could be implemented."[119] That Cattier could couch in such bland terms Belgium's violently exploitative colonization of the Congo's population and natural resources suggests the degree to which he held an imperial perspective on the non-Western countries in which he worked. Pierre Orts too "was instrumental in the annexation by Belgium" of the Congo and helped found the Belgian Ministry of Colonies.[120] Sheridan served in the Congo, and Dauge worked in China soon after he left Siam in 1899.[121] Padoux arrived in Siam

[115] Tips, *Gustave Rolin-Jaequemyns (Chao Phraya Aphai Raja),* 270; and Tips, *Gustave Rolin-Jaequemyns and the Making of Modern Siam,* xvii.

[116] Mr. and Mrs. Émile Jottrand, *Au Siam* (Paris: Librairie Plon, 1905), translated by Walter Tips (rpt.; Bangkok: White Lotus, 1996).

[117] Francis B. Sayre, *Glad Adventure* (New York: Macmillan, 1957).

[118] Louis Duplatre, "Essai sur la condition de la femme au Siam," PhD diss., University of Grenoble, 1922. His dissertation was translated into Thai by Dr. Phairot Kamphusiri and published as *Sathana khong ying mi sami nai prathet sayam* (Bangkok: Thammasat University Press, 1990).

[119] Tips, *Gustave Rolin-Jaequemyns (Chao Phraya Aphai Raja),* 264–65.

[120] Ibid., 271.

[121] Ibid., 274. Tilleke, "Administration of Justice," 96.

after having worked on juridical reforms and courts in French Algeria and Tunisia, and eventually he served in Beijing.[122] Another Frenchman who occasionally adjudicated cases in Siam's Dika Court had worked in French Indochina for five years before that.[123] Briton Skinner Turner, who administered justice at the Dika Court between 1908 and 1915, had spent five years serving on British courts in the East Africa Protectorate, Uganda, Mombassa, and Zanzibar.[124]

Contrast their experiences to that of Siam's royal officials. As mentioned earlier, all of King Chulalongkorn's surviving nineteen sons studied abroad before returning to Siam or continuing their studies elsewhere.[125] Siam's ministers of justice from 1892 to 1913 received their law degrees in England. Siamese judges either studied British legal principles with Prince Ratburi, who taught at Siam's law school, or studied abroad. For example, Khun Luang Phraya Kraisi (Pleng Wephara) graduated from Siam's law school in 1897 and from Oxford.[126] Siamese officials personally or vicariously embarked on an educational pilgrimage that connected them to the hub of empire during the nineteenth century: London. They socialized daily with foreign legal advisers who were employed because of their legal expertise garnered from experience in directly colonized countries.

As participants in a global circulation of legal reform, Siamese and foreign legal advisers linked Siam to a network of ideas that went beyond national boundaries. This is reflected in the translation and transculturation of legal codes. Foreign and Siamese reformers codified criminal and civil codes and procedures. They drafted the penal code first, between 1897 and 1908, because it was relatively short and straightforward compared to the civil code. The civil code consumed a much longer period of time, taking nearly thirty years to complete (1908–35). Typically, more foreign legal advisers than Siamese sat on the commissions formed to draft these codes because of the lack of Siamese with royal pedigrees who were fluent in English and educated in European legal doctrines. All of these advisers emphasized the need to keep the codes culturally Siamese—that is, to incorporate Siamese law from the KTSD to the extent that these laws suited Siam's changed circumstances. However, only in family law were KTSD codes seriously considered. The foreign origins of Thailand's modern law codes are reflected today in law school courses on Thailand's legal history: two-thirds of the semester is

[122] Jens Westengard to Rebecca Westengard, 22 Jan. 1905, Papers of Jens Iverson Westengard, Harvard Law School Library, Box 1, Folder 4.

[123] Tilleke, "Administration of Justice," 96.

[124] Ibid., 95.

[125] Department of Fine Arts, *Ratchasakunwong* (Royal lineage) (Bangkok, 1993), 58–77.

[126] Charles Buls, *Siamese Sketches* (Bangkok: White Lotus, 1994 [1901]), 63. Siam's government continued to send the children of the upper classes to study abroad. As a consequence, the number of foreign legal advisers working in the entire administration began to decline in the 1920s.

spent studying Roman law and one-third (all related to family law) on the KTSD.[127]

The transnationality of Siam's legal reformers had several consequences. At both the levels of codification and linguistics, foreign laws and concepts dominated the reform process, which occurred in English. Siam's modern penal code, promulgated in 1908, demonstrates the radically transnational origins of Siamese law generally. The drafting committee, composed of Siamese, French, Japanese, and British members, researched Siamese laws and compared them to the penal codes of France (1905 version), British India (1886), Belgium (1867), Holland (1881), Italy (1889), Japan (1903 draft), Egypt (1904), Germany, Denmark, and Hungary.[128] The translation and codification of the Penal Code set the tone for the six-volume Civil and Commercial Code (CCC).[129] The CCC, with its 1,755 provisions, was more than four times larger than the Penal Code, which had 398 provisions. The CCC was promulgated in six books covering General Principles (1923), Obligations (1923), Specific Contracts (1924), Property (1931–32), Family (1935), and Inheritance (1935). The Siamese and French legal advisers considered as potential models the civil codes of France, Italy, Spain, Chile, Portugal, Sweden, Japan, and Germany.[130] The final version of Siam's civil code most closely resembled that of Germany, but was not the same in content or even in the six divisions. In any case, divining the origins of Siam's penal and civil codes will not necessarily clarify Siam's modern law at the level of translation or implementation.[131]

Regardless of their country of origin or their degree of proficiency in the Thai language, Siam's legal reformers used English as their lingua franca. Their cosmopolitanism shouts through the archival documentation on codification, much of which is in English or sprinkled with English terms. Committees of Siamese and foreign legal advisers produced Siam's "modern" laws in English and later had them translated into Thai. This was by no means a straightforward process, given the composition of the committees, the varying degrees of fluency in both languages, and the subtle connotations of each term. The English used was not a homogenous language because of the cultural and linguistic backgrounds of the international advisers, for many of whom English was a second language. The Thai used was arguably more ho-

[127] Course on *Prawatisat kotmai thai* (History of Thai Law), Thammasat University Law Faculty. I audited the course in the spring of 1996.

[128] Padoux, "Report on the Proposed Penal Code for the Kingdom of Siam," 583.

[129] Pakdi has written about this process in detail in "Kanchatrang pramuan kotmai."

[130] NA MR6 Yutitham 12.1 Kotmai, Pramuan kotmai phaeng lae phanit, Ruang 2, Letter to Rama VI from the Translation Review Committee, 26 Sept. 1922.

[131] According to most accounts, initially British law and procedural norms exerted dominance but were applied in piecemeal fashion. Continental law began to assert dominance as a model for reforms of the substantive codes when France compelled Siam to hire a French legal adviser, Georges Padoux, in 1904. Sawaeng, *Prawatisat kotmai thai,* 258.

mogenous given the more uniform educational and cultural background of the Siamese working on the translations. Notwithstanding the instabilities of language and the dialectic process by which the translations were generated, the commissions eventually produced a final official translation of the codes.

The composition of the high commission that reviewed the Thai translation of the penal code indicates the priority given to the quality of its translation. It included the four most powerful ministers in the country: Prince Damrong, minister of the interior; Prince Devawongse, minister of foreign affairs; Prince Ratburi;[132] and Prince Naret, minister of local government. Prince Ratburi found the process of translation nearly impossible: "The rhetoric is not very precise since the *farang* [white Westerner] terms and Thai terms are not identical. Each has their own habits and disposition. To select accurately [a term] without excessive or incomplete meanings is, then, a supremely difficult task."[133] He felt it necessary to publish a comparative edition in which he laid out side by side the 1908 official copy of the Penal Code and his own revised "rhetoric" elucidating the original. Siam's modern laws required a Thai-Thai translation. In addition to publishing a guide for central Thai speakers, the government also published the Penal Code in French, northern Thai, and Chinese, but not in Malay. Of these, the central Thai version served as the official one.[134]

Because translation is a power-laden practice that aided and justified imperial authority over colonial populations, its odd trajectory in noncolonial Siam requires attention. In her book *Siting Translation,* Tejaswini Niranjana explains how "translation as a practice shapes, and takes shape within, the asymmetrical relations of power that operate under colonialism. What is at stake here is the representation of the colonized, who need to be produced in such a manner as to justify colonial domination."[135] The translation of a colonized culture into the language of an imperial power gives readers of the imperial language the illusion of privileged access to an authentic original that the process of translation, in fact, creates. Niranjana, like other postcolonial scholars, including Partha Chatterjee and Lata Mani, has argued that the representation of colonized cultures in the language of the colonizer as static objects without a history has justified imperial domination.[136] In representing the colonized culture (in unflattering terms), translation fixes that

[132] Tokichi Masao substituted for Prince Ratburi while the prince was in Europe.

[133] Prince Ratburi, preamble, *Khot aya: chabap luang kap chabap thiap* (Penal Code: Official and Comparative Editions), vol. 1 (Bangkok: Kong Lahuthot, 1910), 1.

[134] These are the only languages in which the code is known to have been produced. If the code was produced in additional languages, this information has been lost.

[135] Tejaswini Niranjana, *Siting Translation: History, Post-Structuralism, and the Colonial Context* (Berkeley: University of California Press, 1992), 2.

[136] Partha Chatterjee, *The Nation and Its Fragments: Colonial and Postcolonial Histories* (Princeton: Princeton University Press, 1993). Lata Mani, "Contentious Traditions: The Debate on SATI in Colonial India," *Cultural Critique* (Fall 1987): 119–56.

culture in time as "traditional" and homogenizes it as monolithic and unvarying. The erasure of the moment of translation essentializes the colonized culture and simultaneously allows the colonizing power to present itself as modern, progressive, and powerfully monolithic.

In Siam the process of translation and the political deployment of its product operated differently. The direction of translation was from English into central Thai, not from Thai into English, which counterintuitively allowed Siam's reforming elites more control over the meaning of the translations, particularly for Siam's domestic population. The elite translators, following Niranjana's theory, may have attempted to stabilize the meanings of the English terms used through their selection of nonanalogous Thai cognates. Unlike the situation in colonized countries, in Siam the individuals in charge of the English-to-Thai translation were not alien colonizers but elite Siamese officials, most of whom were members of the royal family. Their Thai translations of European enlightenment legal concepts reflect, wittingly or not, domestic power hierarchies.

The translation of the English term *liberty* into the Thai term *issaraphap* provides a case in point.[137] *Issaraphap* is commonly translated today as *liberty, independence, freedom,* or *autonomy.* However, its historic meanings, which applied at the turn of the century, stemmed from its usage in Siam's traditional laws. In the KTSD, issaraphap referred to the authority or sovereignty that superiors (referring to people or polities) had over themselves and their subordinates. For subordinates, issaraphap was conceptualized in negative terms; it described the condition of not being subject to the power of a superior.[138] In addition to obvious status asymmetries, the positions of superior and subordinate also incorporated a hierarchical notion of gender relations. Within a given class, men consistently were superior while women were considered subordinate.

When the penal code drafting committee identified liberty with issaraphap, they may have meant to reconceptualize issaraphap as a new right that in theory each individual possessed. The Enlightenment ideal of individuals as equal and born with an inherent right to liberty, however, marked a significant departure from the extant meaning of issaraphap, as well as the conception of rights in Siam.[139] Siam's social system emphasized hierarchy rather

[137] For a full explication of this process, refer to Loos, "Issaraphap."

[138] See for example, "Laksana phua mia" (Laws on Husbands and Wives), Clause 81, vol. 2 (Bangkok: Thammasat University Press, 1938), 43; "Laksana that" (Laws on Slaves), Clauses 3–4, vol. 2 (Bangkok: Thammasat University Press, 1938), 74; "Laksana moradok" (Laws on Inheritance), Clause 20, vol. 2 (Bangkok: Thammasat University Press, 1938), 152. All laws cited come from the KTSD (Bangkok: Thammasat University Press, 1938).

[139] Scholars like Joan Scott have determined that this notion of the universalized, abstract, and supposedly neutral individual was actually based on white, propertied males. Their exposure of the allegedly universal individual for its particular constitution explains how the concept of liberty existed simultaneously with the institutions of slavery in the United States and of coverture in the United States and Europe. Joan Wallach Scott, *Only Paradoxes to Offer: French Feminists and the Rights of Man* (Cambridge: Harvard University Press, 1996), 5.

than equality, demonstrated by individuals' sakdina rankings. In the nineteenth century, only people in positions of power obtained privileges, as opposed to rights, and these privileges were attached to the position, not the individual. The boundaries of issaraphap stop at the level of the self for a lower-class person but can include self and subordinates for the highest elites. Court documents suggest that the greater the intimacy or more immediate the dependency between two individuals, whether as husband and wife, parent and child, and even official and constituent, the greater the control a superior had over a subordinate and the less autonomy the subordinate individual had. Not only does issaraphap imply inequality between two individuals but it suggests that intimacy denied the subordinate issaraphap.

When Siam's translation commission selected *issaraphap,* with its inherent gender and status hierarchies, as the closest Thai cognate for *liberty,* Siam's elites in charge of translating the terms muted the radical potential of liberty as inherent to each individual equally.[140] Royal elites resisted the imposition of the legal concept of equal individual rights and liberties in Siam by indirectly transforming the meanings of Enlightenment law through translation. Simultaneously, Siam's rulers maintained their dominant position in the domestic social hierarchy by regulating through language who had access to the rights and obligations of the newly conceived legal subject. This example suggests the influence of transnationalism as well as its limitations. On the one hand, the concept of liberty is one of many that owed its existence in Siamese modern law to the foreign and foreign-educated legal advisers revising the penal and civil codes. On the other hand, once the work of transnational jurisprudence was localized in language, as well as through practical implementation in courts of law, it underwent a transformation that was not random. The translation into Thai of myriad English legal terms, each replete with their own historical and cultural associations, offered ample opportunity to reshape the meanings of these terms. In the case of liberty, its translation as issaraphap reflected the predispositions of the ruling class.

Domination, however, is never total, especially in language and law. The legal subject became a location of resistance for subordinate members of society who claimed status as legal subjects in order to contest existing power relations. After the promulgation in 1908 of a law protecting individuals against the deprivation of their liberty, lawyers attempted to use the new laws on issaraphap on behalf of servants against their proprietors, commoner women abducted by men, and constituents against officials.[141] In one case from 1911, an army prosecutor brought charges against six men for violating the issaraphap, committing assault, and perpetrating other crimes against Amdaeng Pha.[142] Amdaeng Pha worked for an army officer in Ayutthaya but

[140] For a full explication of this, see Loos, "Issaraphap."

[141] Loos, "Issaraphap."

[142] NA MR5 Yutitham 14.1 *Khamphiphaksa* (*cham-khuk*) (Verdicts [imprisonment]), mai het 46/23864 (Feb. 1914); Loos, Archival Notebooks, vol. 9, 36–59.

was persuaded by acting 2nd Lt. Thong Suk and his wife to move in with and work for them. However, abuse by Thong Suk and his wife and failure to pay wages compelled Amdaeng Pha to move out. Thong Suk, however, ordered his soldiers to capture and forcibly return Amdaeng Pha to his residence, where she was sexually and physically assaulted. The case went from the Dika Court to the desk of King Vajiravudh, who imprisoned Thong Suk for four years and another defendant for three for damaging the honor of the royal army and failing to respect the martial esprit de corps when they appropriated Amdaeng Pha from a fellow officer. The violation of a female servant's issaraphap, the first priority in the lower courts, was omitted at the apex of the judicial system, however. Culture-bound notions of issaraphap as a relative right that did not apply to servants trumped the imported idea of liberty. Amdaeng Pha's case exposes the limits of the legal protection provided by issaraphap, despite lawyers' attempts to use it in new ways. It also reveals the localized application of the law protecting individual liberty.

Several levels of domination and resistance surface in this example that a binary East-West model of colonial conflict obfuscates. Elite resistance to foreign hegemony is only one level on which Siam's leaders "resisted," intentionally or not, the imposition of foreign laws in Siam by guiding the translation and therefore the culturally nuanced meanings of key legal terms.[143] Within Siam, hierarchies of status, gender, age, and religion divided the population in myriad ways. Military officers who attempted to claim advantages that their position once allowed them found their presumptions challenged by subaltern women as well as by the monarch. This, however, does not imply an alliance between the latter two. At stake in these legal battles was nothing less than control over the meaning of national law and its concomitant links to power, protection, and resources.

According to the ethos of nationalism in the post-World War II era, the fact that the Siamese who worked on legal reforms were indigenous nationals gave them a privileged position as heroes of Siam's independence in the historical scholarship. The focus on their indigenousness in relation to foreign imperial powers, as opposed to their elite positions within Siam, has often hindered scholars from critically viewing the domestic impact of such reforms. Domestically, legal reforms stabilized, centralized, and solidified the power of the absolute monarchy even as the reforms introduced seemingly contradictory Enlightenment legal concepts such as the notion of individual rights. The ultimate goal of the reforms was not simply national political independence vis-à-vis foreign powers but the maintenance of existing hierarchies within Siam and the pursuit of imperial expansion on Siam's borders.

[143] For an excellent discussion and critique of resistance studies, see Sherry Ortner, "Resistance and the Problem of Ethnographic Refusal," *Comparative Studies in Society and History* 37, no. 1 (Jan. 1995): 173–93.

The same cosmopolitan leaders in charge of creating a uniform, centralized juridical system and legal code also sought to invent a legal subcolony in areas on the Malay Peninsula that bumped up against British territories. The transformation to modernity encouraged Siam to join the global community on equal terms, which meant engaging in empire.

THREE

Colonial Law and Buddhist Modernity in the Malay Muslim South

I began the previous chapter with the peculiar migration of the *Minhaj et Talibin* from its fifteenth-century Arabic originals through the hands of nineteenth-century Dutch and British colonial administrators to the desk of Islamic judges in southern Thailand today. It is one of many reference sources used by *dato yutitham* or Islamic judges at the Pattani provincial court who decide Muslim inheritance, marriage, and divorce cases.[1] A little-known fact about this Buddhist kingdom is that a pluralistic legal system exists in which national law applies throughout the country except in the four southern provinces of Pattani, Yala, Narathiwat, and Satun. In these areas, Islamic courts dispense Islamic marriage, divorce, and inheritance law in cases between Muslims, while national law applies in all other types of cases.[2] The courts are territorial rather than personal; cases among Muslims originating outside the four provinces cannot be settled in Islamic courts. Moreover, Muslims who live in these four provinces have no recourse to Thai civil courts in disputes relating to marriage, divorce, and inheritance, but must rely on the Islamic courts or resolve their cases outside these official institutions. Today, eight dato yutitham, two in each of the four provinces, handle an annual caseload ranging between two and three hundred, most of which are inheritance disputes.[3]

[1] I am grateful to the judges in Thailand's Islamic family courts, whose names I omit here so that they will in no way be associated with the opinions expressed in this chapter, which are my own.

[2] National law applies in all other civil and criminal cases regardless of the religious affiliation of litigants.

[3] One of the most senior dato yutitham estimated the number of cases. He maintains that no gov-

Photograph 4. Pattani Central Mosque, built in 1963 in Pattani Province.
Tamara Loos, 2003.

As of 2002, about 5 percent (three million) of Thailand's population of sixty-three million profess Islam as their religion (photograph 4).[4] In those four provinces, Muslims outnumber Buddhists, comprising as much as 60 to 80 percent of the population.[5] Muslims have formed the majority of the population there for centuries. Neatly conflating with religious differences are ethnic distinctions: most Muslims in Narathiwat, Pattani, and Yala (though not Satun) are ethnically, culturally, and linguistically Malay.[6] Most Buddhists are ethnic Thai who, as such, occupy a privileged location as more authentic nationals.

---

ernment office collects statistics on the number or types of cases adjudicated annually in the Islamic family court system. I have been unable to find any government statistics.

[4] National Statistical Office 2003, http://www.nso.go.th/eng/ (accessed 10 Jan. 2004).

[5] Chaiwat Satha-Anand, "Islam and Violence: A Case Study of Violent Events in the Four Southern Provinces, Thailand, 1976–1981," Monographs in Religion and Public Policy 2 (Tampa: University of South Florida, 1986), 19; Jaran Maluleem, "The Coming of Islam to Thailand," Occasional Paper 15 (Taipai: Academia Sinica, Program for Southeast Asian Area Studies, 1998), 9; Ryoko Nishii, "Social Memory as It Emerges: A Consideration of the Death of a Young Convert on the West Coast in Southern Thailand," in Shigeharu Tanabe and Charles F. Keyes, eds., *Cultural Crisis and Social Memory* (London: RoutledgeCurzon, 2002), 232.

[6] Satun's Muslims are largely ethnically Thai and Thai-speaking, hence they have a less contentious relationship with the state and are considered Thailand's "model Muslims." Satun has a history dis-

The following history of the establishment of these courts will undoubtedly be interpreted within the twenty-first century context in southern Thailand where a violent struggle has rekindled between Thailand's security forces and various groups, including but not limited to Malay Muslim separatists. The lack of information about politics on the ground in southern Thailand historically and today is the result of governmental and scholarly neglect of the region's local history, particularly as it articulates with Thailand's national history.[7] This history will be rewritten in the post-9/11 world, which has its own contextual biases. Even so, interrogating Siam's imperial past at this moment is absolutely essential, and yet it must be done carefully to distinguish between the resistance by Malay Muslim leaders at the turn of the twentieth century and the struggle engaged in by individuals fighting against Bangkok today. The historical and global contexts, local rationales, and the background of individuals involved in the struggle are different, though there are similarities in Bangkok's policies then and now.

With these considerations in mind, I examine the history of Patani and its Islamic family courts. Patani hereafter refers to the historical areas encompassed by the present day provinces of Pattani, Yala, and Narathiwat. By contrast, Pattani refers to the modern province of Pattani or indicates the view of the area from the perspective of Thai language sources.[8] The existence of what looks like a colonial-style plural legal system in Thailand's southern provinces today raises several issues, the most important of which is the apparent parallel between Thailand and imperial governments. Similar to colonies once possessed by Britain, the Netherlands, and most other imperial nations in the nineteenth and early twentieth centuries, Siam had also created a plural legal system. A hallmark of colonial states, plural legal systems established a hierarchy of legal rights and obligations among various populations founded in theory on the separation of the secular colonial state and religion. This operated in a much more complicated way in Siam, which both suffered under a plural legal system imposed by imperial powers and simultaneously forced a plural legal system on the Muslim population in the south.

On the one hand, Siam was subject to a plural legal system dictated by extraterritoriality clauses in treaties with Japan, the United States, and most European powers that removed from Siamese jurisdiction nearly all Europeans, Americans, Japanese, and their Asian subjects or protégés. Siam experienced

---

tinct from the other three Muslim-majority provinces. The state did not establish Islamic family courts there until 1917, about fifteen years after such courts had been established in Pattani, Yala and Narathiwat.

[7] The National Archives in Bangkok denied me access in the mid-1990s to documents relating to the southern Malay provinces. As a result, I rely heavily on Somchot Ongsakum's 1978 study, which utilizes sources from this archive.

[8] Patani is the Malay spelling, whereas Pattani is the romanized Thai spelling. On their usage, see Thanet Aphornsuvan, "Origins of Malay Muslim 'Separatism' in Southern Thailand," Working Paper Series No. 32 (Singapore: National University of Singapore, Asia Research Institute, 2004), 1, n. 2.

an attenuated form of domestic sovereignty and was placed in an asymmetrical position vis-à-vis the imperial powers.

On the other hand, a second, separate hierarchical legal system existed in Siam, which disrupts the parallels between Siam and colonized states: Siam subjected a segment of its "own" population to a colonial-style legal system. As Siam's leaders incorporated areas on the Malay Peninsula into the modern administrative system, they simultaneously created a separate legal jurisdiction for the Muslim population there. Siam's leaders were not naive or passive victims of imperial pressure; instead, they acquired a sophisticated understanding of British imperial strategies, including its legal systems. In this chapter I explore the rationale behind the establishment of Islamic family courts in the south and the extent to which they paralleled the plural jurisprudence dictated by colonial governments elsewhere. Bangkok's leaders, in a kind of competition with the British in Malaya, considered "their" Malay Muslim states in the south a colonized population and treated them accordingly. Yet, the decisions made by Siam's leaders in Muslim areas must always be understood within the framework of imperialism, which restricted and shaped Bangkok's policy in the south.

There are limitations to comparing Siam to either an imperial state or a colonized state. Although Siam shares the characteristics of a colonized state vis-à-vis the European imperial powers and of an imperial power toward the Muslim south, it cannot be conflated with either one. The comparison produces an irresolvable dialectical tension because Siam is measured against some unarticulated archetype of *the* colonized state and *the* imperial state, both of which have as their endpoint a Eurocentric model of modernity. Modernity is abridged here as rule by secular and rational institutions of the state, law, bureaucracy, and capitalist enterprise. These institutions are regarded as fundamental to the formation of a modern independent nation-state. The degree to which these institutions were, in practice, secular and rational, is an issue of great debate and not discussed here. Allusions herein to the secularity and rationality of this modular form of modernity refer to an *ideal,* not to the quasi-Protestant and often uneven, inconsistent realities of secularism and rationality in modern societies. The ideal, after all, exerted a form of power when colonial officials used it to legitimize policies that had an impact on colonized populations.

Siam, however, did not simply emulate the ideals of colonial modernity. Its form and path were distinct: Siam's monarchs reformed Theravada Buddhism when they created the Thammayut sect in the 1870s and made it an integral part of Siam's modernity. King Mongkut "purified" Buddhist doctrine and practice, which he felt had become tainted by superstition and substandard local practices. Thammayut Buddhism was adopted by all royally patronized temples and by 1902, with the Sangha Act, all of Siam's monasteries were rearranged in a hierarchy that precisely paralleled the new civilian administration. This enabled central control and imposed uniformity on monks, doctrine, and temples throughout Siam.

The conflation of religion and state power runs counter to theories of nationalism, which argue that modern nation-states are not defined in religious terms because they depend on inclusion regardless of race, class, or creed for their legitimacy. If a state adopted a particular religion, it would be exclusive of groups with different religious allegiances.[9] Siam's rulers, however, did not attempt to claim religious neutrality. Instead, Siam's absolute monarchs intensified the connections among religion, the modern state, and nationalism. Theravada Buddhism—Siam's official Thammayut incarnation of it, not canonical Buddhism—and royal power were articulated together, making it difficult to conceive of, let alone articulate, a distinction between monarchical power and Buddhism.[10] In fact, until the 1930s overthrow of the absolute monarchy and creation of a national constitution, the term for religion, *sasana,* was tantamount to *Phutthasasana* or Buddhism rather than to religion as an abstract category.[11] King Mongkut created the Thammayut Buddhist sect of Theravada Buddhism; King Chulalongkorn rationalized and conflated it with the modernizing state; and King Vajiravudh fused it with nationalism. As a result, secularism as a category created in opposition to religion did not resonate with Siam's ruling classes.

State-sponsored Thammayut Buddhism was created in response to Western Christian morality and to "superstitious" forms of Siamese Buddhism, not in response to southern Islam, about which Siam's leaders understood little. Focusing on the integration of the Muslim south into Siam proper and the concomitant creation of Islamic family courts highlights the religiosity of Siam's modernity as well as the centrality of the south to Siam's national history and historiography, which typically treats the Malay Muslim south as peripheral. This chapter is not a history of greater Patani, Islamic law, or reformed Theravada Buddhism as a part of Siam's modernity project, but focuses on the nexus of these three histories, which reveals Siam's distinct trajectory of modernity.

As the governments of Siam and the British in Singapore and Malaya began to clarify the territorial boundaries along their shared border they engaged in a kind of competitive colonialism that was, at best, secondarily interested in the desires of local populations. Siam's leaders were less concerned with Siam's survival, as nationalist historiography so frequently argues, than with demonstrating their status as equals to the British. The following section examines the establishment of Islamic family courts in Patani. Despite the similarities between the policies enacted by Siam and the

[9] van der Veer, *Imperial Encounters,* 19.
[10] On reforms in the Buddhist tradition, see Reynolds, "Buddhist Monkhood."
[11] Yoneo Ishii, "Thai Muslims," 455.

British on the Malay Peninsula, notable differences remained. One key distinction between Siam's alternative modernity and British notions of modern rule as secular was Siam's continued reliance on Siamese conceptions of Buddhism.

Historiography of Siam-Patani Relations

Buddhism, Islamic law, and Siam's modern state-building project collided in the region of Patani.[12] Most histories of Patani detail the political events, rather than social or cultural life, of the area. Ruled by a sultan or raja, Patani was an ethnically Malay and religiously Muslim area that had discontinuously paid tribute as a vassal state to Siamese kingdoms since the Sukhothai era (the thirteenth to the fifteenth centuries). Patani was also the center of Islamic teachings and Malay culture in the northern Malay Peninsula. It had the ability to protect itself militarily against Siam, or at least to wage powerful revolts that were inspired by Islamic leaders and teachings.[13] Whenever the Thai royal capital was weak, Patani's ruler revolted by refusing to send tribute. Once the Thai rulers regrouped, they sent troops south to force the sultan to resume paying tribute, symbolized by presentation of *bunga mas* (gold and silver trees). Rama II (r. 1809–1824) of the Chakri dynasty wanted to end this pattern, so he broke Patani into seven Malay principalities, each with their own ruler.[14] According to one pro-Patani account, Siam's troops violently quelled the Patani Malays, established Siamese laws of governance, and resettled some Siamese there.[15] The seven Malay principalities (*boriwen chet huamuang* or *muang khaek chet huamuang*) included Saiburi, Patani, Yala, Yaring, Ra-ngae, Raman, and Nong Chik. Only Nong Chik had a Thai Buddhist ruler, while the six others were governed by Muslim rajas. The relations between greater Patani and Siam remained fraught with tension that sometimes erupted in war when rajas tested the boundaries of their autonomy from Bangkok.

[12] This condensed summary of the history of Patani is an amalgam of many sources, including Chaiwat, "Islam and Violence"; Peter Chalk, "Militant Islamic Separatism in Southern Thailand," in *Islam in Asia: Changing Political Realities,* ed. Jason F. Isaacson and Colin Rubenstein (New Brunswick, N.J.: Transaction, 2001), 165–86; Kobkua Suwannathat-Pian, *Thai-Malay Relations: Traditional Intraregional Relations from the Seventeenth to the Early Twentieth Centuries* (Singapore: Oxford University Press, 1988); Narong, *Khwampenma;* Prasong Sukhum, *Chak yomarat thung sukhumwit* (From Yomarat to Sukhumwit) (Bangkok: Chulalongkorn University Press, 2000); Somchot, *Kan-patirup.*

[13] Kobkua, *Thai-Malay Relations,* 160.

[14] Some confusion exists over which monarch divided Patani into seven principalities. Kobkua says Rama I subjugated Patani through this divide and rule method, while others claim that Rama II divided Patani in 1817. In any case, both kings increased Bangkok's control over the region. Kobkua, *Thai-Malay Relations,* 161–62.

[15] Ibrahim Syukri [pseud.], *History of the Malay Kingdom of Patani,* trans. Conner Bailey and John N. Miksic, Monographs in International Studies, Southeast Asia Series No. 68 (Athens: Ohio University), 48.

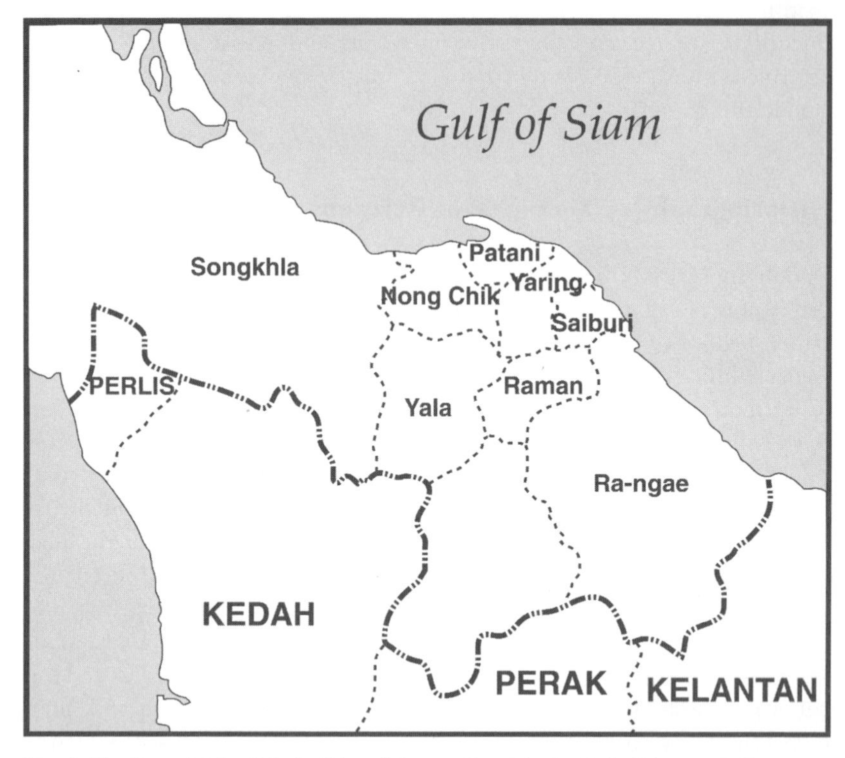

Map 2. The Seven Malay Principalities of Greater Patani in the Early Nineteenth Century
David W. Wyatt, 2005.

Until the 1890s, the seven Malay principalities ruled themselves autonomously in their day-to-day governance, recognizing Bangkok's nominal suzerainty by sending symbolic tribute and drinking the water of allegiance yearly, a ritual that signified their subordination to Siam's king. In the 1890s, Siam's leaders began to incorporate the south into the modern provincial administrative system (*thesaphiban* or "protection over territory" system), created by Prince Damrong, Siam's minister of the interior. By 1906, the once autonomous southern Malay principalities had been reformed into a monthon, the largest administrative unit in the provincial government. In 1931 the area was subdivided into the provinces of Pattani, Yala, and Narathiwat, as they are known today.

The catalyst for Bangkok's centralization of control over territory on all of its ill-defined borders in the 1890s was nineteenth-century European imperialism. Siam's encroachment in greater Patani had its own history and origins, but its administrative techniques had changed. Siam's presence in Patani shifted from a comparatively superficial one, marked by uneven periods of vigilance or neglect, to a more penetrative and permanent administration that used bureaucratic and military techniques associated with Bangkok's modernizing and centralizing state. This was in response to British encroachment in areas that Siam's Chakri dynasty considered within its sphere of influence. This encompassed Patani, Kelantan, Kedah, Trengganu, and Perlis—thousands of square miles that made up over half of the Malay Peninsula. Siam's provincial centralization system aimed at preventing divisions of territory to the detriment of Siam and in favor of imperial powers. The real losers in this context, as elucidated by Thongchai Winichakul in *Siam Mapped* (1994), were local rulers in Patani, Kelantan, Chiang Mai, and elsewhere. Parts of northwest Cambodia and Laos also became subject to an imperial tug-of-war between Siam and the French. However, Bangkok did not establish separate colonial family courts in formerly autonomous areas full of Lao and Khmer subjects, most of whom were Buddhist. Patani is unique in this regard, which is related to perceived religious differences and arguably ethnic distinctions between the Buddhist Siamese and Muslim Malays.

In the region of Patani, the gradual creation of a rational, unified, and centralized system of rule focused on Bangkok deprived provincial elites of autonomy over economic, political, and juridical power, except for Muslim family matters. Malay customary law or *adat,* which was "protected" in British ruled areas, seems to have been conflated with Islamic family concerns—Siamese government documents fail to mention adat as an arena of local elite jurisdiction. The legitimacy of Siam's monarchs was founded in Buddhist doctrine, rendering the categories of secular and religious irrelevant. Instead, Siamese state law and Islamic family law, which encompassed adat, were the only two relevant categories. Islamic law in the Malay states under Siamese control certainly entailed an admixture of Quranic law and local adat law that varied over time and place.[16]

The historiography of the process by which Patani was incorporated permanently into Siam because of foreign encroachment is, however, both frustratingly vague and classically teleological. Did Siam's leaders truly believe that the country's survival required integrating the Malay Muslim south? Did they actually replicate a (British) colonial model? By leaving the answers to these questions imprecise and generalized, historical accounts evade examination of the process by which the monarch used the reforms to centralize and solidify his control over formerly autonomous areas. The decision by Siam's rulers to incorporate certain territories on the Malay Peninsula (Patani) but not others (Kelantan and Trengganu, for example) and the specificities of the reforms were imbued with motives that went far beyond the original concern for Siam's independence, let alone survival. It entailed the

[16] One of the major differences between Islamic law and adat lies in the principles regarding inheritance. Whereas Malay adat favors bilateral descent in the inheritance of property (especially land), Islamic law entitles sons to receive twice the size or value of the shares allotted to daughters. Peletz, *Islamic Modern,* 56–57.

direct administration of hitherto autonomously ruled Malay Muslim states and involved several other measures that appear characteristically imperial.

This political chronology does not simply serve Siam's aggrandizing interests, however. Malay Muslims who desire autonomy from Bangkok have used the same chronology to argue that Siam is a colonial power that annexed Patani.[17] Hence, in addition to being vague, this structure of understanding history is teleological in that both the Siamese state and Malay separatists use the same idiom of national state formation. Both claim they were besieged by foreign powers. Both argue that their very existence was at stake because they could, at any moment, be colonized. This teleology is at the crux of Siam's dilemma: the kingdom appears colonized from the perspective of its asymmetrical relationship with European imperial powers *and* imperial in its relationship to the Malay states in the south. Siam is in a purgatory of in-betweens. Malay Muslims, by contrast, stand firmly on the ground of their victimization at the hands of Siam (and now Thailand), even though the process by which Patani was "colonized" by Siam differed from that of areas directly colonized by Europeans.

Competitive Colonialisms

Siam's in-betweenness has fundamentally to do with historical timing and context. The architects of Siam's modernity in the Malay south applied a preemptive colonization policy—Siam's rulers believed that if they did not aggressively incorporate the Malay principalities the British would. Siam's leaders are comparable to the colonial British, their rivals in the south, in many ways. Bangkok's leaders began implementing modern centralization techniques in earnest in 1896, a few months after Britain formalized its Malay policy by creating the Federated Malay States and the same year that France and Britain signed the Anglo-French Convention (January). The convention guaranteed the territorial integrity of the Menam Valley from colonial confiscation by France or Britain, but it remained silent regarding possession of areas along Siam's southern, northern, and eastern borders. In early 1896 Prince Damrong appointed the highly regarded Phra Wichit Worasat (Pan Sukhum), later renowned as Chao Phraya Yomarat, as special commissioner in charge of integrating the southern territories into Siam proper (see photograph 1, image 4, p. 50).

Chao Phraya Yomarat's initial reports about the Malay principalities reveal that Siam's leaders *did* think of the Malay Muslim population as foreign and

[17] Syukri, *History of the Malay Kingdom of Patani*. See examples from IslamOnline.net such as Iqbal Ragataf, "Thailand: Hunting Muslims to Death," 13 Feb. 2000, www.islamonline.net (accessed 3 Apr. 2003).

backward compared to Bangkok, which are key characteristics of a colonial state's rationale for rule. Siam's view of Malay Muslims as uncivilized and foreign may have had its origins in native elitism, but the attitude toward these differences was newly deployed to Siam's advantage. The "barbarity" of the Muslim areas compared to Bangkok's civilized methods of rule positioned Bangkok as relatively modern and thus comparable to European colonial powers. Siam's Malay Muslims were "others within" Siam's domestic social hierarchy, similar to the Senoi peoples on the Malay Peninsula (Orang Asli) described by Thongchai Winichakul.[18] However, these Muslims were also "others without" in being culturally located irrevocably outside the boundaries of Siam's national citizenry because of their ethnic and religious differences—differences that were the source of active local dissent and rebellion. In this way, they allowed Siam's leaders to prove to imperial Britain that Siam was a colonial power equally capable of colonizing a foreign population, modernizing its administration, and protecting its distinct religion and culture from change by providing special legal courts.

Chao Phraya Yomarat noted the foreign nature of the Malay population in his confidential reports to Prince Damrong, the man who created the provincial administrative system. Chao Phraya Yomarat observed that the population was *khaek malayu* or Malay Muslim, not Thai, in their own eyes as well as his. However, he initially believed they would identify as Thai once they received an education, experienced economic security, and were employed in the government.[19] His optimism quickly proved unfounded. After Siam's centralization policies were met with local resistance that ground the reforms to a halt for several years, Chao Phraya Yomarat began referring to these areas as *muang pa-pa* or semibarbaric states, replicating colonial civilizing discourse.[20] Siamese officials and ruling elite (and some historians) who narrated the incorporation of outlying areas into Siam proper wrote about the local elite as abusive, inefficient, corrupt, nepotistic, and oppressive to the "people."[21] By describing the preexisting "traditional" conditions in this way, King Chulalongkorn appears to have been compelled to intervene as the hero who protects the nation from being swallowed by imperial powers and saves the local population from the tyranny of the rajas ruling the Malay principalities.

[18] Thongchai Winichakul, "The Others Within: Travel and Ethno-Spatial Differentiation of Siamese Subjects, 1885–1910," in *Civility and Savagery: Social Identity in Thai States,* ed. Andrew Turton (Richmond, Surrey: Curzon Press, 2000), 38–62.

[19] Prasong, *Chak yomarat,* 167–68, 176–77.

[20] Somchot, *Kan-patirup,* 134. The discourse of civility and savagery is not the exclusive province of nineteenth-century European imperialism but can be found in early modern Siamese state discourses about populations not under oaths of allegiance to its leadership. Yomarat may well have tapped into older Siamese "othering" discourses, as well as those he was exposed to in nineteenth-century imperial discourses.

[21] Tej Bunnag, *Provincial Administration of Siam;* Somchot, *Kan-patirup,* 77, 87–93, 118–19.

The royalist narrative that dominates Thai historiography is grounded in the events surrounding Bangkok's incorporation of Patani. The logic by which King Chulalongkorn "saved" the kingdom from colonial intervention by modernizing and centralizing state power insists that the incorporation of the Muslim Malay south was crucial to Siam's very survival as an independent country. However, a closer look at the confidential reports by Chao Phraya Yomarat suggests that Siam's survival was hardly at stake. He wrote in February 1896 to Prince Damrong: "At this time, the British are itching to obtain all of the *khaek* [Muslim] states in *muang malayu* [the Malay principalities]. . . . If we do nothing and fail to manage to make them prosper, I fear that the British will find cause to seize them, deploying a ruse."[22] This is echoed in confidential reports at the highest levels of rule by Prince Damrong to King Chulalongkorn, who agreed on the need to "catch up" with British-controlled Malay areas. This discourse about Patani never expressed a *fear of extinction* but revealed instead a desire to be considered *an equal to European colonial states* in the region.

Tellingly, the 1896 reforms by Prince Damrong look remarkably like those promulgated in 1895 by the British in their newly created Federated Malay States.[23] The 1895 reforms formalized changes introduced in the Pangkor Treaty—the blueprint for British rule—by establishing a British "resident" in the Malay states of Perak, then subsequently in Selangor, Pahang, and Negri Sembilan. The British resident "advised" the local sultan or raja in all matters except "those touching Malay religion and custom."[24] This phrase regarding noninterference found its way into all future treaties with Malay authorities. Frank Swettenham, the resident in Perak in 1895, vigorously supported this system of indirect rule by negotiating an agreement with Malay rulers from the four states. Unsurprisingly, he became the first resident general of the Federated Malay States in July 1896.

Many of Siam's reforms in Patani closely resembled those initiated by the British. For example, both Siam's leaders and the British appointed a government representative to oversee the administration in their respective Malay states. Both allowed the existing Malay rajas to keep their positions but deprived them of political and fiscal autonomy. Both attempted to buy off rajas with state pensions. And finally, both allowed the Malay states a form of limited judicial autonomy over customary or Islamic concerns, narrowed to mean inheritance and marital matters. In practice, the British and Siamese severely constricted the jurisdiction of religious courts and authorities and intervened in them substantively. In other ways, Siam surpassed the British

[22] NA MR5 Mahathai 49/28 *Phrawichit ruan sat krap thun krom mun damrong ratchanuphap,* 42196, 26 Feb. 114 [1896], quoted in Somchot, *Kan-patirup,* 86, 132.

[23] M. B. Hooker, *Islamic Law in South-East Asia* (Singapore: Oxford University Press, 1984), 131.

[24] Barbara Andaya and Leonard Andaya, *A History of Malaysia,* 2nd ed. (Honolulu: University of Hawai'i Press, 2001), 158.

in the austerity and finality of the reforms. Siam's Malay rajas were not replaced when they died, were forbidden from conducting official affairs in their personal residences, and were no longer allowed control over any aspect of law including Islamic family law. Only Islamic legal experts could do that. Siam's official policy either integrated rajas into the modern administrative system or gradually removed them if they hindered the state's centralization policies.[25]

From the beginning, leaders of the Malay states resented and resisted Bangkok's presence. In 1896, Bangkok officials informed the rajas that they could continue to rule their localities as usual but must first receive the approval and accept the oversight of two Siamese officials, one of whom would live locally. Bangkok's presence would no longer remain at its usual geographic distance. The local rajas, in particular the raja of Pattani, opposed Bangkok's plans. He ordered everyone in Pattani to refuse to work for the Bangkok representative, who consequently had to paddle his own boat for lack of oarsmen and rent his own residence.[26] Humiliated and unable to accomplish anything, Bangkok's representative was recalled, and Siam's leaders, concerned about British intervention on the side of "oppressed" Pattani residents, waited before pressing their reforms.

The Anglo-Siamese Secret Convention signed in 1897 promised Siam's suzerainty over Trengganu and Kelantan if Siam promised not to alienate land in these two states to a foreign power without first consulting the British.[27] Bangkok's efforts to control Patani's leaders intensified. In July 1898, when the raja of Pattani died, King Chulalongkorn did not rubber-stamp the succession of the raja's son, Tengku (Prince) Abdul Kadir, but "appointed" him as temporary "acting governor." As Siam's leaders had feared, Tengku Abdul Kadir appealed to the British in Singapore for assistance on the grounds that the Siamese were bent on destroying Islam and local culture by preventing the normal succession from father to eldest son.[28] The accusation of destroying local Malay culture as a way to invite British intervention was a dangerous one and had to be dealt with immediately, so Chao Phraya Yomarat met with Mr. Anderson, the Thai consul in Singapore. He explained that it was King Chulalongkorn's prerogative to appoint local *chaomuang* or governors, not simply to authorize successors who might not have the educational background or administrative ability to carry out modernizing reforms. Still, Bangkok allowed the full appointment of Tengku Abdul Kadir

[25] Somchot, *Kan-patirup,* 135–56, 195–96.

[26] Ibid., 133.

[27] Andaya and Andaya, *History of Malaysia,* 198–200. In 1896, the British had formalized the Federated Malay States (out of Perak, Selangor, Negri Sembilan, and Pahang) and appointed a British resident who ruled through the shell of the preexisting Malay administrative system. This left Kedah, Perlis, Kelantan, and Trengganu in an ambiguous position between Siam and Britain (which acquired them in 1909).

[28] Somchot, *Kan-patirup,* 136.

as Pattani's "governor" (not raja) so long as he adhered to the new administrative regulations.

In August 1901 Tengku Abdul Kadir wrote to the British governor of the Straits Settlements, Frank Swettenham, that Siamese men were seducing and abducting Pattani women, persuading these women to cut their hair and convert to Buddhism.[29] He appealed to the British on religious grounds and in gendered terms, which were often effective means of securing "protective" intervention. In neighboring Kelantan, a famously anti-Siamese Briton similarly complained in 1900 that Siamese soldiers and officials had displaced over one hundred Malays and assaulted Malay women.[30] Chao Phraya Yomarat, who was also in charge of the Siamese mission in Kelantan, visited Kelantan in 1900 to try to convince the raja to submit to Bangkok's demand that he hand over the administration of the state to them in return for a monthly salary. These communications may have prompted Swettenham into action.

By 1901 Swettenham had become governor of the Straits Settlements and high commissioner for the Malay States. He desired British expansion into Kelantan and Trengganu so he proposed to help the Siamese obtain written agreements from Kelantan and Trengganu to give Bangkok de jure status there in return for having British nationals work for the Siamese government in Kelantan as advisers.[31] As these negotiations proceeded, a Siamese official met with each ruler of the seven Malay principalities and secured their signatures on a contract that promised they would abide by a set of centralizing reforms in local administration. Understanding that these reforms had been formally agreed to by the rajas, King Chulalongkorn promulgated his controversial Regulations Governing the Administration of the Seven Malay Principalities in December 1901. These reforms established a ruling committee in each of the Malay principalities of which the raja was simply one part, thus depriving him of political, juridical, and economic sources of power.[32]

Despite having signed the regulations, the vocal and charismatic raja of Pattani, Tengku Abdul Kadir, led the rajas of at least three other Malay principalities, Ra-ngae, Raman, and Saiburi, to thwart Bangkok's commissioner in his attempts to implement the reforms. Abdul Kadir's success in halting the reform process and his overt and regular contact with British officials in the Straits Settlements catalyzed Siam's leaders to send a warship to the mouth of the Pattani River in February 1902 to end Abdul Kadir's attempts to fo-

[29] Kobkua, *Thai-Malay Relations,* 215 n. 16.

[30] Mohamed B. Nik Mohd. Salleh, "Kelantan in Transition: 1891–1900," in William R. Roff, ed., *Kelantan: Religion, Society and Politics in a Malay State* (Kuala Lumpur: Oxford University Press, 1974), 36, note 54.

[31] Ibid., 40.

[32] Somchot, *Kan-patirup,* 146–48.

ment opposition to Bangkok's sweeping reforms.[33] Abdul Kadir was arrested and shipped to Phitsanulok, where he was placed under house arrest and stripped of authority over Pattani.[34] Bangkok's action in Pattani is similar to the Paknam incident of 1893, when the French sent two gunboats up the Chaophraya River to Bangkok and demanded all Lao territories east of the Mekong River. In both cases, a foreign power threatened the autonomy of a local power, and the British were considered a potential foreign ally to the local powers.

The dismissal of Tengku Abdul Kadir caused a diplomatic uproar. Frank Swettenham asked the British Colonial Office (in India) to intervene on behalf of the deposed raja. However, after intense negotiations in Bangkok, the British agreed to desist from intervening in Pattani. The settlement must have involved a quid pro quo in Kelantan and Trengganu, the two areas to which the British turned their full attention, because they did not refer again to Pattani. The Anglo-Siamese Treaty of 1902 required Siam to appoint two British nationals: William A. Graham, as Siam's adviser in Kelantan and Trengganu, and H. W. Thomson, a former officer in the Federated Malay States (FMS), as the assistant adviser.[35] The treaty, like others before it, required the rajas to accept advice in all matters except those pertaining to Islam and Malay custom. According to one source, Siam had to obtain the British government's consent when it selected or removed Kelantan's "Siamese" advisers or renewed their contracts.[36] This ambiguous situation was resolved only in 1909, when Siam and Britain signed a new treaty that transferred Kelantan, Trengganu, Perlis, and Kedah to the British in return for the removal of extraterritoriality protections for most of Britain's Asian subjects and for a loan at 4 percent interest to Siam's government from the Federated Malay States to build a railway in southern Siam.[37]

The Siamese negotiators in 1902 may have understood the intentions behind Swettenham's scheme of employing British nationals in areas nominally under Siam's suzerainty, but they signed the treaty for reasons of their own. In return for agreeing to British advisers, Siam received British support in controlling the seven Malay principalities that comprised Patani.[38] By May

[33] Ibid., 189–190.

[34] He was released in 1904, after he pledged to not intervene in the local administration or politics again. However, he continued to lead the resistance to Siamese rule until his death in 1933. Kobkua, *Thai-Malay Relations,* 178–81.

[35] According to one source, Graham arrived in Kelantan with his own detachment of troops suggesting the lack of local support for his initiatives. Clive S. Kessler, *Islam and Politics in a Malay State: Kelantan, 1838–1969* (Ithaca: Cornell University Press, 1978), 50; Salleh, "Kelantan in Transition," 41.

[36] Salleh, "Kelantan in Transition," 41. Given the controversial status of Graham among British officials in Malaya and the strong defense of him by Prince Damrong, one cannot assume that Graham worked for British interests in Kelantan, but his nationality set a trend.

[37] Salleh, 55–57; Thornely, *Siam in Transition,* 200–219.

[38] Moreover, Siam agreed in 1899 to give the British territory near Raman as a way to smooth

1902, Siam's officials in the south were able to implement reforms with less apprehension of British interference.

After Bangkok resorted to force, arrested the ringleader from Pattani, and proved that the British would not intervene, the remaining resistance fell apart. The rajas of Yala and Yaring decided to send their children to study government service with Chao Phraya Yomarat.[39] Ra-ngae's raja "volunteered" to study methods of government administration in Songkhla with Chao Phraya Yomarat. Tuanmat, the son of the supervisor of Raman (Phra Narongwangsa), who approved of Bangkok's reforms, took the place of the raja of Ra-ngae. In Muang Raman, many officials who opposed Bangkok's reforms were dismissed and the salaries of those remaining were increased. Chao Phraya Yomarat went to Raman in 1902 where he arrested Luang Raya (Thai transliteration of raja) Phakdi, the son of the raja of Raman, for murder.[40] The year 1902 was a turning point in Siamese-British relations. Chao Phraya Yomarat, Prince Damrong, and King Chulalongkorn had been aware of Luang Raya Phakdi's crime for over a year. They had discovered in March 1901 that Phakdi had ordered the death of a woman who had arranged an adulterous affair between his wife and a Malay Muslim man.[41] King Chulalongkorn opined that the khaek punishment for adultery was severe but that Siam had "great power" (*rao mi amnat mak*), meaning sovereign jurisdiction, over the case. However, he cautioned against any action that might invite British meddling. Only after tensions with the British and southern Malay leaders had been relieved in 1902 could Bangkok's representative enforce new laws. Luang Raya Phakdi received a twenty-year prison term.

In sum, Bangkok dealt with local resistance by arresting and exiling dissident rajas; co-opting rajas and community leaders by offering pensions or prestigious positions in the Siamese local administration; sending Siamese troops, police, and the royal navy to intimidate local opposition; creating a spy unit in May 1902 to keep abreast of movements in the south; and enlisting the British to refuse to support rebellious rajas.[42] Militarily, Siam's lead-

---

relations and gain leverage to proceed unhindered with Siam's reforms in the south. Kobkua, *Thai-Malay Relations,* 176.

[39] Somchot, *Kan-patirup,* 156–58.

[40] Ibid., 157.

[41] NA MR5 Mahathai 50/2 Nakhon Srithammarat, case 47/16, mai het 17/321, "Ruang luang raya phakdi kha amdaeng mae-ae sae tai doi ha wa pen su chak phanraya luang raya phakdi pai hai kap khaek mae rae kratham chukan" (The case of Luang Raya Phakdi's murder of Miss Mae-ae Sai, who he accused of being a go-between in the adulterous liaison between the wife of Luang Raya Phakdi and the Khaek Mae Rae), R.S. 119 [March 1901]; Loos, Archival Notebooks, vol. 6, 107–10.

[42] Somchot lists what chaomuang were paid by the Siamese government to compensate them when they were deprived of their taxation privileges. Chaomuang were paid an annual salary plus a "bonus." In 1905–6, they received the following amounts and they and their relatives were exempt from paying any government taxes: Pattani, 12,000 baht; Nong Chik, 12,000 baht; Yaring, 11,000; Saiburi, 14,000; Ra-ngae, 10,000; Raman, 8,000; and Yala, 10,000. Somchot, *Kan-patirup,* 179–80, 187–90.

ers used a regional ethnic and religious minority—Buddhist Siamese—to counterbalance or regulate a majority population—the Muslim Malays in the south. Before his posting there, Chao Phraya Yomarat learned of this technique while in British Burma, where the British used Indians to help administer Burma. This caused some Burmese to hate khaek (in this case, ethnic South Asians).[43] Later, when King Chulalongkorn instituted national military conscription in 1909, the Ministry of Interior refused to arm and train local populations in the south because of their ethnic difference.[44] The Siamese government did not trust the Malays with arms. Instead, an ethnic Thai military force patrolled the south, paralleling the British deployment of Indian soldiers and police in British Burma and the Malay states. In all, these strategies offer overwhelming evidence that Siam's leaders thought very consciously like those of an imperial state.

After 1902, Bangkok's representatives aggressively implemented reforms, which included the creation of four new administrative posts in each of the seven principalities: the *chaomuang,* which is the name by which rajas were referred and thereby incorporated in a subordinate position within the Siamese government system; deputy chaomuang, who was usually a Bangkokian; a *yokrabatmuang* with duties involving law and order; and an assistant who would advise this muang-level council on laws and reforms. The raja, as chaomuang, was required to conduct all government business out of a newly constructed government office, rather than out of his personal residence. If he failed to show up, the Bangkokian deputy chaomuang ran governmental affairs in his stead.[45] Above this local ruling committee was a regular commissioner (*kha luang yai pracham*), and above him was the special commissioner of Nakhon Sri Thammarat (occupied then by Chao Phraya Yomarat).

Siam's leaders began to articulate "their" Malay states as sites of competitive colonial modernity. Having reached some clarity regarding possession of the border areas, Siam's leaders shifted their policy in the Malay states to one of competition with British-controlled areas on the peninsula. King Chulalongkorn wanted Siam "to catch up with" the British in modernizing the political and economic administration of the Malay areas, especially Kelantan and areas directly bordering Siam's territories; otherwise, the British would believe that they could better modernize the region.[46] King Chulalongkorn had long been keeping track of British assessments of Siam's ability to govern the Malay principalities. He had collected articles written in the British papers in Singapore and Penang that criticized the Siamese gov-

[43] Prasong, *Chak yomarat,* 84.

[44] Krasuang mahat-thai, *Thesaphiban,* vol. 24, map 24 (Bangkok: Mar. 1908), and PKPS 21: 330–31, cited in Somchot Ongsakun, *Kan-patirup,* 202.

[45] Somchot, *Kan-patirup,* 138.

[46] MR 5 Mahathai 49/25, number 26/924, "Kromluang damrong ratchanupha krap bankhom thuk R. 5," 27 Apr. 1904, cited in Somchot, *Kan-patirup,* 183.

ernment's administration of the seven Malay states. The articles suggested that the Siamese government was incapable of creating a prosperous or efficient local government equal to that organized by the British in their Malay states.[47]

Siam's Malay states became a showcase of Siam's ability to modernize local administration, rather than an area with natural resources to exploit. This is best evidenced by the official financial statements proving that Bangkok failed to earn revenue from the seven Malay principalities. Instead, they exerted a drain on the royal treasury. This stands in stark contrast to claims made by one Malay separatist, writing in the late 1940s, who argued that Siamese officials drained Patani of its revenues, all of which enriched Siamese officials and Bangkok, rather than being used for the welfare of the local population.[48] Both may have been true. Patani's economic infrastructure may have been unable to support the new administrative apparatus even after the collection of taxes, causing Bangkok to send additional funds to develop the local administration so they could visibly demonstrate to the British that Siam could cultivate these areas as well as the British could. If true, then Siam was not investing in the Malay states exclusively for economic profit or for territorial aggrandizement but to prove to imperial powers that Siam was a capable equal. The few government sources that exist do not suggest that Bangkok highly prioritized the welfare of the local population, who may have had cause to resent the new administration.

Islamic Family Courts in Southern Siam

Perhaps the most important display in the "showcase" of Siam's colonial modernity was the Islamic family court system established in the south. These courts reveal most clearly Siam's attempt to compete with the British in creating a model colony that ran efficiently and was "just" to the "native" population, at least on paper. The model for the reformed Islamic laws and courts is clearly British. King Chulalongkorn himself suggested sending someone to investigate the laws that the English used in their Malay possessions and consider modifying them for use in Siam's Malay states.[49] In the years after 1902, Siamese centralized state courts were established in the south alongside Islamic courts. Both courts were inventions of the modern Siamese state system. The Muslim courts were created and systematized, which removed juridical power from local rajas, and Bangkok's representatives selected a cadre of Islamic judges from respected local religious figures.

[47] Somchot, *Kan-patirup,* 119.

[48] Syukri, *History of the Malay Kingdom of Patani,* 63.

[49] NA MR5 Mahathai 49/27, Confidential correspondence 187/696, "Ruang phonprayot muang nongchik lae muang khaek 7 huamuang, phraratcha-hatlekha r. 5 thung kromamun damrong ratchanuphap," 6 Mar. 1896, cited in Somchot, *Kan-patirup,* 128.

Regarding the legal "autonomy" that both the Siamese and the British allowed in Malay Muslim areas, the decision to establish autonomous Islamic courts and law rather than imposing foreign law could be interpreted as a positive result of colonization. Muslims were allowed to practice their faith unhindered. In practice, however, the British and Siamese severely constricted the authority of religious courts and authorities, reshaping their function, power, and relevance. Not only did Siamese and British officials subsume Islamic authority under that of their respective governments but they intervened substantively in Islamic codes and procedures in an effort to restructure Islamic institutions within their modern bureaucratized legal regimes.

In his chapter on the colonial history of Islamic courts in British Malaya, Michael Peletz emphasizes that "the British imperial bias toward written codes and substantive law as opposed to, say, more informal, unwritten modes of operation, including, especially, those bearing on procedure and the cultural logic of judicial process, means that we do not know much about actual judicial process in the *kadi*'s [Islamic judge] courts during any period of colonial rule."[50] Even less is known about local Islamic judges, law, and society in areas administered by Siam's representatives, who, unlike their neighboring British colonialists, were neither systematic in their collection of information about the south nor in their production of voluminous Orientalist texts. For example, none of Siam's officials (aside from the monarch who wrote travel diaries) wrote about their experiences officiating in the south, whereas British officials such a Swettenham and Clifford wrote copiously, and even Graham wrote a comprehensive study of Kelantan during his six-year stint there.

For Patani, the main documents extant for that period are ephemeral Thai language reports written by the officials who came predisposed to interpret the methods of local administration as barbaric, thus requiring righteous Siamese intervention. Given the colonial attitude of Siamese officials, it is especially regrettable that no Siamese documents on the Muslim practice of polygyny exist from this period. Both the Siamese Buddhists and Malay Muslims allowed polygyny, but in different ways and for different reasons. It is unlikely that this practice was regarded as a shared one by either community, given their hierarchical relationship and the distinct reasons for the practice by each religion.

Because of a lack of sources about turn-of-the-century Patani, sources on Kelantan are used to speculate about social and religious life in Patani. If Patani was anything like its neighbor, then village social life revolved around the *surao,* or prayer house and ritual center. There the imam, who presided over the surao, also acted as the religious leader of the community as a whole. He was responsible for the proper conduct of Friday prayer, ensured that

[50] Michael Peletz, *Islamic Modern,* 48.

Shari'a laws on marriage and divorce were implemented, performed funeral rights, and resolved disputes relating to the interpretation of law, especially about the division of landed property.[51] Both Islamic and Malay customary law applied in criminal, civil, and religious disputes, but the relative significance of adat as opposed to Islamic law varied over time. A Shari'a court (an Islamic court with jurisdiction over Islamic matrimonial, personal law, property law, and violations of Islamic moral law) existed in Kelantan but not in any other British-protected Malay state and probably not in Patani either.[52] Even in Kelantan, where the Shari'a court suggests the dominance of Islam over adat, Graham noted in 1908 that people did not strictly adhere to Sunni Islam, but followed Malay customs and animistic practices as much or more so. There, in a state known for its relatively strict adherence to Islamic law, Graham claims that "animistic superstition" is "thinly covered by a veneer of Mohammedanism and ready to crop up at any moment of stress, not only amongst the peasantry but in the highest quarters."[53] Men were described as inveterate gamblers, not with dice or cards, but with bulls, buffalo, cocks, and fish. Kelantanese women, he wrote, follow the

> customs of their Siamese, Burmese, Cambodian and other Mongolian neighbours rather than the sterner precepts of their adopted religion. The women move about with perfect freedom, buying and selling in the markets and in their shops, visiting their friends and assisting their husbands in their agricultural pursuits, and except for the wearing of the Kelumbong [loose shawl used to cover the head, face, and shoulders], which burlesque is the only concession to Islam, their habits and manners are scarcely to be distinguished from the usually modest behaviour of the females of the other Indo-Chinese races. (Graham, *Kelantan,* 24–25)

It is not a stretch to imagine that in Patani, men and women interpreted and practiced a localized form of Islam that reflected customary practices, and that Islamic law too was practiced in less doctrinal forms than in the Middle East.

Chao Phraya Yomarat's descriptions of social life in Patani are nonexistent, but he comments extensively on local jurisprudence prior to the 1890s reforms. He views the situation in the Patani region through the distorting prism of modernity that motivated colonial-style reforms. He writes that the political structure of the seven Malay principalities included a governor (chaomuang), a council of city fathers (*sri tawan kromakan*), and a committee

[51] William Roff, "The Origin and Early Years of the Majlis Ugama," in *Kelantan: Religion, Society and Politics in a Malay State,* ed. William R. Roff (Kuala Lumpur: Oxford University Press, 1974), 104–5.

[52] Ibid., 120.

[53] Graham, *Kelantan,* 32.

of judges (to-kali), which may correspond to kadi, the Malay term for Islamic judges. Their official duties overlapped, as there was no functional division of labor. For instance, within each of the seven principalities, several different judges existed, each with their own jurisdiction. One kind of judge called the dato (Malay term for "elder," used as an honorific title for a nonroyal official) arbitrated all cases relating to taxation, while to-kali (Islamic judges) handled cases of a more strictly religious nature. *Mae kong* or *to khwaeng* (*to' kweng* or *penghulu* in Malay) or district headmen dealt with conflicts that incurred no more than a five *rian* penalty.[54] The position of to khwaeng is Siamese, which indicates that Siam had already introduced changes in the local administration. To khwaeng represented Siamese attempts to wrest some authority from local imams in Kelantan, and that may also have been the case in Patani.

In all, Chao Phraya Yomarat observed at least three types of judges whose jurisdiction depended on a combination of the gravity of the penalty and the nature of the infraction. However, the raja or chaomuang could deprive the existing hierarchy of judges of any power because he exercised complete and arbitrary control over all cases. Moreover, because there was no written code for deciding cases, the raja exercised total authority over decisions, fines, the severity of punishment, and the success of appeals.[55]

According to Chao Phraya Yomarat, the chaomuang's excesses manifested in two ways, both of which were related to family law. First, local rulers had usurped jurisdiction over any profitable cases of inheritance and marriage that clearly should have fallen within the purview of Islamic judges (to- kali). The chaomuang decided cases in ways that profited his entourage, rather than investigating the accusations of the plaintiff. Second, not only had the chaomuang overstepped their jurisdictional boundaries in terms of religious authority but they had also, in the eyes of Bangkok, grossly exaggerated the punishment for adultery. In adultery cases, the chaomuang would bury the accused man to his neck and order passersby to stone him to death.[56] In Siam, no one but the monarch in Bangkok had legitimate control over the life and death of Siam's subjects, so the power of execution exercised by rajas directly infringed on and challenged the authority of the king.

Chao Phraya Yomarat understood the severity and barbarity of the punishment meted out by the chaomuang as an instance of spectacular despotism driven by the objectives of personal enrichment and fanatical barbarity. The population of the Muslim south required Siamese government intervention, according to this logic, to protect them from the arbitrary exercise of unlimited power by local autocrats. There is no sense that Chao Phraya

[54] Somchot, *Kan-patirup,* 73–74.
[55] Ibid., 75.
[56] Ibid., 77.

Yomarat understood the local interpretation and application of Islamic laws regarding adultery in the context of the south. Instead, it was imminently deployable to symbolize Muslim Malays' difference from and relative backwardness compared to the Buddhist Siamese. Significantly, this line of reasoning precisely parallels the rationale used by (Christian) imperial powers to intervene in their colonies and to impose extraterritoriality clauses on Siam. It was used by King Chulalongkorn to describe Siam's traditional justice to justify the modernizing, centralizing reforms, and it was used by W. A. Graham in his 1908 description of the chronic infighting among members of the ruling classes in Kelantan.[57]

To rectify the perceived abuse of power by rajas, the Siamese government initiated a new set of administrative reforms in December 1901. The regulations required the implementation of the 1896 Constitution of the Provincial Courts. Three levels of (non-Islamic) state courts were created: *khwaeng* or lowest-level courts were established in Muang Ra-ngae and Raman; muang-level courts were set up in Saiburi and Yala; and a *boriwen* or monthon court of the highest-level provincial court was created in Pattani.[58] It also stipulated that Islamic courts would be established to resolve civil disputes regarding marriage, divorce, and inheritance among Muslims living in the newly incorporated territories. This required a distinction between religious law and jurisdiction and Siam's state law and jurisdiction. When Chao Phraya Yomarat reported on religious courts in the south in 1897, he said that a religious court called a san to-kali existed in six of the seven principalities where Islamic experts decided cases according to Islamic law.[59] Presumably, the newly defined Islamic family courts were built upon the preexisting ones, whose jurisdiction was narrowed.

It is not known what kind of law was used to resolve disputes in the Malay Muslim south whose population, like other Muslims in Southeast Asia, adhered to the Shafii school of Islam. Nor is it known whether any written codes existed in the Patani region in 1901. The December 1901 regulation stipulated the use of the Quran in the Islamic family courts. According to one of the few books on the subject, Islamic laws used in the south derived from the Quran, *hadith* (a secondary body of Islamic scripture attributed to the Prophet Muhammad that provides religious guidance and describes law and customs), and *kitab* (texts that explain and expand on the Quran and hadith).[60] These books were written in Arabic and Malay (both in romanized script and in Jawi, the Malay language written in Arabic script), even though very few could read Arabic.

Within a year, the Ministry of the Interior further intervened in Islamic

[57] Graham, *Kelantan,* 50–54.

[58] Somchot, *Kan-patirup,* 172–73. A severe shortage of judges during these early years meant that the Ministry of Interior had to appoint local Malay officials as judges in the nonreligious state courts.

[59] Somchot, *Kan-patirup,* 131.

[60] Narong, *Khwampenma,* 21.

law by issuing a new set of rules because the to-kali "did not clearly know Muslim law."[61] Chao Phraya Yomarat called a meeting in October 1902 of all existing to-kali, to-hayi (a reference to haji, individuals who had completed a pilgrimage to Mecca), and other Islamic religious experts. They agreed to a new set of regulations (*san-tra*) issued by the Ministry of the Interior in December 1902 which empowered the chaomuang to select six haji, who were also religious experts, to be to-kali. The regular and special commissioners had veto power over their appointments, a secular court judge approved their decisions, and the to-kali had to follow the civil and criminal procedural rules issued by the Ministry of Justice.[62] This did not solve the issue of the substantive content of the law, however. According to reports from 1903, there were persistent problems resolving family disputes among Muslims because the to-kali did not have an adequate grasp of the kitab texts, which purported to explain the law.

Bangkok intervened extensively in the substantive and procedural laws regulating Patani's Islamic courts and personnel, despite promises to the contrary. In Kelantan as well, Graham intervened in the Shari'a court by securing the passage of regulations that dealt with marriage and divorce, set Islamic court procedures, established rules of evidence, standardized penalties, and so on. In addition, in Kelantan, the imam's authority and function was bureaucratized and disciplined, bringing this position under central control in the capital, Kota Baharu.[63]

Over time, the Islamic courts, the process of selecting Islamic judges, and the laws used were systematized and codified. By the 1910s, stricter requirements for selecting dato yutitham, as to-kali were then called, were instituted. Bangkok established greater control over the appointment of judges who had to pledge affection (*namchai*) and steadfast loyalty (*chong-rak phakdi*) to the Siamese monarch.[64] According to other sources, by the late 1920s the judges were selected by qualified Muslims and imam who would then seek the approval by the chief judge of the provincial (monthon) court and the king.[65] Astoundingly, the laws were not fully systematized (from dozens of Arabic and Malay language kitab) and translated into Thai until 1941.

If Siam's leaders were not concerned with the content of Islamic law, signified by their lack of interest in having it translated into Thai for nearly fifty years, why did they establish Islamic courts? Islamic family courts were not maintained because local Muslims agitated for them but, in part, because

[61] Ibid., 48.

[62] Somchot, *Kan-patirup,* 169–72.

[63] Roff, "Origin and Early Years of the Majlis Ugama," 113–16.

[64] Narong, *Khwampenma,* 62, 67. By the 1950s, Islamic judges also had to be over twenty-five and able to read and speak Thai.

[65] NA MR6 Yutitham 4 Sanhuamuang 12, maihet 25/52, "Ruang santokali lae tang dato yutitham pen phuphiphaksa chamra khwam satsana itsalam" (Documents regarding the to-kali courts and establishing Dato Yutitham as judges to clear up Islamic court cases), Apr. 1916–Nov. 1925. See also Narong, *Khwampenma,* 67–68.

Siam's officials believed that if they did not have religious family courts, the Muslims would protest, which might invite foreign intervention and would certainly suggest Siam's inability to rule. It was a preemptive policy based on the colonial models of law that King Chulalongkorn, Prince Damrong, and others saw in colonial states on their borders. There is, however, a more profound reason behind the transformation of Islamic jurisprudence in Siam. Siam, like colonial governments elsewhere, considered practices related to family and religion sources of local cultural authenticity and, therefore, necessary to preserve in some form. By contrast, laws that supported the development of the capitalist state and economy, including commercial laws, contract law, and administrative regulations, were treated as if they reflected universal, natural practices of competition. As it turns out, this bifurcation was fictional rather than actual in both the Siamese and the British Malay instances.

The power of claims to authenticity and tradition, however, lent credibility and power to the reconstructed spaces of Islamic courts to such a degree that the idea of abolishing them today is inconceivable. When Field Marshall Phibun Songkhram abolished the office of the dato yutitham and the use of Islamic family law courts in the four southern provinces in the early 1940s, Malay Muslims in Patani protested these revocations and other abuses by Phibun's administration.[66] Haji Sulong, the head of the Islamic Council, and other Muslim leaders submitted demands to Bangkok that included the reinstatement of Islamic courts, laws, and justices that would, moreover, no longer be subsumed within the Thai civil court system.[67] Phibun fell from power in 1944, after which more sympathetic governments took over and attempted to address the Muslim protesters. By 1946, the Islamic courts and justices had been reinstated.

Siam's Buddhist Modernity

Euro-American colonial states were nonsectarian in publicly articulating a policy of noninterference in "native" religious practices, even though they regularly disregarded this policy.[68] Similarly, most modern histories of Siam claim that Siam was (and is) tolerant of all religions and is officially nonsectarian. Yet Buddhism and state power are conflated throughout the reigns of Siam's modernizing kings (Mongkut, Chulalongkorn, Vajiravudh, and even the currently reigning King Bhumipol), who have ruled since the 1850s. Here, Siam departs again from the European model of colonial modernity.

[66] Thanet Aphornsuvan, "Origins of Malay Muslim 'Separatism,'" 25–26.
[67] Syukri, *History of the Malay Kingdom of Patani*, 71–72.
[68] Peter van der Veer problematizes this secularization in *Imperial Encounters.*

Siam did not publicly articulate a nonsectarian policy. Instead, Siam's leaders conjoined Buddhism and state rule, which is perhaps best exemplified in their interpretation of the 1902 *phumibun* (holy man) rebellions in Siam's northeast, a response to Bangkok's centralization policies. These were regarded as superstitious movements by Siam's ruling elites and foreign colonial powers alike because, for instance, the rebels believed that amulets would protect them from bullets. However, Siam's rulers did not counterpose "superstition" to secular rationality, as it is in the Enlightenment understanding of the concept. Instead, it was counterposed to a Buddhist rationality that characterized the Thammayut sect of Theravada Buddhism, which was created by King Mongkut and "rationalized" by King Chulalongkorn. Although the royally sponsored Thammayut sect distinguished itself from foreign religions such as Islam and Christianity, it even more intensely separated itself from less doctrinal forms of Buddhism. When King Chulalongkorn traveled throughout his territory, he refused to enter and thereby endorse certain Buddhist temples because of their unorthodox practices.[69] So, the absolute monarchy's antagonism to the Malay Muslim areas was not a simplistic antagonism between two monoliths—Buddhism and Islam. Patani's Islam was far from doctrinal. In addition, Siam was in the process of modernizing and refining the kind of Buddhism that informed state policies and principles.

Siam's modernity is imbued with a form of Buddhism practiced by royal elites. Although it permeated the reforms everywhere, it had an especially detrimental impact in the Muslim south, which was rejected as foreign and structurally barred from complete integration into the state through the institutionalization (in the Islamic family court system) of its differences. No other ethnic or religious group in Siam was treated this way by Siam's government, because the others either practiced a form of Buddhism (ethnic Lao, Khmer, and Burmans) or their religion did not map onto ethnic and territorial claims (Christians).

There are many examples of how King Chulalongkorn devoutly practiced his faith and conflated it as a matter of course with modern state rule in the Muslim areas. Evidence used here comes from King Chulalongkorn's journal of his first official trip to the Malay Peninsula, in 1888, as a fully empowered monarch. After disembarking on Samui Island in the Gulf of Siam, the vigorous thirty-something King Chulalongkorn visited one Buddhist temple after another: from Wat Kham to Wat Maraet to a newly constructed temple replete with four impressions of the Buddha's footprints. From Samui, the king went to Muang Songkhla where, after meeting briefly with some local Malay Muslim (khaek) officials, he visited Wat Machanimawat, the cen-

[69] Kamala Tiyavanich, *Forest Recollections: Wandering Monks in Twentieth-Century Thailand* (Honolulu: University of Hawai'i Press, 1997), and *The Buddha in the Jungle* (Seattle: University of Washington Press, 2003).

tral temple for Thammayut monks. At Yo Island he climbed to Wat Laemkrapho and visited a Chinese garden. An energetic traveler, he reboarded the boat and disembarked in Pattani, where he was greeted by the city elders and their children, wives, and relatives. He met briefly with the raja of Pattani before visiting Wat Tani, the town's central Buddhist temple, where he donated funds to the *kapitan chin,* the leader of the Chinese community, to build a pavilion at the temple. The pavilion, he decreed, would become an education center for monks to teach Buddhism, where local people would receive an education to qualify them to work in the local government administration, and where the raja of Tani and other city elders would henceforth drink the oath of allegiance to Siam's king.[70]

This summary of relevant passages from his travel diary suggests that King Chulalongkorn made his presence felt in the south by carving a peculiar path, endorsing certain sites but bypassing others. It looks like a Buddhist pilgrimage (*thiao wat*) to certain Buddhist temples sprinkled with brief visits to the local markets, Chinese sites of commerce and production, and the homes of local dignitaries. However, his travel itinerary did not include stops at significant Islamic sites, even though he was aware that Songkhla and Pattani were largely Muslim cities and that Muslim rajas ruled most of the areas he visited.[71] Most important, the king's decision to continue to require that Muslim officials participate in the ritualistic drinking of the water of allegiance—a Brahmanic ritual incorporated by Siam's Buddhist monarchy—to a conspicuously Buddhist ruler in a Buddhist temple appears to defy the logic of secular modernity. He was clearly not attempting to create a neutral secular context for conducting government affairs or for training new officials. The king's selection of a Buddhist temple for the training of future officials drawn from the local population unsurprisingly failed to attract Muslim candidates. As a consequence, Malay Muslims rarely obtained the kind of education that would enable them to qualify for work in Siam's administration in the southern provinces.

Clifford Geertz discusses in another context how monarchs take symbolic possession of their realm through rituals, ceremonies, and royal processions: "When kings journey around the countryside, making appearances, attending fêtes, conferring honors, exchanging gifts, or defying rivals, they mark it like some wolf or tiger spreading his scent through his territory as almost physically part of them."[72] King Chulalongkorn journeyed to the Malay Peninsula at least six times within little more than a decade—in 1888, 1889,

[70] Prince Sommot Ammoraphan, *Raya thang sadet praphat laem malayu nai ratchakan thi 5 ruam 3 khrao* (Itineraries of three royal trips to the Malay Peninsula by Rama V) (Bangkok: Sophanaphiphanthanathon, 1920), 3–4, 12–13.

[71] Sommot, *Raya thang,* 4.

[72] Clifford Geertz, "Centers, Kings, and Charisma: Reflections on the Symbolics of Power," in his *Local Knowledge* (New York: Basic Books, 1983), 125.

1890, 1896, 1898, and 1901. The frequency and timing of these trips and the particular sites visited manifest a symbolics of power of a political-religious sort: politics and Buddhism were indistinguishable in Siam. When the king "marked" his territory through "numinous peregrinations," he imbued Buddhist sites with state power and ignored Muslim mosques or other sites of significance in the local Muslim landscape. This was a defensive move, however, because the very frequency of "marking" or visiting the southern Malay areas suggests that these areas were contested not just by the British but by local Muslim rajas as well. The king returned repeatedly to make it known that he desired possession of those areas. Tellingly, the royal processions occurred during the period when Bangkok began to incorporate the south into Siam's modern administrative polity—a process, begun in the 1890s, that became official by 1902. His last visit was in 1901.

Another incident that reveals that Siam's modernity was Buddhist occurred in 1896. That year King Chulalongkorn traveled to Java and returned to Bangkok via the Malay Peninsula.[73] He studied colonial systems of administration, including provincial control in Malaya, India, Java, and Singapore. However, this view takes the mysterious out of it all—Siam's rule becomes squarely about control and profit devoid of the numinous symbolism of power. The king certainly left Java with material ideas about modernity. He and his entourage, including the future minister of justice, Prince Ratburi, and minister of the interior, Prince Damrong, had visited and studied prisons, police organization, irrigation systems, and administrative techniques. But the king also returned with material evidence of his continued status as a Buddhist monarch, including several Buddhist statues from one of Southeast Asia's most venerated Buddhist temples, Borobudor in Java. In the Theravadin world, there is great significance attached to certain symbolic Buddhist relics (such as the Emerald Buddha). The significance of Buddhist statues from Java—an area ruled by a European power—was not lost on King Chulalongkorn, who displayed these relics in Bangkok's most powerful royal temples such as Wat Phra Kaeo and Wat Bowoniwet.

Another way in which Siam's modernity was undeniably Buddhist is manifest in the person of Chao Phraya Yomarat. He was the first and the single most important official sent by Bangkok to integrate the southern Malay territories into Siam. Chao Phraya Yomarat was also a consummate Siamese Buddhist: he spent at least fifteen years from the ages of five to twenty-one in a Buddhist temple. He was the first monk in fourteen years to pass the third level of Buddhist exams, indicating his erudition and bringing him to royal attention. After he left the monkhood at the age of twenty-one, he was hired by Prince Damrong to tutor several royal princes in England for ten

[73] King Chulalongkorn, *Itineraire d'un Voyage à Java en 1896,* intro. Chanatip Kesavadhana (Paris: Cahier d'Archipel 20, 1993).

years, during which he traveled throughout Europe, the United States, Russia, Turkey, Japan, British Burma, and British India. On his return in 1895, he was appointed superintendent commissioner of monthon Nakhon Sri Thammarat, which was administered by him in Songkhla, and charged with modernizing the provincial administration of the southern territories.[74] He held this position for the next ten years. His networks of power and recruitment strategies for the construction of public works in the south involved the local Buddhist abbots and their religious communities, which unwittingly excluded Muslims.[75] In sum, the most authoritative Siamese figure in the Malay Muslim south was profoundly dedicated to Buddhist principles and was the kingdom's leading lay expert in Buddhological relics.[76] As such, he neatly represented Bangkok in its amalgamated state and religious power.

In all, these strategies employed by Siam's Buddhist administration and the Malay Muslim resistance to them reinforce an understanding of Bangkok as an occupying force, and of the relationship between the south and Bangkok as colonial.[77] The incorporation of the Malay Muslim territories into the Kingdom of Siam occurred in the context of high imperialism in Southeast Asia—an imperialism that Siam's leaders also practiced, for reasons they understood as imperative. Siam's actions in the Malay Muslim states demonstrate Siam's position at the nexus of colonialism and imperialism in the nineteenth and early twentieth centuries, as simultaneously wary of imperial intervention and entertaining imperial ambitions of its own. The Malay areas incorporated into Siam became the sites where Siam's leaders worked out Siam's form of legal modernity with a clear awareness of British stratagems of imperial intervention. Although Bangkok's leaders were conscious of the religious, ethnic, cultural, and customary distinctions between the Malay Muslims and the Siamese, they were remarkably ignorant of their own position in the south as anything other than universal or the norm, another trait they shared with European and American colonial powers.

Siam did not replicate European modular modernity, however. In terms of law, the implementation of a national legal system in the Malay Muslim south narrowed the formerly comprehensive jurisdiction and authority of lo-

[74] Prasong, *Chak yomarat,* 40, 58–65, 83–84, 138, 153.

[75] For example, he needed to recruit a volunteer labor force to construct a site where King Chulalongkorn would stop on his travels through Songkhla in 1896. Chao Phraya Yomarat called on a local Buddhist monk famous for his ability to recruit members of the local community. The monk, Achan Pan, successfully appealed to the wealthy to donate funds and the poor to donate their labor. Prasong, *Chak yomarat,* 157–59.

[76] King Chulalongkorn called on him to go in his stead in 1898 to Lord Curzon's India to verify the authenticity of a Buddhist relic dug up there. Prasong, *Chak yomarat,* 182–83.

[77] IslamOnline.net draws parallels regularly between the Thai government and colonial regimes. For example, one article compares Thailand's "annexation" of the south to Indonesia's "annexation" of East Timor. Others publicize the grievances of the Pattani United Liberation Organization, one of the separatist organizations that now operate out of Malaysia. Iqbal Ragataf, "Thailand: Hunting Muslims to Death," 13 Feb. 2000, www.islamonline.net (accessed 3 Apr. 2003).

cal Islamic authorities. In terms of translation, Siamese officials appear to have been less concerned than European colonial magistrates with controlling the substantive content and translation of Islamic law, so long as these codes did not usurp powers outside the bounds of Islamic law's newly delimited authority. Finally, Siam's form of modernity differed in its refusal of secularity, even nominally. The promiscuous and overt commingling of Buddhism and state power made Siam's "annexation" of the south unique, unlike colonial rule by European powers. Buddhism also became a touchstone for a cultural defense of polygyny as a modern Siamese practice in contradistinction to Christian European monogamy.

FOUR

The Imperialism of Monogamy in Family Law

No clearer manifestation of the similarities between Siam and imperial powers exists than Bangkok's establishment of a colonial-style plural legal system in Siam's southern Muslim provinces. There Siam's leaders created a distinct set of laws and courts for resolving Islamic family and religious disputes, thereby replicating the structure of colonial jurisprudence that existed across the globe. The juridical affinities between Siam and European imperial powers ends and Siam's similarities with directly colonized states begins with the family law reforms that applied to Siam's population outside the southern Muslim provinces. As in directly colonized countries, jurisdiction over Siam's Buddhist-derived laws on divorce, polygynous marriage, adultery, and inheritance was protected from Westernized legal intervention. However, the same practices that were sheltered from change because they reflected the allegedly authentic cultural identity of the Siamese were ideologically deployed by foreign powers as evidence of Siam's uncivilized status. This justified the perpetuation of a plural legal system, which granted legal and economic privileges to many foreigners, Asian and European, in Siam.

The institutions of the family and marriage were interpreted as sources of national, cultural authenticity in nineteenth-century imperial (and protoethnographic) discourse, which considered monogamous heterosexual marriage the paradigmatic standard. Monogamous marriage anchored the family as a civilized institution. Societies that allowed marital practices that deviated from monogamous marriage were located lower down on the evolutionary scale of progress, which had enormous legal repercussions. Regimes of law in many European colonies maintained distinctions among ethnically polyglot members of the populations on the basis of the marital form and kinship organization of those individuals. For example, according to scholar Peter Burns, in the Netherlands East Indies the legal category of "Europeans" included "all Japanese and other peoples (e.g. Americans, Argentineans, Australians) who came from states in which substantially the same *family law* was observed as that which held good in Holland." Following the same logic, the category of "Foreign Orientals" encompassed all non-Europeans and non-natives on the basis of their observance of "polygamous family law."[1]

In Siam, the legal repercussions of nonmonogamous sexual relations were similarly significant. The practice of polygyny by Siam's politically and economically powerful classes evidenced Siam's backwardness to many nineteenth-century Europeans who otherwise might have had to recognize Siam's status as an independent and legally equal state. It also enabled the association of polygyny with Buddhism, a source of Siam's alternative modernity, even though Buddhism did not favor any type of marriage over another.

By focusing on polygyny, I will show that the Christian system of monogamous marriage, which was projected globally by imperial countries through law, was hegemonic. A country that did not at least formally adopt heterosexual, monogamous marriage as the basis for its modern family system was not considered fully modern by other powerful countries, most of which were Western, Christian, and imperialist. This placed non-Western, noncolonized countries such as Siam, China, Turkey, and Japan in a slightly different position than directly colonized countries whose traditions, such as polygyny or arranged marriages, were "preserved." Japan, the only non-Western country that signed unequal treaties with Siam, had discarded polygyny and adopted monogamy as its legal marital standard in the Meiji civil code. Reformers in early twentieth-century Turkey also eventually secured the abolition of polygyny, which they castigated as a remnant of traditionalism that opposed the values of modern civilization.[2] The People's Republic of China also adopted a monogamy law in 1950, much later than other noncolonized Asian states perhaps because the politically tumultuous first half of the twentieth century prevented its earlier promulgation and because of Mao's communist ideology that supported sexual equality. The examples of noncolonized, non-Western countries offer a unique opportunity to study the impact of imperial civilizational ideology, precisely because they did not have their social policies dictated to them.

Siam's sovereignty was fundamentally a gender and legal issue as much as it was a political and economic one, as indicated by the centrality of debates about marriage. Siam would not be free of burdensome extraterritoriality

[1] Peter Burns, "The Netherlands East Indies," in *Laws of South-East Asia,* vol. 2, ed. M. B. Hooker (Singapore: Butterworth and Co., 1988), 246, 261. Emphasis added.

[2] Nilufer Göle, *Forbidden Modern,* 30–33, 74–77.

clauses until it "modernized" its legal system, which ultimately meant adopting a "modern" family law on monogamous marriage. As if to test this hypothesis, the government promulgated a law on monogamous marriage in 1935. Within three years, all remaining extraterritoriality clauses and unequal commercial provisions hindering Siam's legal and fiscal autonomy were rescinded. It appears from chronology alone that gaining full sovereignty was contingent on adopting monogamy as a marital standard.

Even though Siam's leaders had ultimately to adopt monogamy as the country's legal standard of marriage to regain full sovereignty, why did they endure nearly a century of extraterritoriality and other unequal treaty impositions before they formally disavowed the practice of polygyny? Therein lies a conundrum. The pressure to adopt monogamy existed as early as the 1850s, when King Mongkut first considered it. Moreover, because Siam's leaders were aware that polygyny could serve as a justification for foreign intervention, they could have adopted monogamy as early as 1855. They chose not to do so until 1935 despite costly imperial condemnation of polygyny, a massive backlog of court cases caused by indecision about a marital standard, and eventually domestic advocacy for monogamy.

In this chapter I explore why Siam's leaders did not adopt a monogamy law sooner. The historical, cultural meanings and political functions of polygyny far exceeded the narrow colonial conception of it as a sexual and immoral practice. Polygyny performed vital political work in Siam, integrating the kingdom's powerful political rivals and manifesting the association between masculinity and power. Outlawing polygyny in favor of monogamy was anathema to Siamese elite political and cultural norms. Trading in on the discourse of imperial civilization, Siam's elite began to advocate polygyny as central to that kingdom's distinct form of Buddhist modernity, in explicit juxtaposition to Christian European modernity.

Although polygyny was deployed discursively as a source of national identity, it nonetheless occupied an increasingly ambiguous location in Siam's cultural repertoire. Monarchs and officials had defended polygyny since the 1860s, but they did not proactively pass a modern law in favor of it nor have they ever abolished it. Polygyny, unlike any other "customary" practice, was the rock upon which domestic legal reform foundered for decades. Legal reforms and the resolution of court cases about inheritance, divorce, parentage and illegitimate children, marital property, and adultery required a legal definition of marriage. The indecision about passing a law on a marital standard, regardless of whether it was polygyny or monogamy, held up the completion of the entire civil code and the adjudication of thousands of court cases. In their debates about polygyny, Siam's ruling elite and lawmakers failed to reach consensus until 1935, three years after the overthrow of the absolute monarchy, when the newly formed National Assembly passed a law adopting monogamy as the legal form of marriage. At that point, the Assembly promulgated Book V (on family) and Book VI (on inheritance), thus completing Siam's modern Civil and Commercial Code.

Siam's leaders and people reconfigured their moral and political landscape through debates about polygyny. The particular meanings and direction of the fiery debates about marital reform was left up to Siamese statesmen and intellectuals rather than to foreign legal advisers. However, these debates were fundamentally informed by and strategically deployed within an asymmetrical imperial context that set the standard for modern marriage as heterosexual and monogamous. The discourses on the differences between monogamy and polygyny were utilized by various groups within Siam who harnessed these transnational languages of modernity to their own purposes. Polygyny symbolized the kingdom's international status as ambiguously modern.

The question about the relationship between polygyny and extraterritoriality will be answered in three parts. First, I consider imperial ethnography's emphasis on "family" and marital form as an index of a culture's level of civilization, and the practical manifestation of this ideology in Siam's legal reform process. This section demonstrates the concrete links among imperialism, law, and polygyny in Siam. The second section offers a historical account of the institution of polygyny in Siam, against which later transformations in its meaning and function are juxtaposed. Both sections establish a framework for understanding how it became possible to deploy polygyny in domestic debates over national identity and political authority. Polygyny, through this process, was articulated as a site of Siam's alternative modernity. The third section explains the domestic discord about polygyny that was argued in the popular press and behind the scenes, as it were, in private high-level cabinet meetings. It ends with the politics behind the promulgation of the monogamy law in 1935.

Imperial Hegemony and the Colonized Family

Outside Siam, polygyny played a political role in the ideology of colonial powers, which made a connection between colonial domination and imperial conceptions of monogamous marriage as the most legitimate form of sexual relations. Much of the scholarship on imperial ethnography as well as on Islam and modernity supports the argument that monogamy was equated with civilization and Enlightenment notions of progress.[3] Feminist scholars such as Ann Stoler and Anne McClintock have exposed the parallels between

[3] Elman Service, *A Century of Controversy: Ethnological Issues from 1860 to 1960* (Orlando, Fla.: Academic Press, 1985), 99–101; Göle, *Forbidden Modern;* Loos, "Gender Adjudicated."

the ideology of civilization that justified colonialism and the location of heterosexual, monogamous marriage at the apex of that hierarchy.[4] Any sexual practice that deviated from the norm of heterosexual marital monogamy, preferably between partners of the same race and class, was located at a point lower on the civilizational hierarchy. The hierarchy theorized heterosexual monogamous marital sex as the most egalitarian, legitimate, and civilized form of sexual union. All other "primitive" forms of "fornication," including homosexual sex, prostitution, concubinage, and polygyny, existed at various locations on the barbarous and illegitimate end of the imperial sexual spectrum.

The engagement by Europeans in the very practices they most fiercely condemned constitutes the dark underbelly of the ideology promoting monogamy as civilization's ideal. Western men indulged in concubinage, prostitution, mixed-race marriages, and even polygyny with Southeast Asian women (and men) throughout the colonies and in Siam. Louis, the son of Anna Leonowens, was married but frequented the "harem" of his friend, a former American missionary named Dr. Cheek.[5] Long-time Bangkok resident and American missionary Dan Beach Bradley noted in the mid-nineteenth century that European and American men purchased local women as mistresses, thereby practicing a form of sexual slavery, according to colonial ideology.[6] Katherine Grindrod, writing in Siam in 1894, noted that "nearly all the Europeans here keep Siamese women—the lower sort."[7] Grindrod also discussed the situation of Miss Inn, a European woman who voluntarily joined the wives of Prince Devawongse, the minister of foreign affairs.[8]

The degree of offense taken by Europeans and Americans to these practices generally was linked to the numbers of white men ("nearly all" of those in Siam, according to one British woman), and even some women, who engaged in polygyny.[9] The practice of polygyny by Europeans and Americans undermined the ideological basis for the civilizing project that legitimized Euro-American cultural "guidance" in Siam. Despite, or perhaps because of this, imperial ideologies about family and sexuality served to discipline the sexual behavior of those non-Western individuals and polities that aspired to climb up the colonial-era power hierarchy, which determined their inclusion in the category of ruler rather than ruled. One notable distinction in

[4] Ann Stoler, "Sexual Affronts and Racial Frontiers," *Comparative Studies in Society and History* 34, no. 3 (July 1992): 514–51; Stoler, *Carnal Knowledge and Imperial Power;* McClintock, *Imperial Leather.*

[5] Prakai Nonthawasi, "Siao nung khong mo chik" (One Aspect of Dr. Cheek), *Sinlapa Wathanatham* 5 (Mar. 1992): 120–25; W. S. Bristowe, *Louis and the King of Siam* (New York: Thai-American Publishers, 1976), esp. 82–88.

[6] William L. Bradley, *Siam Then: The Foreign Colony in Bangkok before and after Anna* (Pasadena, Calif.: William Carey Library, 1981), 105, cited in Lysa Hong, "'Stranger within the Gates,'" 332.

[7] Katherine Grindrod, "Siam," Personal Diary, vol. 1 (23 May–Dec. 1892) (Hong Kong: University of Hong Kong, 1982), 30–31.

[8] Ibid., vol. 1, 30–31, vol. 2, 102–3.

[9] Ibid., vol. 1, 30–31.

the discourses about sexual behavior in Siam is the lack of public debate about the offspring produced by mixed race unions, which were not uncommon in Siam, especially between Chinese and Siamese. The number of mixed Siamese-*farang* (white Westerner) offspring remained relatively insignificant, however, because of the small number of foreigners in Siam compared to foreigners in colonized countries, such as the Netherlands East Indies, British India, and French Indochina. In addition, the need to manage racial boundaries to prevent the blurring between ruler and ruled populations did not apply in Siam, where the Siamese, rather than Europeans, ruled the kingdom. By contrast, many Siamese voices contributed to the discussion of these issues.

Differences in official policies and discourses regarding race, sexuality, and mixed-race children exist between Siam and colonized countries as a result of their distinct relationships to European imperialism. Nonetheless, imperial discourses had an impact on popular and elite conceptions of proper sexuality and the configuration of modern kinship relations in Siam. Imperial ideologies considered the "family," regardless of its actual referent, the source of a country's cultural specificity and authentic national identity in two interrelated ways: through imperial ethnography and colonial jurisprudence. First, imperial ethnography, which the colonial endeavor funded, constructed the family as the location of a society's cultural uniqueness. Ethnographic discourse and the ideology of the Enlightenment both understood kin and family structures as offering a window onto the degree of civilization of a given society. Nineteenth-century theories about the origins and nature of human society—by such ethnologists as Lewis H. Morgan, Sir Henry S. Maine, Johann Bachofen, John F. McLennan, Numa Denis Fustel de Coulanges, and Friedrich Engels—understood kinship structures and marital institutions as the foundation of each society's governmental organization and of its relative degree of civilization.[10] Seeking to explain what they saw as the evolutionary transformation from primitive to civilized society, they deployed the language of science to categorize human communities: family, gentes, phratries, tribes, clans, and so on.[11]

Kinship and family constituted *the* primary objects of study for early ethnologists because kinship and family indicated where a given society would be placed on an evolutionary scale of progressively more civilized societies. By privileging the family as an object of study, late-nineteenth-century

[10] Service, *Century of Controversy*, 3–12.

[11] Ibid., 9, 36. Morgan, perhaps the most famous of the early ethnologists, linked technological changes to various stages of social organization and inspired, in part, works on this point written by Marx and Engels. Friedrich Engels, *The Origin of the Family, Private Property, and the State* (New York: International Publishers, 1972 [1884]), and Karl Marx, *The Ethnological Notebooks of Karl Marx (Studies of Morgan, Phear, Maine, Lubbock)*, trans., ed., intro. Lawrence Krader (Assen, Neth.: Van Gorcum, 1974). For the definitive book on Morgan, see Thomas R. Trautmann, *Lewis Henry Morgan and the Invention of Kinship* (Berkeley: University of California Press, 1987).

ethnographic discourse overdetermined the significance of the family as the litmus test of a society's place on the evolutionary scale of progress.[12] This evolutionary hierarchy of societies located European and American whites at the zenith, providing the ideological foundation that sanctioned Euro-American colonization of so-called primitive societies.

In noncolonized Siam, the emphasis in imperial discourse on the family politicized it to a degree hitherto unknown. The term *polygyny* did not exist in the Thai language at the time. Even today *polygyny* is not encapsulated in a single word as it is in English but must be described as in "the principle of having many wives simultaneously" (*lathi mi mia lai khon nai wela phromkan*).[13] Polygyny—not as a practice, but as an ethnographic concept—was a foreign import to Siam.

In addition to imperial ethnography, a second way in which family became a site of cultural and national authenticity was through the structure of colonial jurisprudence. The emphasis in nineteenth-century imperial ideology on family, religion, and custom as spaces of cultural authenticity and distinction consequently removed them from the jurisdiction of the colonial state and placed them at least nominally under the control of indigenous authorities. The previous chapter demonstrated the implementation of this form of colonial law in Siam's Muslim Malay south. In Siam proper, treaties with foreign powers explicitly excluded family law from the requirement of general legal reform, even as imperialism paradoxically provided the model for the modern, civilized family. This was defined as sex for reproductive purposes within the confines of a patriarchal monogamous marriage. Foreign legal advisers hired by Siam's monarch drafted new laws in all arenas except for those related to inheritance, religion, and marriage. Despite this protection, domestic legal reform of family law occurred, and in fact became an area of innovation and nationalist rhetoric for Siam's ruling elites. In this way, legal reform in Siam aimed to appease an international (largely European and American) constituency that transformed domestic family, class, and gender relations through the process of segregating it, even though Siam was never directly colonized. Siam was a noncolonized country that paradoxically transformed its legal and familial systems in ways that paralleled those of its colonized neighbors.

The international imperial context compelled Siam's leaders to adopt a Western-style legal system and commercial codes, but the content of laws related to family and religious life were more subtly negotiated. Siam's reformers had greater latitude in family than in contract, criminal, or procedural law, but this did not mean that family law was more authentic or static.

[12] This helps explain why home, family, and other "domestic" spaces became crucial to articulations of anticolonial nationalisms. See, for instance, Chatterjee, *Nation and Its Fragments,* 116–34.

[13] So Sethaputra, ed. *New Model Thai-English Dictionary* (Bangkok: Thai Watanaphanit, 1991), 507.

Instead, family law became the site of intense dispute in domestic debates about Siamese national identity. Moreover, the disputes were not hermetically sealed from the larger imperial context. They necessarily engaged imperial hegemonic definitions of family in ways that contributed to or detracted from arguments about Siam's status as a modern nation.

The exemption of family law from legal reform was anomalous given that the "advice" from foreign legal advisers was otherwise wide-ranging and comprehensive. It is the most striking exception to Siam's legal negotiations with foreign legal advisers and signatory powers. The atypical treatment that laws regarding familial relations received began in 1897, when a treaty between Siam and Japan gave Siam's leaders concrete, if onerous, objectives by which they could jettison the unequal clauses of the treaty and enter into a relationship with Japan on the basis of equality, as a sovereign state.[14] The treaty specified that

> Japanese consular officers shall exercise jurisdiction over Japanese subjects in Siam, until the judicial reforms in Siam shall have been completed, that is until a criminal code, a code of criminal procedure, a civil code (*with the exception of law of marriage and succession*), a code of civil procedure, and a law of constitution of the courts of justice will come into force. (Ministry of Foreign Affairs, *Sonthisanya,* 160; emphasis added)

Other foreign treaty powers eventually agreed to observe this guarantee by which Siamese laws on marriage, succession, and related matters such as divorce and inheritance were segregated from the process of legal reform throughout the late nineteenth and early twentieth centuries. The treaty with Japan, the first that included a process by which Siam could abrogate unequal treaties, served as a prototype, even though it was never directly acknowledged as such by Siam's (American) general adviser, Francis B. Sayre, who helped renegotiate the treaties in the 1920s.

Under the supervision of two Frenchmen—Georges Padoux, the legislative adviser in Siam from 1904 to 1913, and René Guyon, who worked for Siam's government from 1908 until his death in 1963—all criminal and civil laws except the codes on inheritance and marriage were promulgated between the years of 1908 and 1931.[15] The debate over Siam's legally sanc-

[14] The treaty was ratified in 1898. Ministry of Foreign Affairs, Thailand, *Sonthisanya lae khwamtoklong thawiphaki rawang prathet thai kap tang prathet lae ongkan rawang prathet* (Bilateral Treaties and Agreements between Thailand and Foreign Countries and International Organizations), vol. 2 (1870–1919) (Bangkok: Ministry of Foreign Affairs, Treaty and Legal Department, 1969), 160. See also M. B. Hooker, "The 'Europeanization' of Siam's Law 1855–1908," in *Laws of South-East Asia,* ed. M. B. Hooker (Singapore: Butterworth and Co., 1986), 554.

[15] New codes on inheritance, marriage, and other secular family laws were drafted at this time but not promulgated.

tioned form of marriage, which began in legal circles in 1912, took decades to resolve.

Contrary to assumptions about outsiders pressuring Siam to reform marriage laws, the foreign legal advisers hired by Kings Chulalongkorn (r. 1868–1910), Vajiravudh (r. 1910–1925), and Prajadhipok (r. 1925–1935) repeatedly stressed as late as 1931 that reforms in family, marriage, and inheritance laws fell squarely in the laps of Siam's officials. The foreign and Siamese legal advisers working on the civil code had the contradictory objectives of preserving Siamese customs and adjusting Siamese laws to correspond with modern legal principles of foreign countries. Émile Jottrand, a Belgian legal adviser to King Chulalongkorn, wrote in his diary on 23 September 1900 that "The European judical advisors have limited themselves to encouraging it [polygyny], because it existed before we arrived."[16] With the notable exception of the Japanese legal adviser, Tokichi Masao, all historical records by foreign legal advisers in Siam indicate that they would support legislation that allowed polygyny.[17] This was true even in instances in which foreign treaties forced Siam to hire certain legal advisers. Although the government voluntarily and proactively hired many foreign advisers to aid in Siam's administrative and economic restructuring, the hiring of French legal advisers was not a matter of choice. The French government forced King Chulalongkorn to hire a French legal adviser, Georges Padoux, in 1904. Despite the circumstances of his employment, Padoux was an advocate of polygyny in Siam *if* that was what Siamese elites wanted. Guyon, who replaced Padoux, went so far as to publish books in Europe about what he termed "sexual freedom," suggesting that Siam's sexual regime had an impact on Guyon's conceptions of monogamy as a repressive sexual practice.[18] In Padoux's memo to King Vajiravudh in 1913, Padoux reiterated the unique place that family law had in the process of reform.[19]

> I was—and I am still—strongly of [the] opinion that the initiative of fundamental reforms in questions of marriage, divorce, parentage, inheritance, must lie only with the Siamese Statesmen and legal men. Europeans, however long they may have lived in this country never know sufficiently the Siamese customs and the Siamese life to be in a position to make authoritative suggestions on the matter. The Siamese Government alone can know what Siam may require and how far the old rules of the Siamese Family Law may be altered. I

[16] Jottrand, *In Siam,* 309.

[17] Rungsaeng, "The Origins of Thailand's Modern Ministry of Justice," 260–61.

[18] René Guyon, *Sexual Freedom,* trans. Eden and Cedar Paul (London: John Land and the Bodley Head, 1949 [1939]).

[19] His memo is largely reproduced in Adul Wichiencharoen and Luang Chamroon Netisastra, "Some Main Features of Modernization of Ancient Family Law in Thailand," in *Family Law and Customary Law in Asia: A Contemporary Legal Perspective,* ed. by David C. Buxbaum (The Hague: Martinus Nijhoff, 1968), 97.

> say that not because we are afraid to take responsibilities, but because this is a matter on which I feel we are not qualified to submit proposals to the Government. . . . We would have been of course quite prepared to substitute monogamy for polygamy in the draft, if instructed by the Government to do so. But it would have been mere presumption on our part even to simply raise the point. It seems very difficult for a man who has been born and brought up in one of the systems to form an independent opinion as to whether monogamy is superior to polygamy or not. (Padoux in Adul and Luang Chamroon, "Some Main Features," 97)

The very reticence of foreign legal advisers to give advice on Siam's family law is extraordinary compared to the alacrity with which foreign officials advocated changes in Siam's commercial and criminal law. Those men closest to the legal reform process adamantly refused to intervene directly in or alter Siam's familial practices. Moreover, no law on monogamy was passed until 1935 despite the overwhelming international judgment that the practice of polygyny was backward and despite the strong desire on the part of Siam's leaders to be perceived as a cultural and political equal to other European nations.

Foreigners would not force a change in Siam's marital practices because, according to Padoux, it required the epistemological and cultural insight afforded only to Siamese. This racialized privileging of location and knowledge about family law for Siamese had a flipside: it justified the involvement of foreigners in other areas of Siam's domestic law in which foreigners had privileged knowledge. Padoux's epistemological argument that Europeans would never understand sufficiently Siamese marital and kinship institutions rings false given the thousands of codes on criminal, civil, and procedural matters that Europeans (and Siamese) did not hesitate to uproot and replace with ones more amenable to their jurisprudence. This included laws supporting capitalist development, which were seen as merely formalizing natural, universal competition among equal parties.

In any case, the juridical reform process elucidated above makes the argument that Siam adopted monogamy in order to rid itself of unequal treaty clauses seem too simplistically straightforward. If Siam's leaders had ultimately to adopt monogamy as the country's legal standard of marriage, why did they wait so long before passing a monogamy law? Why did foreign legal advisers, who led the legal reform process, refuse to discard Siam's polygynous family model in favor of a Western, Christian monogamous model? Some argue that polygyny was not abandoned sooner because it was intimately associated with absolutism, so its demise was delayed until the overthrow of the absolute monarchy in 1932.[20] This line of reasoning falters when we consider that all

[20] Scot Barmé, *Woman, Man, Bangkok* (Lanham, Md.: Rowman and Littlefield, 2002), chap. 6.

kings from Rama VI (1910) on, including two absolute monarchs, either expressed indifference to both systems or practiced monogamy.[21] Why, if some absolute monarchs repudiated polygyny, did they refuse to adopt a monogamy law sooner, particularly given the overwhelming importance of regaining full sovereignty? The answers to these questions are found in the significance of polygyny historically to Siam's political culture.

Polygynous Politics

Polygyny existed as Siam's source of distinction in the eyes of imperial powers and as a crucible through which the country would prove, through the abolition of polygyny and the adoption of monogamy, its transition to modernity. Polygyny, indeed, was a practice that made Siam's form of modernity palpably alternative. However, to focus on polygyny as the main issue at stake privileges concerns about Siam's image in the eyes of foreigners over domestic social transformations that concerned Siam's denizens. The exclusive focus on polygyny occludes the nature of the crisis, which was much broader than simply debating the moral merits of polygyny as a form of marriage. This account of polygyny in Siam is not meant to defend it or romanticize its role in the past but to explain why Siam's statesmen were unable to come to a consensus about the legitimacy of polygyny for nearly eighty years (from 1855 to the 1930s), despite costly imperial condemnation.

Historically, polygyny performed political work that spilled over the boundaries of its definition as a mere marital category. It functioned to integrate geographically disparate settlements into the kingdom, to provide the monarch with numerous male relatives to govern the kingdom, and to construct Siam's masculine political culture. Women's bodies mediated political loyalty, integrated powerful groups throughout the kingdom by linking them to the monarch in the capital, and maintained this connection through the reproduction of children. The relationship between a powerful monarch and his subordinate rulers was highly personalized in Siam and elsewhere in Southeast Asia prior to the colonial period. These ties were often initiated and maintained through polygynous marriages between kings and the female relatives of other subordinate rulers or powerful men.

The "state" of Siam was constituted less by formal institutions than by royal-blooded men, nobles, and provincial elites, all of whom intermarried.

[21] King Vajiravudh was personally indifferent to either marital standard. Barmé suggests this may have been an instance in which King Vajiravudh hinted at his sexual preference for men. Barmé, *Woman, Man, Bangkok*, 160. The focus on King Vajiravudh's alleged homosexuality in the absence of a discussion of the vigorous heterosexual practices of Siam's polygynous kings inaccurately treats homosexuality as the causal factor in decisions about polygyny. See Tamara Loos, "Sex in the Inner City: The Fidelity between Sex and Politics in Siam," *Journal of Asian Studies* 64, no. 4 (Nov. 2005). Portions of this chapter appear in a revised form in this article.

Tony Day has argued in the regional context of Southeast Asia that the state was not an institution or structure distinct from social relations.[22] In particular, kinship relations made and unmade kings. Lineage-based claims through descent from a particular male or female were not particularly important in determining who would ascend the throne. Instead, competition arose among powerful families for the right to appoint the next king, who obtained the throne (during times of peace) through a complex negotiation among important families.

Charnvit Kasetsiri, Sunait Chutintaranond, and David Wyatt have also demonstrated the significance of polygyny and kinship relations since the thirteenth century in the kingdoms now considered part of Thailand.[23] Wyatt, who studied the origins of the currently reigning Chakri dynasty, demonstrated how multiple powerful families "made" kings from the seventeenth to the nineteenth century in Siam. He argues that four major ministerial families (all of whom were non-Thai in origin but had intermarried with local Thai over several generations) had by the late eighteenth century intermarried with one important Thai family, which emerged as the Chakri dynasty in 1782. Chakri dynastic rule was made possible by the institution of the Inner Palace—often glossed as the "harem." The Inner Palace or Inner City was founded on the gifting of women, which cemented bonds among powerful men ruling throughout the disparate settlements that constituted Siam. The state was linked not solely through tribute exchanges and kingly gifts of men (as soldiers or laborers) but also personally through polygyny and gifts of female relatives.

Polygyny differed from other forms of political networking because it, as marriage, was a relationship in process rather than a singular event: it enabled political alliances that could be negotiated, altered, and deepened (or dissolved) over time. Until the reign of King Vajiravudh, Siam's monarchs literally reproduced the state through the allegiances and children born of polygynous marriages. Phonsiri Bunranakhet powerfully details the composition of King Chulalongkorn's Inner City, which accommodated female royalty, the monarch's royal wives, female officials administering the Inner City, servants, and slaves (photograph 5).[24] She traces the genealogy of fifty out of the king's 153 wives who are representative of the types of families that presented women to the monarch. Wives typically came from five categories of

[22] Tony Day, "Ties That (Un)Bind: Families and States in Premodern Southeast Asia," *Journal of Asian Studies,* 55, no. 2 (May 1996): 384–409, and *Fluid Iron* (Honolulu: University of Hawai'i Press, 2002), chap. 2.

[23] Charnvit Kasetsiri, *The Rise of Ayudhya* (Kuala Lumpur: Oxford University Press, 1976); Sunait Chutintaranond, "Political Kinship Relations in Early Thai History," MA thesis, Cornell University, 1982; David Wyatt, "Family Politics in Seventeenth and Eighteenth Century Siam," in *Studies in Thai History* (Chiang Mai: Silkworm Books, 1994).

[24] I have written elsewhere about the politics of the Inner Palace. See Loos, "Sex in the Inner City."

Photograph 5. Siamese woman (purportedly a servant of one of King Chulalongkorn's queens) in Western dress in the 1860s.
John Thomson, Photograph Album of Siam 1900, Collection 4863, Box 9, Image 2. Courtesy of Kroch Library Rare and Manuscript Collection.

families: politically influential lineages whose male members held high office; branches of the royal family; wealthy Chinese tax-farming families; ruling families of provincial areas and tributary states; and families related to powerful women already residing in the Inner City.[25]

Since at least the seventeenth century, then, polygynous marital ties between the king and provincial and urban elite families provided a concrete and continuous connection of blood, communication, and loyalty between the monarch and powerful groups.[26] Local, less powerful rulers sent daughters or sisters to the king in order to establish and maintain ties over time. For example, a proclamation issued by King Mongkut acknowledged the long-standing tradition in which provincial administrators and officials of all ranks sent a female relative, usually a daughter, to serve in the Inner Palace and to act as a kind of collateral, ensuring the loyalty of the official to the monarch.[27] In return, monarchs conferred gifts appropriate to the rank of the government official. In settlements bordering enemy kingdoms, the gifting of women was arguably of greatest significance as a symbol of fealty. Allegiance to Siam's king was proven in part through the presentation of female family members to the king's Inner Palace. Far from being an institution parasitical or peripheral to political history, polygyny was a system that helped integrate the kingdom socially and politically.[28]

The second function of the institution of polygyny was no less significant. In addition to cementing bonds between ruling families, polygynous liaisons with the monarch also ensured that there would be sufficient numbers of male elite to fill the highest posts in the government, which they did until the overthrow of the absolute monarchy and establishment of a constitutional one in 1932.[29] This process helped maintain sociopolitical hierarchies by ensuring that royal and aristocratic men remained in positions of rule. Stacking officialdom with royalty was possible only because of polygynous procreation, which provided 324 children to the first five kings (and 176 mothers) of the Chakri dynasty.[30] All of the important ministries created by King Chulalongkorn's reforms were headed by his brothers, half-brothers,

[25] Phonsiri Bunranakhet, *Nangnai: Chiwit thang sangkhom lae botbat nai sangkhom thai samai ratchakan thi 5* (Inner Palace Women: Social Lives and Roles in Thai Society during the Reign of Rama V), MA thesis, Thammasat University, 1997, 109–70.

[26] Wyatt, "Family Politics," 1994.

[27] NL R4, "Prakat ruang thwai but ying pai tham ratchakan nai phraratchawang" (Proclamation on presenting daughters for service in royal palaces), no date; Loos, Archival Notebooks, vol. 1, 174–79.

[28] Phonsiri, "Nangnai"; Susan Morgan, *Place Matters: Gendered Geography in Victorian Women's Travel Books about Southeast Asia* (New Brunswick, N.J.: Rutgers University Press), 228–35; Day, "Ties That (Un)Bind" and *Fluid Iron,* chap. 2.

[29] In fact, this was one of the most powerful motivations of those who led the coup. Coup leaders came from commoner rather than royal or aristocratic families but had the same educational qualifications (or better) than the royal scions who headed the military and civilian administrations.

[30] Pasuk and Baker, *Thailand,* 235; Robert Jones, *Thai Titles and Ranks: Including a Translation of Traditions of Royal Lineage in Siam by King Chulalongkorn,* Data Paper 81 (Ithaca: Cornell University, Southeast Asia Program, 1971), 4.

and sons; nine of twelve cabinet posts were held by royal family members in 1906; royal sons filled nine of the sixteen most senior posts in the army and all generals were of royal blood in 1910; and royal and aristocratic men were located throughout the upper ranks of the central bureaucracy and provincial governments.[31]

The third function of the institution of polygyny was its role in Siam's political culture and construction of masculine authority, expressed through the number of a man's wives, the reproduction of children, and his ability to control the sexuality of the women in his household.[32] The type of masculinity associated with political power defined a man without wives as incomplete—not fully a man. This did not bar him, necessarily, from having sexual relations with other men, but same-sex relations without heterosexual relations would not "complete" him. Polygynous marriages culturally enhanced the *barami* (merit, charisma, and virtue) of men because the number of a man's wives and children expressed his masculinity, virility, and capacity to lead. Just as the number of a man's wives implied his skills as a leader, so too a wife's infidelity signified weakness in her husband's capacity as a man and leader. This notion of masculine power applied not just to the king but to other royal men and nonroyal elite officials.[33]

This facet of Siam's political culture helps make sense of an otherwise puzzling incident. In 1863 King Mongkut engaged in a public exchange with the American missionary editors of the English-language newspaper, the *Bangkok Calendar.* The king took issue with an article critical of the widespread practice of polygyny among elites that listed the monarch as possessing over sixty wives and the monarch's brother (the Front Palace King, Phra Pin Klao) as having about twenty-five.[34] King Mongkut was not angry because the editors publicly broadcast details of his polygynous household. Instead, and inexplicably to the editors of the *Bangkok Calendar,* King Mongkut published an angry response in which he demanded the editors correct their accounting of the Front Palace King's wives. King Mongkut criticized the Front Palace King for having accumulated over 120 wives, which was more than that of the monarch himself and therefore worthy of censure.[35] The king's response makes sense from the perspective of Siam's political culture in which masculinity and sexual prowess were correlated with political au-

[31] Pasuk and Baker, *Thailand,* 236.

[32] Craig J. Reynolds, "A Nineteenth Century Thai Buddhist Defense of Polygamy and Some Remarks on the Social History of Women in Thailand." Paper presented for the 7th Conference of the International Association of Historians of Asia. Chulalongkorn University, Bangkok, August 1977, 936–39.

[33] Arguably, this form of masculinity expressed through the ability to attract numerous women applied to and was practiced by lower class men as well, when feasible.

[34] Malcolm Smith, *A Physician at the Court of Siam* (Kuala Lumpur: Oxford University Press, 1982 [1947]), 37–40.

[35] Phonsiri, "Nangnai," 44–45; Smith, *Physician at the Court of Siam,* 39–40.

thority. King Mongkut wrote elsewhere about the Front Palace King's physical prowess and magnetic appeal that compelled ruling elite in the provinces and elsewhere to offer beautiful women to him.[36] Mongkut criticized his brother for too intensely concentrating on accumulating desirable women, suggesting not simply envy but also anxiety that the Front Palace King was successfully competing with King Mongkut by manifesting increased levels of barami and masculine authority.

King Mongkut reached the throne at age forty-six. He had false teeth and was paralyzed on one side of his face. This may have negatively affected his confidence in public perceptions of his masculine virility, ability to attract women, and capacity to rule.[37] These anxieties reveal themselves in his proclamations. In a legal ruling issued in 1858, King Mongkut wrote that it pleased him when local political elites presented beautiful women to him because it would "become widely known that the king is not yet too decrepit."[38] It also helps make sense of the king's oft-cited 1861 proclamation that allowed women to leave the Inner Palace. One issuance of this proclamation is explicit about how government officials should go about requesting the withdrawal of their daughters from the Inner City. These officials could not mention as a reason for reclaiming their daughters any reference to the king's age (*phra chara*). This would, according to the proclamation, incur the monarch's extreme ire and displeasure.[39]

King Chulalongkorn appears to have been more confident about his barami, perhaps because he ascended the throne at a much earlier age, was a father at fifteen, and was presented with over three times as many wives as King Mongkut. Over his forty-two-year reign, more than 150 women were gifted to him as *chaochom* (minor wives), compared to fifty women presented to King Mongkut, who received the second largest number of women of any Chakri king.[40] The number of his consorts intimidated even the most radical group of royal and aristocratic reformers who had access to power in the 1880s. A group of the highest-ranking princes studying in Europe presented a sixty-page petition to King Chulalongkorn asking, among other things, for a constitutional monarchy instead of an absolute one. The authors of the petition wanted to include a request to abolish polygyny as well but did not dare because of the number and significance of the monarch's polygynous relationships.[41] Remarkably, they believed they could request a shift to a con-

[36] Phonsiri "Nangnai," 44–45.

[37] Smith, *Physician at the Court of Siam,* 43.

[38] Cited in Phonsiri, "Nangnai," 46.

[39] NL R4, "Prakat ruang thwai but ying pai tham ratchakan nai phraratchawang," no date; Loos, Archival Notebooks, vol. 1, 174–79.

[40] These numbers do not include female royal family members, female officials, servants and slaves who also lived in the Inner Palace.

[41] Kullada Kesboonchoo Mead, *The Rise and Decline of Thai Absolutism* (London: Taylor and Francis, 2004), chap. 4.

stitutional monarchy but could not openly request the end of polygyny. King Chulalongkorn nonetheless was informed of this by Prince Devawongse. Prince Svasti Sobhon,[42] one of the petition signatories and a half-brother to the king, presented a "memorial" to the king in 1891 expressing his view of polygyny as a social ill.[43] Arguably, part of the reason why he was more or less out of favor for much of King Chulalongkorn's reign was because of this.

In stark contrast to both King Mongkut and King Chulalongkorn, King Vajiravudh refused to marry until he was forty-two and was likely a homosexual. His homosexuality per se, however, is not the cause for his unpopularity both during his life and in some histories of his reign. When evaluated by the standards of Siam's masculine political culture, his reign reflected a kind of political as well as conjugal impotence.[44] Instead of building personal alliances through marriages and appointments of relatives, King Vajiravudh disdained marriage and gradually replaced many royal-blooded government officials with commoners.[45] His feuds with some of the highest-ranking princes were a consequence also of his personal disavowal of polygynous politics and his private stance on marriage. (The monarch publicly defended polygyny as a Buddhist custom, despite his private efforts to end polygynous politics.)

One reason he had a falling out in 1915 with Prince Damrong (minister of the interior between 1892 and 1915 and probably the most important political leader next to the king) was Rama VI's repeated refusal to marry one of Prince Damrong's daughters.[46] The king's dispute with his eldest full brother, Prince Chakrabongse, is also telling. While his Russian wife was away, Prince Chakrabongse (who was in charge of the army) had an affair with unmarried Princess Chawalit, the daughter of Prince Ratburi (minister of justice from 1897 to 1910 and minister of agriculture after 1910), which caused his Russian wife to divorce the prince. When Prince Chakrabongse requested the king's permission to marry the princess, as was required by law, King Vajiravudh refused. This shocked everyone because the "affair" was simply polygynous politics in practice and the princess was high ranking and thus a good match.[47] Lastly, the king and Prince Svasti agreed that polygyny had to go and advocated monogamy but disagreed intensely over its implementation. This disagreement caused a nearly irrevocable split between the

[42] Prince Svasti was also the full brother of Prince Devawongse, president of the Dika Court, former minister of justice in 1892, and otherwise one of the highest-ranking and highest-positioned princes.

[43] "The Late Prince Svasti," *Bangkok Times Weekly Mail* (12 Dec. 1935), 11–12.

[44] I address the impact of King Vajiravudh's purported homosexuality in Loos, "Sex in the Inner City."

[45] Stephen Greene, *Absolute Dreams: Thai Government under Rama VI, 1910–1925* (Bangkok: White Lotus, 1999), 33, 73–81.

[46] Greene, *Absolute Dreams,* 92.

[47] Ibid., 126–27.

two men in the late 1910s. Even though King Vajiravudh eventually obtained four wives in quick succession in order to produce an heir, he had only one child—a daughter. His marriages were a last-ditch effort to provide a male heir to the throne rather than an attempt to show that he personally supported polygyny.

For a variety of related reasons over the period that these three kings ruled, the significance of polygyny as a foundation of Siam's political culture began to shift. Economic historians differ in their emphasis on internal versus external forces, but they agree that the nineteenth century marks the beginning of major structural changes in Siam's polity and economy. Under King Mongkut, Siam opened its economy to international trade after signing the Bowring Treaty in 1855. This began a long transformation in the structure of Siam's domestic economy from subsistence agriculture to a more diversified, increasingly monetized economy that traded in various natural resources then in demand by European powers.[48] The material basis and manifestations of political authority changed as well.

By the 1880s, the need for drastic institutional change had made itself clear, and the individuals who had previously obstructed reforms had died, opening the way for King Chulalongkorn's reforms. As a result of King Chulalongkorn's creation of a territorially based administrative bureaucracy, the geographic map and the outreach of the bureaucracy into distant provinces began to signify political inclusion in the kingdom.[49] It was no longer necessary for provincial elites to send a proxy, in the form of a daughter, to the king to establish political affiliation. Moreover, after the introduction of the rule of primogeniture in 1886, individual monarchs were no longer as beholden to elite families, who had traditionally determined kingly successors.[50] Yet, the Inner Palace population expanded under Siam's famously modernizing King Chulalongkorn to become the largest under any Chakri monarch. The reign of King Chulalongkorn, Thailand's most cherished monarch, has been densely studied by historians, but no one has critically discussed the fact that the Inner Palace population was the largest of all Chakri monarchs at the same time that polygyny ceased to serve its integrative function and, moreover, was widely regarded by contemporaries (foreign and increasingly Siamese as well) as a sign of Siam's "backwardness." By taking into account Siam's masculine political culture, one can understand why polygyny continued to function as a sign of power even after its integrative functions had been replicated by administrative structures.

[48] Pasuk and Baker, *Thailand,* chaps. 3, 4, and 12; Ingram, *Economic Change in Thailand,* 1971, chap. 3.

[49] Thongchai, *Siam Mapped;* Tej, *Provincial Administration.*

[50] These changes had legal ramifications: the class status of aristocrats and royalty was no longer effectively performed through the strict regulation of elite female sexuality. On primogeniture, see Greene, *Absolute Dreams,* 2.

Foreign Critiques of Polygyny

The increasing presence of foreigners in Siam starting in the 1850s opened Siamese cultural practices, such as polygyny, to criticism. Dr. Dan B. Bradley, an American missionary, doctor, and printer living in Siam from 1835 to 1873, commented in his publication, the *Bangkok Calendar,* that "virtue can never have much sway in Siam, nor any true prosperity until polygamy is made a crime by the Government."[51] Most famous and (now) controversial among foreign observers was Anna Leonowens, who cemented the interpretation of polygyny as slavery in the popular imagination of Europeans and Americans. Her books, *The English Governess at the Siamese Court* (1870) and *Siamese Harem Life* (1873), were well-nigh required reading by Westerners, particularly women, heading to Siam as missionaries, travelers, and wives of men working in Siam.[52] Leonowens's friendship with Harriet Beecher Stowe undoubtedly influenced her treatment of polygyny as a form of bondage. Emancipation, freedom, independence—concepts that became foundational to Siam's national identity—were defined early on as the antithesis of "sexual slavery."[53] Monogamy was, in Leonowens's writings, the next step toward freeing women from enslavement as minor wives.

References in English to the "harem" of King Mongkut and to his sheer number of "concubines" were used to condemn the king as depraved and sexually excessive.[54] For example, Townsend Harris, the first American consul and minister to Japan, spent several months in Siam in 1856. He commented on King Mongkut's "affairs" of state. In a moment of bumptious frustration after having his meeting with the king postponed, Harris wrote: "His Majesty is pedantic beyond belief, and that too on a very small capital of knowledge. Add to this the fact that he is much given to women, and a solution is found for the delay of all useful business. It may be said that [he] resembles Solomon only in the chapter of wives and concubines."[55] Dis-

[51] Abbot Low Moffat, *Mongkut, King of Siam* (Ithaca: Cornell University Press, 1961), 135, cited in Craig Reynolds, "A Nineteenth Century Thai Buddhist Defense of Polygamy," 940.

[52] Mary Backus, ed., *Siam and Laos: As Seen by Our American Missionaries* (Philadelphia: Presbyterian Board of Publication Backus, 1884); Florence Caddy, *To Siam and Malay in the Duke of Sutherland's Yacht, 'Sans Peur'* (London: Hurst and Blackett, 1889); Mary Lovina Cort, *Siam: Or, The Heart of Farther India* (New York: Anson D. F. Randolph, 1886); and Grindrod (1982 [1882]) were among the Western female authors who read Anna Leonowens's books. The two most relevant are Anna Leonowens, *The English Governess at the Siamese Court* (Singapore: Oxford University Press, 1988 [1870]), and *Siamese Harem Life* (New York: E. P. Dutton, 1953 [1873].

[53] For an insightful treatment of the association between Thailand's national identity and the idea of freedom, see Thanet Aphornsuvan, "Slavery and Modernity: Freedom in the Making of Modern Siam," in *Asian Freedoms: The Idea of Freedom in East and Southeast Asia,* ed. David Kelly and Anthony Reid (Cambridge: Cambridge University Press, 1998), 161–86.

[54] *Bangkok Calendar* (Bangkok), 1863; Sir John Bowring, *The Kingdom and People of Siam,* vol. 2 (London: John W. Parker and Son, 1857), 319–20; Leonowens, *English Governess,* 43–48, 94, 103–15.

[55] *The Complete Journal of Townsend Harris,* intro. Mario Emilio Cosenza, preface Douglas MacArthur II, rev. ed. (Rutland, Vt.: Charles E. Tuttle, 1959), 145.

courses produced by Leonowens, Bradley, Harris, and others construct an image of Siamese women enslaved for sexual purposes by Siam's ruling men, and therefore in need of rescue by "enlightened" Europeans and Americans. This move is paradigmatic of colonial discourses elsewhere, as Lata Mani has demonstrated in the case of British reformulations of sati and Leila Ahmed has discussed in relation to European discourses about Middle Eastern women.[56]

Their narrow castigation of polygyny as a sexual perversion, an injustice to women, and a sign of an uncivilized nation, reframes polygyny within Euro-American imperial discourses of civilization and denies the political work performed by the institution of polygyny in Siam up to the late nineteenth century. European and American visitors understood the purpose of the "harem" as exclusively a sexual outlet for monarchs rather than seeing its wider role in political alliance formation and integration and as a reflection of masculinity and power. As a result of unequal treaties with over a dozen foreign powers, foreigners in Siam gained economic and extraterritorial legal privileges after 1855. The consequent political, economic, and, increasingly, legal power of foreigners gave additional disciplinary weight to their "opinions" about the "uncivilized" practice of "polygyny." The Inner Palace—forbidden to outsiders and the location of personalized political loyalties—contradicted modern standards of professionalized, meritocratic administration. The lack of transparency of the "harem" as a political institution signified to foreigners an irrational, disorderly mode of power.

The foreign critique of polygyny had an impact on the Siamese elite, even causing King Mongkut to consider including a treaty clause that would abolish polygyny for Siam's monarchs in the 1856 agreement with the United States. Yet, the Inner Palace was not restructured or disbanded. Instead, it was defended as a Buddhist practice. Alongside the establishment by the 1890s of modern political institutions, Siam's leaders preserved aspects of local political culture, especially those that supported the existing social hierarchy.[57] In other words, the integrative, alliance-making, and legitimating functions of the Inner Palace continued to operate under Kings Mongkut and Chulalongkorn. As one scholar, Leslie Peirce, has noted in a different context, "Functionally ascribed authority—authority devolving from one's office—certainly existed, but more important was the web of individual relations—of patronage and clientele, of teacher and student, of kinship and marriage—that brought one to that office and that one used in the exercise of one's official power."[58]

The abrupt and dramatic cessation of polygynous political marriages oc-

[56] Lata Mani, "Contentious Traditions"; Leila Ahmed, *Women and Gender in Islam: Historical Roots of a Modern Debate* (New Haven: Yale University Press, 1992).

[57] Loos, "Sex in the Inner City."

[58] Leslie Peirce, *The Imperial Harem: Women and Sovereignty in the Ottoman Empire* (New York: Oxford University Press, 1993), 149.

curred in 1910, the year that King Chulalongkorn's son, Vajiravudh, ascended the throne. Although it is tempting to explain the cessation of polygyny as a political institution by resorting to King Vajiravudh's alleged sexual preferences for men, this is an insufficient explanation. It is more fully explained as the result of King Vajiravudh's refusal to perpetuate certain crucial aspects of Siam's masculinist political culture. This does not mean that King Vajiravudh's form of nationalism was not masculine—he stressed militarism and patriarchal familial values and policies.[59] Although King Vajiravudh refused to engage in polygynous alliances throughout most of his reign, he did not promulgate a law on monogamy as Siam's marital standard.

The Domestic Politics of Polygyny

The special status of polygyny lies in the logic of reform internal to politics within Siam. Siam's reformers and educated elites sifted through liberal ideas from Europe, selected ones that suited their needs, and significantly transformed the meaning of the reforms in the process of localizing them in the context of Siam. Various factions of Siam's political elites selected different reforms to further their distinct and often conflicting political aims. In this context, polygyny served as a lightening rod for domestic conflict. It became a politically polarizing issue that positioned one on either end of the political spectrum. On one end was the cultural nativist who defended polygyny as a Siamese Buddhist practice that offered an alternative form of modernity in contradistinction to the Christian West. On the other end stood the political reformer who advocated equality between the sexes as modern, progressive, and necessary before Siam could advance geopolitically. In these ways, rhetoric about the family, gender relations, and sexual practices was located within the larger framework of Siam's domestic politics, even as it was constantly in dialogue with the hegemonic cultures of imperial powers.

Domestic debates about polygyny arose from two distinct sources: official discourses produced by legal advisers, cabinet members (comprised of royal and high-ranking nonroyal officials), and kings; and popular discourses in newspapers and court case testimonies that provide a glimpse at the lived experience and popular understandings of polygyny. Despite differences within and between the two sources, they all share the same ideological and temporal contingencies. Domestic debates on polygyny occurred during the era of high imperialism in which ideas and bodies increasingly crossed national boundaries. Siam's royal-noble elite, particularly those men revising Siam's laws, went to England and France to study jurisprudence. Similarly, over forty foreign legal advisers—many of whom had experience in colonial settings—

[59] On militarism, see chaps. 3 and 5 in Vella, *Chaiyo!*

worked in Siam's Ministry of Justice, on its international courts, and on committees that drafted modern laws.

Nearly all of Siam's legal codes were drafted initially in English, not Thai. Ideas about morality, based on radically different religious and philosophical traditions, could not help but intermingle and collide. The asymmetrical power relations between Siam and European nations meant that such collisions required adaptation or defense by the Siamese. Within this framework, Siam's leaders and urban population deliberated on the complex question of marital reform.

At the level of publicized official discourse and legislation, kings and statesmen from the 1850s until 1910 refused to discard polygyny as Siam's marital standard, even as they privately debated its merits. They articulated in religious terms a Buddhist "defense" of polygyny as early as 1867, when King Mongkut's minister of foreign affairs, Chao Phraya Thiphakorawong [Kham Bunnag] published *Kitchanukit* (A Book Explaining Various Things).[60] In it, he sought a legitimate basis for polygyny in Buddhism, which he claimed sanctioned the custom by not explicitly forbidding it. Buddhism, he argued, forbade polyandry because women were inherently predisposed to play favorites among their husbands, a game that might result in the murder of all but their favorite man. Unlike Islam, which Chao Phraya Thipakurawong understood as allowing polygyny for the irreligious reason of man's sexual convenience, Buddhism allowed a man to practice polygyny because it forestalled him from forcing a woman to engage in sexual intercourse against her will, which would cause him to lose merit.[61] It is no coincidence that the author was the minister who negotiated the Bowring Treaty on behalf of King Mongkut in 1855.[62] King Mongkut may have seen certain strategic advantages in ending polygyny, which he briefly considered doing in the 1856 treaty with the United States, but he stopped short of this. King Mongkut issued a proclamation suggesting the decline in importance of "gifting" one's daughter to the Inner Palace and also allowed certain women to leave the Inner Palace. However, he ultimately decided against interfering with existing marital customs.

Although the idea that the tradition of polygyny is rooted in a Buddhist worldview is cited occasionally into the early twentieth century, Chao Phraya Thiphakorawong was perhaps the last high-ranking official to defend it publicly, though it continued to be practiced and defended by elites in private government meetings. In the first decade of the new century, King Chula-

[60] Chao Phraya Thiphakorawong, *Nangsu sadaeng kitchanukit* (Bangkok: Khuru Sapha, 1971), first published in 1867. For an analysis of the book in the context of Buddhist cosmography and Siam's social history, see Reynolds (1976 and 1977).

[61] Chao Phraya Thiphakorawong, *Nangsu sadaeng kitchanukit,* 220–22, 226; Reynolds, *A Nineteenth Century Thai Buddhist Defense of Polygamy,* 947–48, 962–63.

[62] Sukit Nimmanhemin, "Khamnam" (introduction) to *Nangsu sadaeng kitchanukit.*

longkorn suggested taking a survey of men who practiced polygyny to help legal advisers determine whether monogamy or polygyny should constitute the legal standard, but no survey was taken.[63] The king did not publish an official opinion on polygyny.

In contrast to King Chulalongkorn's silence on polygyny is the relative explosion of official discourses on polygyny, most of which were not publicly circulated, after the king died in 1910 and King Vajiravudh succeeded him on the throne. Between 1910 and 1935, when the state passed a monogamy law, the all-Siamese Cabinet Council (*senabodi sapha*) that advised the monarchy made authoritative decisions regarding polygyny and other legal issues. Georges Padoux catalyzed discussion of polygyny in 1912 when he asked the Cabinet Council to determine Siam's legal definition of marriage so that he could proceed with drafting a new national inheritance law. This provoked a stream of memos and meetings of the Cabinet Council in 1912 and 1913, which discussed polygyny at theoretical and practical levels. The council critiqued the harmful and fallacious deployment of polygyny as the source of moral and religious difference between Siam and Europe. One member argued that polygyny was old-fashioned and that if Siam passed a polygyny law, then foreigners would use it against Siam by claiming that Siam failed to meet Western standards.[64] King Vajiravudh responded as follows:

> It is stated that if it were set down in our Law that if we allowed man to have more than one wife, it would amount to a confession that we were on a lower moral plane than that of the Western Nations. I can not agree with this statement, because the monogamous system of the Europeans is the result of their religion, which ordains that a man may have only one wife and a woman only one husband, and that married people who have connection with others than their own spouses are said to commit adultery. (King Vajiravudh in Adul and Luang Chamroon, "Some Main Features," 93–94)

He states further that Buddhism does not limit the number of wives a man has, does not forbid polygyny, and does not condemn polygyny as immoral unless a man seeks connection with the wife of another man, which counts as covetousness.

> This being so, it cannot be said that the Siamese who has several wives is on a lower moral plane than the European with only one wife, because to admit such a proposition would mean that we shall have also to admit that the Buddhist Religion itself is also on a lower moral plane than the Christian Religion, which naturally I for one *cannot* admit. . . . I have brought this matter up

[63] Rungsaeng, "Origins of Thailand's Modern Ministry of Justice," 261.
[64] Adul and Luang Chamroon, "Some Main Features," 97.

> in order to demonstrate that our moral plane and that of the Europeans could not very well be compared with fairness, because they are so different, and it is most difficult to judge who is on the higher moral plane and who on the lower. Therefore to drag the subject of Moral Planes into the drafting of Marriage Law appears to me to be rather inapt. (King Vajiravudh in Adul and *Luang* Chamroon, "Some Main Features, 94)

The remaining meeting minutes that deal with polygyny from 1912 and the memos from 1913 focus on practical legal issues that result from the lack of a marital standard in the law. Namely, the council was concerned that passing a law on monogamy would create illegitimate children, paternity confusion, and inheritance problems. Some argued that men would ignore a monogamy law, would deceive women into marrying them, and thus the law would ultimately fail to protect women. For these reasons, and because no consensus was reached by Cabinet Council members, King Vajiravudh pushed for a law that would at the very least require the registration of marriage(s) so the state could regulate what he considered promiscuous liaisons.[65] Although he could not push through a national marriage law, he did promulgate laws regarding marital registration for state officials.

Ultimately, no law adopting monogamy or polygyny as a marital form was passed despite high-level recognition of a dire need for a legal standard. The issue was dropped after 1912 because of the agonistic nature of the debate among the elite, because lawmakers focused their attention on preparing books one through four of the Civil and Commercial Code (Books V and VI were on family and inheritance, respectively), and because the person who catalyzed the discussion, Padoux, returned to Paris.[66]

The Cabinet Council did not revisit the marriage issue until 1926, under King Prajadhipok, who suggested passing a law allowing the registration of many minor wives but only one major wife. Before he could promulgate this law, the Cabinet Council met again to discuss a marital standard in October 1928.[67] They voted 8–6 in favor of polygyny. Their concerns were similar to those raised earlier by King Vajiravudh's Cabinet Council: a polygyny law would reveal too starkly Siam's difference from other countries, but a monogamy law would lead to increased problems regarding illegitimate children and would fail to protect women. King Prajadhipok, like King Vajiravudh, simultaneously raised the specter of foreign judgment as he enjoined councilors to take pride in their decision to maintain polygyny: "After deciding in favor of polygyny, we do not have to be ashamed before farang [white Westerners]."[68] The codification committee drafted a law on polyg-

[65] Ibid., 92–93; Pakdi, "Kanchatrang pramuan kotmai," 99.
[66] Pakdi, "Kanchatrang pramuan kotmai," 99–100.
[67] Ibid., 99–101.
[68] Ibid., 102.

yny in December 1928, but it was rescinded for budgetary reasons before it was implemented.[69] The inability of pro-monogamy monarchs to press ahead with marital reform demonstrates that monarchical power was, by this time, far from absolute.

The years between 1931 and 1935 were troubled ones economically (as a result of the Great Depression) and politically. A coup staged by civilian and military officials in 1932 overthrew King Prajadhipok and established a constitutional monarchy. Still, lawmakers continued to draft the remaining laws as if the shift in political regime made no difference. The final books, V (family) and VI (inheritance), of the Civil and Commercial Code were passed by parliament in 1935. Monogamy was adopted as the legal form of marriage, which recognized couples as married only if they registered with their local district offices.[70] Polygyny was not, however, criminalized. Moreover, while a man could legally register but one wife, he could legitimate children born outside of wedlock by legally acknowledging them. Foreign treaty powers rescinded the remaining extraterritoriality clauses by 1939.

It appears that Siam had to pass a marriage law in order to rid the country of extraterritorial treaties. That it ended up supporting a monogamy law that invited polygyny in through the back door is no coincidence. The marriage law was the stumbling block to promulgating the Civil and Commercial Code, which was the last set of laws foreign powers required Siam to pass before all extraterritorial rights were abrogated. The selection of polygyny as the sticking point was the result of domestic and international historical contingencies, which collided on the issue of polygyny.

In many ways the official debates about marriage were hermetically sealed from popular discourses and experiences of it because high-level debates were not made accessible to the public. Imperial discourses about modernity, morality, and marriage framed both popular and official discourses on marriage reform, thereby linking them together. Officials and kings concerned themselves with defending polygyny as a Buddhist and Siamese customary practice that was equal to but different from European, Christian morals and notions of the modern. By contrast, intellectuals and urbanites writing for the press used the imperial norm of monogamous marriage to challenge the

[69] The law stated that husbands could register only one major wife, who was the only wife entitled to a portion of marital property upon divorce by mutual consent. It did not forbid marriage to minor wives. "Phraratchabanyat kaekhai phoemtoem kotmai laksana phuamia" (Royal Act Revising and Supplementing the Law on Husbands and Wives), 20 Feb. 1931, 43 PKPS 323–35; "Ngot kanchai phraratchabanyat kaekhai phoemtoem kotmai laksana phuamia" (Suspending the Implementation of the Royal Act Revising and Supplementing the Law on Husbands and Wives), 18 Nov. 1931, 44 PKPS 322–33.

[70] On the 1935 law on monogamy, see "Phraratchabanyat chot thabian khropkhrua," (Royal Act on Registering Families) Sept. 1935, 48 pt. 1, PKPS 354–93. Clause 1451 very subtly states that if an individual has already registered a marriage that individual cannot register another marriage unless the first marriage has ended by death, divorce, or cancellation by the court.

legitimacy of the absolutist state. They claimed that polygyny indexed the abuses of officialdom and the backwardness of the state.

The public debates regarding polygyny as expressed in the print media, including private newspapers and journals as well as those that served as outlets for the monarch's essays, have been treated thoroughly by Scot Barmé.[71] The following discussion highlights major themes and provides the social context for understanding how heterosexual sexuality and gender were redeployed in early twentieth century law and court cases. Court records and laws regarding sexual relations, including polygyny, prostitution, citizenship, and family are treated separately in the following chapters.

Analyses of the print media in Siam by Matthew Copeland and Scot Barmé have demonstrated the extensive use of newspapers and journals by middle class intellectuals to develop a distinct voice of political opposition to the absolutist monarchical system.[72] Their excellent studies have demonstrated that vibrant antimonarchical political dissent existed in early twentieth century Siam. Barmé, in particular, brings this political stance to bear on gender issues. He scoured early twentieth century Thai-language newspapers for articles and political cartoons that targeted royal and aristocratic officials for the wastefulness and abuse engendered by polygyny.[73]

The earliest example is Thianwan (T. W. S. Wannapho, 1842–1915), a politically progressive male commoner intellectual who published magazine articles in 1905 criticizing polygyny as economically wasteful and harmful to a man's health.[74] By the 1910s and 1920s, these kinds of arguments became common. Middle class men and women writing for the press blamed the decadence of royal family members and aristocrats for the persistence of polygyny. Elite polygynous men were ridiculed and critiqued in the press. They are seen as "living an idle, licentious existence, immersed in pleasure while contributing nothing to the wider community" and as individuals whose "sexual peccadilloes" caused them, and by extension the nation, financial ruin.[75] Foreign-educated members of Siam's elite in particular were portrayed as lascivious, womanizing, and corrupt men who were contemptuous of their fellow citizens. Their Western-inspired office hours were described as interrupted by their daily visits to their "daytime wives."[76]

Barmé translates portions of a serialized novel, *Dancing,* written by Chamnong Wongkhaluang for the popular newspaper *Thai thai* (1931), in which

[71] Barmé, *Woman, Man, Bangkok,* chaps. 5 and 6.

[72] Matthew Copeland, "Contested Nationalism and the 1932 Overthrow of the Absolute Monarchy in Siam," PhD diss., Australian National University, 1993; Barmé, *Woman, Man, Bangkok.*

[73] Barmé, *Woman, Man, Bangkok,* 120–29, 157–75.

[74] Scot Barmé, "Protofeminist Discourses in Early Twentieth-Century Siam," in *Genders and Sexualities in Modern Thailand,* ed. Peter A. Jackson and Nerida M. Cook (Chiang Mai: Silkworm Books, 1999), 134–53.

[75] Barmé, *Woman, Man, Bangkok,* 125.

[76] Ibid., 126.

high-ranking government officials are mocked in a passage relaying one official's description of his experience with polygyny:

> I've got wives in almost every street in the capital. . . . I use my money to lure them. . . . The law in Siam doesn't limit the number of wives a man can have. If you've got the money you can take as many as you like. . . . Go and visit the homes of *Chaokhun* [a title used to refer to a high-ranking man] so-and-so or *Khun Phra* [official title] whoever, and you'll see it's no different from a Turkish harem: their houses are jam packed with women. (Barmé, *Woman, Man, Bangkok,* 123)

Members of the middle class writing for the popular press held absolutism and its political administration responsible for Siam's backward ways, symbolized by polygyny, and questioned their moral fitness to rule.

Women as well as men wrote scathing critiques of polygyny. One female author wrote in 1922 that the government is the source of the problem because it gave men the right to have multiple wives. She linked the existing law on marriage to the male behavior it sanctioned—it allowed men to abandon their wives (and children) for younger women, which in turn caused daughters to engage in prostitution and promoted similar behavior in sons. She called on the government to stop advocating inequality between the sexes, which was clearly disruptive to family life, by promulgating a monogamy law.[77]

Barmé's research also turned up articles by men in the popular press that qualified their support of monogamy (first women must be better educated) or endorsed polygyny outright (it increased the population, which was seen as good for the nation).[78] One female author took a softer stance on polygyny but persisted in linking it to official practices. Her article emphasized the connection between an official's work in the bureaucracy and his behavior at home, including his treatment of his wives, children, and female servants. This article stressed, rather patriotically, that officials must love their home in order to love the nation.[79]

Barmé's decision to use exclusively popular sources of public opinion to counter the normative privileging of royal writings to write history is laudable. However, both the public and King Vajiravudh (Rama VI)—who wrote extensively on gender issues in the press—worked within the same discursive, political, and social domain. Royal elite and urban commoner intellectuals deployed rhetoric that was remarkably similar in content and flavor (sentimental, dramatic), even when these two groups used the discourse of progress and

[77] Ibid., 165.
[78] Ibid., 167–71.
[79] Ibid., 163.

civilization to radically different political ends. In Rama VI's writings, ideas about women as wives and mothers of the nation offer him ammunition against middle-class men who were critical of the monarchy. However, Thianwan deployed the same arguments as part of his larger political critique of absolutism. In both cases, the goal is either antiabsolutism or absolutism, not a better understanding of women's social or political integration into the state. Ideas about women, family, and "progress" had become central to national ideology regardless of one's location on the political spectrum.

It also suggests that attitudes regarding polygyny, prostitution, wives, and gender relations were not as grounded in one's class status as Barmé argues. Officials associated with absolutism *and* middle-class intellectuals published antipolygynous articles in the press. As noted above, a few middle-class writers even signaled their favorable stance toward polygyny. By the early twentieth century, the practice of one man engaging sexually with multiple female partners did not consistently map onto one's class position or political stance on absolutism.

It did, however, map onto officialdom. As the number of men from commoner backgrounds who worked in the administration increased, so too did the practice of having multiple wives. This threatened to cloud the distinction between traditional elites and the middle class, a distinction that had blurred by the 1910s and 1920s when these debates reached their highest pitch. In fact, there is evidence to suggest that polygyny had paradoxically become "democratized." King Chulalongkorn's reforms engendered a salaried middle class of Siamese men. Between 1892 and 1925, the bureaucracy grew sevenfold in size.[80] The expansion of the bureaucracy and introduction of salaried positions meant that nonelite men, in addition to royal elites, obtained positions in Siam's administration and were receiving a cash salary. A salaried bureaucracy composed entirely of young Siamese men combined with other social changes, including increased opportunities for contact between the sexes. As a result, nonelite men had more opportunities to engage in polygyny and to pay for commercial sex, two institutions causally linked in the popular press and increasingly difficult to distinguish. The example of K. S. R. Kulap is a case in point. A commoner born in 1834 and still alive in 1913, Kulap received an extraordinary education that paralleled that of royal princes. He had twelve wives and eighteen children.[81]

Although it is impossible to provide a quantitative analysis of the numbers of polygynous unions and the rank of the men involved, the number of court cases involving officials of middling to high rank who had more than one wife suggests that polygyny continued to be associated with official power.

[80] Batson, *End of the Absolute Monarchy,* 45, n. 40.

[81] Craig Reynolds, "The Case of K. S. R. Kulap: A Challenge to Royal Historical Writing in Late Nineteenth Century Thailand," *Journal of the Siam Society* 61, no. 2 (July 1973): 71. Kulap's lifestyle and education blurred boundaries between royalty and commoners.

Masculine authority continued to manifest through polygynous relations. As the class base from which officials were drawn expanded, so too did the practice of polygyny among members of the new middle classes. Because polygyny was legal, no cases directly contesting polygyny exist. However, the evidence from divorce cases and suits contesting marital property suggests that officials from commoner as well as aristocratic backgrounds commonly engaged in polygyny.

A more obvious source of evidence that polygyny had been "democratized" to include commoner men exists in the eruption of discourse about *illegitimate wives* in law and royal writings. What could the category of illegitimate wife mean in a country where polygyny was legal? The definition of legitimate wives began to depend on which class of men obtained wives and the circumstances under which they had sexual intercourse. At this point, the discourse about sexual relations—monogamous, polygynous, and commercial—began to be used to police class boundaries. Tellingly, at the same time that polygyny was "democratized," the definition of legitimate marriage or a legitimate wife was narrowed in law and in the courts. The collection of mistresses (as opposed to legitimate wives) was not considered a sign of prestige, wealth, or transcendent virtue (barami) in the eyes of the king and laws of the courts.

The fact that Siam was not colonized meant that Siamese "traditional" practices, such as polygyny, did not become an unambiguous symbol of Siam's national identity that required defending in the face of a foreign overlord. Instead, Siam's domestic sovereignty over cultural practices within an imperial context meant that practices like polygyny were subject to polarizing politics. Polygyny as a sign (of Buddhist authenticity or of barbarous incivility) was endlessly deployable. In fact, King Vajiravudh argued at one time that because Buddhism sanctioned polygyny, it could not be discarded without implying that Christianity was a superior religion. In another instance, he contradicted himself. He inadvertently likened "Thai nobles" (*phu di thai*) who practiced polygyny to "savages" (*khon pa*) in Borneo and Africa when he suggested that they both treat their women like livestock.[82] In the essay, he romanticized and eulogized Siamese peasants for practicing sexual equality, claiming that the tradition of polygyny was not indigenous to Siam but was an alien Indic custom introduced centuries earlier:

> We don't have to look as far as any country of white Westerners [for an example of men treating women equally]. I invite you Thai nobles to go to the villages of Siam itself, where you will see examples of monogamous families.

[82] Suphatra Singloka, Khunying, ed., *Khruangmai haeng khwamrungruang khu saphap haeng satri* (A Symbol of Civilization: The Status of Women) (Bangkok: Somakhom banthit satri thang kotmai haeng prathet thai, 1992), 1, 3–4.

> You will see not just one or two such households, [but] many. . . . I therefore think our Thai villagers are genuinely closer to being civilized than people in Bangkok or large cities! (King Vajiravudh in Khunying Suphatra Singloka, ed., "A Symbol of Civilization," 3–4)

King Vajiravudh's emphasis on the equality, in terms of romantic love and labor, of relations among men and women in Siam's farming population allowed him to contend that Siam had a core tradition of equality and monogamy despite the practice of polygyny among some elites in urban areas. In contrast to nationalist ideologies that grew out of a direct colonial encounter, Siam's "backward" customs, such as polygyny, did not consistently become part of a "tradition" used by local indigenous elites against a colonial overlord.

The contradictory yet politically charged uses to which polygyny was put derived its potency from imperial ideologies that treated the institution of marriage as the source of a nation's core identity. Because colonial jurisprudence heightened the significance of family and marital form for national identity, marriage became the vehicle by which Siam would signify its form of national modernity. As a result, polygyny's former political function of integrating the kingdom was drastically flipped: now it served to dis-integrate the nation. In the press, polygyny's sexual connotations were emphasized, moralized, and politicized while its former role in state affairs was depoliticized, disavowed, or omitted altogether. Whereas it once served to stabilize, unite, and literally reproduce the kingdom's administration, by the twentieth century polygyny had become a political minefield.

Legal resolution to marital reform did not come until 1935. Arguments about adopting polygyny or monogamy as Siam's marital standard led up to and continued after the overthrow of the absolute monarchy by a group of mid-level military officers and civilian officials in June 1932. These men aimed to rectify what they saw as the excesses of an absolute monarchical political system. In the larger debate over the direction and identity of the nation, the voices of the newly empowered advocated for a nation of free and equal citizens who had an active role in the government. Polygyny was a contradiction for many, not only because it was practiced by former elites but because it repudiated the discourse of equality among citizens. Monogamy, for some, had come to represent a form of gender equality.

Polygyny was not, however, a contradiction for all. Although the ideology of the new ruling elites contained the idea of egalitarianism, it is difficult to gauge the degree to which this ideology transformed gender practices in Siam. Certainly the practice of accumulating multiple wives has continued after 1935. The shifting function and meanings of polygyny also set in motion a crisis in wifedom as well as novel reforms in male sexual practices.

FIVE

Crisis of Wifedom

King Vajiravudh's 1915 statement about the indeterminability of *mia* or wives serves as a touchstone for a crisis of wifedom, which was in full swing by the 1910s:

> Young men enjoy speaking of all women that they have been involved with—even if it was just one time—as *wife* [*mia*]. I'm really embarrassed by the fact that I must ask if they're speaking of their wife by marriage, their minor wife, or their mistress. When they respond that they're talking about that woman, giving a name of one who is well-known as a harlot or sometimes even a prostitute, it makes it even worse! (King Vajiravudh, "Khlon tit Lo" [Clog on Our Wheels], 109, emphasis in original)

The early twentieth century bombards observers, past and present, with the sheer volume of material about wives: their definition, their role in the nation, their legal protections, and (less often) their voices. It compelled the attention of social commentators, lawyers, judges, and the monarch, who all waged a debate of epic proportions in newspapers, legal manuals, law codes, court cases, and literary essays over "the status of women," prostitution, and polygyny. Much of the popular debate in the print media was covered in the previous chapter. All three of these issues hinged on the meaning of a legitimate wife, whose identity was subject to a legal, social, and official war of definition. The debate revolved around nationalism, masculine power, and material wealth as much as it did around a woman's identity in the family.

The early twentieth century was a ground-shifting period for gender and nationalism in Siam. Although the definition of wife and family was perpetually subject to redefinition, this period was particularly important because of economic shifts, the enthronement of a series of nonpolygynous monarchs after the death of profusely polygynous King Chulalongkorn, the "democratization" of polygyny among nonelite men, and the ambiguous legal definition of wife, which had consequences for the orderly transfer of wealth and status. Delinked from its former legitimacy, polygyny had become a focal point for debate about national identity. Framing and informing the subnational debate were imperial hegemonic definitions of modernity that linked civilized status to monogamous marriage. Both the global and national discourse on marriage, polygyny, and women had consequences for women in law and society.

Legal reformers and King Vajiravudh (Rama VI, r. 1910–25) attempted to shape cultural practices by stabilizing and standardizing Siam's institution of the family through the print media and legal codes. As legislators came closer and closer to completing a comprehensive civil code and as the court system became more consistent in applying legal standards rather than ad hoc judgments, judicial personnel found that the hitherto flexible definition of marital unions confounded the application of laws on divorce and inheritance.[1] They appealed repeatedly to the monarch and the ministerial-level Cabinet Council (*senabodi sapha*) to promulgate a legal standard defining marriage so that they could adjudicate cases on inheritance, divorce, and adultery. However, Siam's ruling elites, most of whom practiced polygynous politics, could not agree on a formal definition of marriage as polygynous or monogamous.

In meetings held in 1912 and 1913, the Cabinet Council was incapable of deciding on monogamy or polygyny, but it agreed that polygyny could not be outlawed. Even King Vajiravudh concurred, but not because he supported polygynists. He worried about alienating Muslims: "I do not wish to do anything, which would force my Malay subjects of Patani and Satul [Satun] to run away from the harshness of our law, to seek refuge under the more equitable laws of the English, who (very wisely) do not interfere with the marriage customs of their subjects."[2] His support for Malays extended to the introduction of an additional Islamic family court in Satun Province in 1917, the year of his second royal tour of the south (the first was in 1915). The new court regulations, however, maintained Thai control over the court by requiring the signature of a Siamese state judge (*phuphiphaksa*) on all of

[1] NA MR6 Yutitham 12.1 Kotmai, Pramuan phaeng lae phanit, "Raingan senabodi sapha," 22 Jan. 1912, and King Vajiravudh, "Khlon tit lo" (Clogs on Our Wheels)," in *Plukchai suapa lae khlon tit lo* (Instilling the Wild Tiger Spirit and Clogs on Our Wheels) (Bangkok, 1951 [1915]), 108.

[2] NA R6 file 204, notes on the marriage laws, 3 June 1913, and additional notes, 5 June 1913, cited in Vella, *Chaiyo!,* 156.

the decisions meted out by dato yutitham, who had to pledge loyalty to Siam's king.[3] The official policy of noninterference in Muslim family matters justified, in this sense, further meddling in the Islamic courts.

Tinkering on a much more extensive scale occurred in Siam's "national" family during King Vajiravudh's reign. And like Malay Muslims in the south, who eventually rebelled against Siamese state interventions (in education) in 1922, members of the Siamese population began to voice their opposition to the way the government sought to incorporate them into the nation. King Vajiravudh, Siamese judges, and Siamese lawyers working on family law bridged the thirty-year gap between usage of the outmoded KTSD laws on family and the modern law on family and inheritance promulgated in 1935. Monarchial essays, judicial verdicts, and legal texts reflect the consequences of this indecision about a national marital standard. Rather than simply promulgate a monogamy law, Siamese of all stripes used the increasingly ambiguous definition of marriage to promote alternative visions of a modern Thai family.

In this chapter I address the moral and legal conundrums regarding who could become a wife and how new laws positioned wives in the family. King Vajiravudh attempted to shore up the inadequacies of laws on the Siamese family by linking the term for *nation* to that of *family* in laws on citizenship and surnames. In turn, these laws required a method for distinguishing between legitimate and illegitimate wives before determining issues of citizenship, divorce, and inheritance. When lawyers referred to the *Three Seals Laws,* however, they discovered that Siam's social and economic transformations had hopelessly muddled the KTSD's wifely status hierarchy. Traditional laws, for example, allowed sexual intercourse to translate into marriage. Given the rise in prostitution and the increasing mobility of men and women, lenient laws on sex acts had to change. Standardized modern law regarding the transference of property required clearer distinctions between wives and casual or less formal sexual partners. Siam's monarch attempted to address the legal indeterminacy of who could be a wife that resulted from the lack of a national marital standard by creating a new taxonomy of wives in the 1910s. He began with the female sexual partners of his own male officials.

Chat as Family and Nation

King Vajiravudh distinguished honorable women from disreputable women through his moral discourse on family and nation:

> The [sexual] comportment [of officials] in violation of the king's wishes . . . is not as important as the issue of having a family, because honorable women are

[3] Narong, *Khwampenma,* 62.

> naturally the bliss of men while evil women of course bring ruin to their mates. It is difficult to find something equally abominable. (King Vajiravudh, 27 PKPS 256, August 1914)

The historical development of family law as an exception to general treaty revisions combined with colonial ethnographic discourse that considered family structures the source of a society's uniqueness to make "family" an overdetermined site of Siam's authentic national identity. King Vajiravudh tapped into the enormous political capital offered by the concept of the family. In fact, the Thai term for nation, *chat,* also refers to the extended family. Chat was a rich, multivalent concept, one reason it was selected as the translation of nation.[4] Etymologically, *chat* derives from the Sanskrit term *jati,* whose meaning encapsulates a sense of birth, as in a life in the Buddhist cycle of rebirth, as well as caste, origin, and lineage.[5] Its combination with other terms indicates its "powerful resonances of blood-ties and, most importantly of all, shared descent."[6] The history of chat is layered over time: its Buddhalogical substratum is tempered first with familial and then with modern political meanings.[7]

When Rama VI popularized chat as the closest Thai term for nation, it encompassed these multivalent connotations. Through his numerous essays on nationality, he shaped its meaning, discarding some of its connotations while emphasizing others.[8] Most historians of this period rightly analyze chat for its ethnic implications for the Chinese and Sino-Thai population in Siam.[9] However, chat's familial connotations have been ignored despite their obvious role in the historical formation of the meaning of chat as nation. Rama VI made the association between chat-as-nation and chat-as-family clear in preambles to legal reforms.

For instance, on 22 March 1913, King Vajiravudh employed national law to construct the Siamese national family. He promulgated Siam's first citizenship (*sanchat* or *sanyachat*) law on the same day as the first modern family

[4] Eiji Murashima makes many of the same points about the origin of the term *chat,* but he does not mention its familial connotations. King Chulalongkorn used the term to refer to the Siamese nation, but King Vajiravudh formalized it. Eiji Murashima, "The Origin of Modern Official State Ideology in Thailand," *Journal of Southeast Asian Studies* 19, no. 1 (Mar. 1988): 81–82, 88–89.

[5] *Pathanukrom bali thai angkrit sansakrit* (Pali-English-Thai-Sanskrit Dictionary), comp. Prince Kitiyakara (Bangkok, 1970), 310.

[6] Charles F. Keyes, "Towards a New Formulation of the Concept of Ethnic Group," *Ethnicity* 3 (1976), 206, cited in Reynolds, *National Identity,* 23–24.

[7] For an extended discussion of *chat*'s historical meanings, see Loos, "Gender Adjudicated," chap. 6.

[8] Rama VI's essay, "Khwampenchat doi thetching" (True Nationhood), is cited as evidence that people were interpreting *chat* in ways that did not conform to Rama VI's definition. Copeland, "Contested Nationalism."

[9] See, for example, Reynolds, ed., *National Identity,* 23–25; Vella, *Chaiyo!,* 187–96; and Copeland, "Contested Nationalism."

law (Surname Act) in March 1913.[10] Both laws operated according to the principle of patronymic descent: fathers passed their nationality and family names to children, and wives adopted their husbands' citizenship and surnames. Rama VI cited administrative efficiency as the immediate impetus behind the promulgation of the acts, explaining in the preamble that Siam had a method of registering births and deaths, but that individuals must also be identifiable by a personal and a family name in order to verify their family background.

The citizenship law claimed as Siamese citizens all persons born in Siam; all persons born to a Siamese father regardless of birthplace; all persons born to Siamese mothers when the father was unknown; and all foreign women married to Siamese subjects. The law privileged fatherhood in considerations of nationality: it proactively considered as Siamese all children born to a male Siamese citizen, regardless of their birthplace and of the nationality of the mother. If parents gave birth to a child outside the boundaries of legitimate marriage, then the Siamese father had the authority to claim or disregard the child as his own and, thus, to inscribe the child as a Siamese national. Mothers, by contrast, had no comparable power to pass on citizenship. The law only allowed a woman to pass on her nationality to her children in the absence of a father/husband. Furthermore, the authority of a Siamese male's citizenship negated his wife's nationality, making her Siamese regardless of her original citizenship.

The citizenship (1913) and naturalization (1912) laws have been appraised as proassimilationist because they placed few obstacles before male individuals, particularly Chinese men, who wanted to claim Siamese subject status.[11] However, if one analyzes these laws for their dynamic of inclusion or exclusion on the basis of gender, one observes an obvious discrepancy. The gender hierarchy in citizenship laws has its antecedents in Siam as well as in the nationality laws of foreign countries, where women similarly acquired the nationality of their husband but had to give up their own. Modern law, like the traditional *Three Seals Laws,* continued to incorporate women into the state indirectly, through their male relatives.

King Vajiravudh inflected most of his opinions about family and marriage with ethnic overtones.[12] Although no anti-Chinese laws were passed during

[10] "Phraratchabanyat sanyachat p. s. 2456" (Nationality Law of 1913), 22 Mar. 1913, 25 PKPS 256–259; "Phraratchabanyat khanan nam sakun p.s. 2456" (Law on Designating Surnames 1913), 22 Mar. 1913, 25 PKPS 259–62.

[11] For an in-depth analysis of this process and how it related to immigration/emigration statistics and the Qing dynasty's nationality act of 1909, see G. William Skinner, *Chinese Society in Thailand* (Ithaca: Cornell University Press, 1957), 126–28, 159, 165.

[12] King Vajiravudh targeted the Chinese in many of his essays written under the pen name as Asvabahu. See Asvabahu [King Vajiravudh], *Phuak yiu haeng buraphathit* (Jews of the East) (Bangkok: Krom Sinlapakon, 1985); Asvabahu, *The Jews of the Orient* (Bangkok: Siam Observer Press, no date). Originally serialized in the *Siam Observer* in July 1914.

his reign, King Vajiravudh relentlessly targeted the Chinese in his polemical essays, including the one that justified the 1913 Surname Act.[13] King Vajiravudh's objectives in passing the Surname Act were explained in his essay "A Comparison of Surnames with [Chinese] Clan Names."[14] In it, he responded to critics of the Surname Act by associating nuclear family structures with modern, civilized nations. King Vajiravudh masterfully utilized the discourse of modern ethnography against an other—in this case the Chinese—within Siam. He found useful the concept of evolutionary progress: each society would eventually pass through the same stages of development and social organization. In this particular essay, the blood-related family sat at the apex of the evolutionary hierarchy, above the clan, tribe, totem, and most important, the Chinese *sae,* which he characterized as being equivalent to the (Scottish) clan.[15] Regardless of the academic accuracy of his definition of the clan or sae as a fictive family as opposed to a "real" blood-related unit, King Vajiravudh defined sae to accommodate his own political agenda. By promulgating an act on family surnames that linked members together through patronymic descent and blood ties, Rama VI caused the Siamese to "soar ahead" of the Chinese, who continued to build group solidarity on the basis of less progressive and less stable grounds than consanguinity.[16] King Vajiravudh ascended the throne in 1910, the same year that leaders of the sizable Chinese population in Siam organized a strike that paralyzed Bangkok for days. He was wary of their economic power and loyalties.

The king's essay evidences the need to analyze the racialized discourse of nationalism alongside its familial content. To Rama VI, the blood-related family governed by the principles of patronymic descent symbolized civilization, modernity, and nationhood. He regarded the consanguineous family as a model for the nation because it was bound by natural ties of affection, rather than by fear of danger, which he associated with the Chinese sae.[17] For him, this love translated into respect and reverence on the part of subordinates (*phu noi*) for family elders, and into kindness toward subordinate family members by elders. As such, the family established the foundation for loyalty that extended to the paternal ruler of the nation.[18] The model of blood-related families served as a prototype for the modern nation.

Because the discourse of nationalism was couched in the language of family values, it had consequences for individuals based on their gender. Rama

[13] "Phraratchabanyat khanan nam sakun 2456" (Surname Act), 22 Mar. 1913, 25 PKPS 259–262.

[14] King Vajiravudh, "Priap nam sakun kap chu sae" (A Comparison of Surnames with Clan Names), in *Pramuan bot phraratchaniphon (phak pakinnaka suan thi 2) nai phrabatsomdet phra mongkutklao chaoyuhua* (Compilation of the Writings of King Vajiravudh [Miscellaneous Pieces, Part 2]) (Bangkok: Sirisan, 1961), 45–53.

[15] Vajiravudh, "Priap nam sakun kap chu sae," 45–48.

[16] Ibid., 48.

[17] Ibid., 51.

[18] Ibid., 52–53.

VI's family ideology affected men because it emphasized the harmful potential of men to undermine the stability of family life by engaging in the sale of female relatives into slavery or servitude, irresponsible parenting, and discrediting the meaning of wifedom by associating indiscriminately with all types of women. The instability caused by men's sexual practices was likened to treason against the state. Rama VI, by intervening on the side of honorable women against caddish men, became the protector of women. However, his protection came at the cost of establishing a powerful artificial distinction between moral and immoral women. Only "moral" women could be considered wives, who operated as a reflection of a properly bourgeois family and as a symbol of Siam as solidly modern and civilized. Wives served as the ideological glue holding together the modern Thai family as a microcosm for the nation.

In both law and court cases, a new taxonomy of wives came into being that displaced former categories of wives, the meanings of sexual intercourse, and marriage. Determining the status of a woman as a wife (and then, what kind of wife) was critical to applying the law and adjudicating cases about marriage, divorce, and inheritance. To ensure the orderly transmission of property and social status, there first had to be a way to distinguish legitimate from illegitimate heirs. In Siam, where long-term stable pairings or "marriage" coexisted with and blended into polygyny, adultery, and fornication, the law was used increasingly to distinguish legal marriage from other sexual liaisons. Of course, because polygyny was still a legal form of marriage, Siam's lawmakers had a complicated task before them.

Cases and law show that the hitherto flexible definition of marriage was becoming increasingly ossified. In the law, marriage narrowed to refer to a permanent, patriarchal family structure in which citizenship and family surnames subordinated a woman's identity to that of her husband rather than carving out an individual space for her as an autonomous citizen of the nation. Despite its vociferously pro-women rhetoric, backed by imperial hegemonic conceptions of the modern family as monogamous rather than polygynous, modern law provided no greater security or legal protection for many Siamese women than had the traditional law codes. Instead, it provided a different kind of legal security and rationale for the rights of women as an inescapably gendered but modern legal subject.

Legitimate Wives

Legal definitions from the *Three Seals Laws* (KTSD), which were the operative codes on family, marriage, and inheritance until 1935, provided the firm grounding for *how* one became a wife, but said little about *who* could become a wife. Every female, except those already married, was a potential wife, so legally regulating the moral character or sexual past of a woman fell outside the domain of law. The law focused more on the method by which one became a wife, because that determined a wife's rank in polygynous households and reflected the rank of her natal family. The KTSD describes three general categories of wives in the Laws on Husbands and Wives: *mia klang muang,* or major wife; *mia klang nok,* or minor wife; and *mia that,* slave wife. Importantly, the differences among them originated in the method by which they became a wife. A woman was considered a major wife when a man had a respected intermediary (*thaokae*) request her as a wife from her parents, who should be of comparable rank and wealth to his own family.[19] After the initial agreement, the thaokae from both sides negotiated the amount of bridewealth (*sinsot* and *khanmak*)[20] to exchange for the bride. On an auspicious day, the groom's thaokae presented the betrothal gifts to the woman's parents or guardians who accepted them as a guarantee of the groom's family's promise of marriage. Then they set a date for the wedding ceremony and the groom's family built a matrimonial home with material provided by the bride's family. After the wedding ceremony, at which Buddhist monks presided and the groom's family gave more khanmak, the couple was considered married in the eyes of the community and the law.

Of the 134 laws on marriage in the KTSD, forty or so dealt with instances in which a groom or bride did not follow this series of traditional exchanges and negotiations, indicating that many broke with custom.[21] If the woman's guardians would not permit the marriage, the suitor could not afford the brideprice, or the suitor feared that the woman he desired would be married to another, he had at least two alternatives.[22] The man could surreptitiously have intercourse with the woman in the home of her guardians, where she lived, and then formally apologize to her guardians. Or the suitor could *lakpha* the woman, meaning he would abduct her from her guardians' house and take her elsewhere. Typically, after several days the suitor in either situation would send thaokae to apologize ceremonially and beg her guardians to per-

[19] Taken from Prince Damrong Rajanubhab, "Praphaeni taengngan baosao" (Tradition of Marrying Young Men and Women), in *Latthi thamniam tang tang* (Miscellaneous Traditional Practices), comp. Phraya Ratchawaranukun [Ouam], vol. 1 (Bangkok: Department of Fine Arts, 1961; 5th ed., 1972), 111–14.

[20] *Sinsot* referred to money given to the bride's parents by the groom's parents at the engagement ceremony; *khanmak* referred to betel, areca, gold, and other presents from the groom's family arranged on ceremonial trays for the bride's parents.

[21] See, for example, the following clauses in the *Laksana phumia* (Laws on Husbands and Wives) [LPM] that deal directly with those who break traditional engagement customs: LPM Clauses 76–77, 81–90, 95–103, 106–9, 122–23, 126–28, 133, in KTSD, vol. 2 (Bangkok: Thammasat University Press, 1938).

[22] Sumalee Bumroongsook, *Love and Marriage,* 152–53.

mit the marriage. If the guardians accepted the apology, then the law considered the couple legitimately married.[23] If her guardians refused to grant their forgiveness or permit the woman to become his wife, then the law similarly refused to legitimate the union.[24] The laws in the KTSD assert directly and indirectly that the consent of a woman's guardians, usually her parents, defined legitimate marriage.[25]

If a man directly asked a woman to be his wife, without an intermediary or ceremony or the permission of her parents, she was considered an *anuphanraya* or minor wife. Minor wives included those obtained through sexual intercourse, short-term liaison, and cohabitation, even in some cases in which the woman did not consent. Finally, a woman redeemed from indebtedness and supported materially as a wife was the least prestigious type of wife: a slave wife.[26]

In the KTSD, distinctions between the three types of wives are clear and important, for they had great consequences for each wife's authority, privileges, protections, and wealth, and for their children's lives. This proved especially important for women from elite families who were likely to be part of a polygynous household yet desirous of maintaining their relatively elite status. A wife's rank in a polygynous household determined the amount of her inheritance when her husband died, the amount of property (*sinsomrot*) received upon divorce, the rank of her children, and the degree of penalty for her sexual transgressions. Typically, the higher the rank of the wife, the steeper the punishment for adultery and rape, the greater her portion of inheritance, and the more prestigious the rank of her children. A wife of higher rank also exercised considerable power over other wives.

For these reasons, when guardians (usually her parents or elder relatives) arranged a woman's marriage they tried to follow standard marital customs by which they would formally give her to her husband, because this would place her in a more powerful, prestigious, and secure position. The method by which a wife was obtained—through a formal ceremony, abduction or elopement, purchase, or simply by having an on-going sexual relationship—established her rank within polygynous households, her wifely classification

[23] Examples in the KTSD that take this for granted include LPM Clauses 86, 87, 96, 106, 116, 119, 122, in KTSD, vol. 2 (Bangkok: Thammasat University Press, 1938).

[24] For laws that relate to the issue of parental consent, see LPM Clauses 44, 77, 81, 82–87, 102–11, and 126–28 in KTSD. Nai Rutt, "Particulars of Consent of the Girl's Parents" in "Report on the Siamese Law Relating to the Family," 22 Mar. 1913 to 12 June 1915; photocopy of Dika 389. By not legitimating the union, the law also promised that it would not treat the woman as his wife. So if the man attempted to charge another man with engaging in an adulterous relationship with his "wife," the courts would not accept the case.

[25] Nai Rutt, "Particulars of Consent of the Girl's Parents."

[26] In addition, two minor categories of wives applied to relatively few women: wives given to a man by the king as a reward and women given to the king by one of his subjects. The former is the highest-ranking wife of all five categories, then the major wife, the wife given by a loyal subject, the minor wife, and finally the slave wife.

in nonpolygynous households, and her ability to claim inheritance or marital property upon divorce. The role of a woman's natal family in arranging her marriage was a necessary factor in her becoming a major wife or in annulling a "marriage" even after sexual intercourse had occurred.

The KTSD laws on wives allegedly date from the fifteenth century, yet they were still operative, that is, judges still applied them (albeit erratically) in court cases five centuries later. However, a great many legal changes had occurred by the 1910s, including the introduction of a new penal code, codes on the organization of the courts, a civil procedural code, and a criminal procedural code. The social and economic environment had also transformed the ways in which young men and women were interacting. No longer were young people as intensely subjected to parental or village surveillance as Bangkok's urban population began its exponential growth. The legal stasis of the Laws on Husbands and Wives compared to dramatic social change in gender relations made their coexistence incompatible. Legal "hangovers," such as the classification of wives into three general categories, were out of step with early twentieth century Siam. While the position of major wife still existed, men could have more than one major wife, thus diluting the authority of the position.[27] Moreover, the differences among minor wives were no longer obvious, and the abolition of slavery rendered obsolete the category "slave wife," at least in law. Yet polygyny survived and arguably even prospered as it trickled down the class hierarchy to be practiced by middle-class men. The seeming clarity of a wifely status hierarchy had become irrevocably muddled by the early twentieth century, which is evident in myriad ways and had important consequences for men, women, their children, and ultimately for national identity. A major and continuing dilemma for lawyers, judges, and litigants was the legal definition of marriage, which in part depended on determining the meaning of sexual intercourse.

Fornication as Marriage

Even though the KTSD provided loose standards by which one could be deemed married—for instance, a single act of sexual intercourse could be interpreted as a legitimate marriage if the woman's guardians consented—the legal circumstances of twentieth-century Siam demanded a more precise and uniform definition. The courts in particular required this before judges could adjudicate cases of prostitution, rape, adultery, divorce, and inheritance, all of which hinged on the interpretation of the sex act. As mentioned, in January

[27] It appears that prior to the twentieth century this was not an issue. However, legal manuals from the 1910s point out that it was not illegal to have more than one major wife, suggesting that this had become an issue in need of legal clarification.

1912 King Vajiravudh stated that the lack of a marital standard was hindering reformers from drafting a law on inheritance. He also complained about the "great many" inheritance cases in arrears because it was impossible to prove or disprove that a marriage existed.[28]

This confusion prompted lawyers to produce legal manuals to assist in the interpretation and adjudication of cases related to marriage, divorce, and inheritance. These were published in the 1910s when most lawyers and judges still had limited access to copies of the KTSD laws on family relations. The manuals were, according to their prefaces, in great demand by judges and lawyers, particularly those working in provincial courts too far from Bangkok to attend the law school lectures held at the Ministry of Justice beginning in the 1890s.

Mr. Siang, a barrister-at-law, compiled two manuals, one on inheritance law and the other on marital law (1913).[29] Luang Phisalaisan wrote a similar manual in August 1913, which was reprinted in 1915 due to the high demand for it by lawyers and judges.[30] He was a first level barrister-at-law who had experience as a teacher at Siam's only law school and as a judge at the district, monthon, and international courts. Significantly, both authors began their manuals by disputing the commonsensical definition of marriage, which used sexual intercourse as the standard by which one might consider a couple married.[31] Their examples of common situations—sex with prostitutes and female servants—indicate that class and gender hierarchies were involved in defining legitimate marriages.

Luang Phisalaisan explains that using sexual intercourse as the standard to define marriage would in effect "marry" every man to every woman with whom he slept, including prostitutes. If a man requests a woman to be his servant in exchange for supporting her, and he sleeps with her but does not make this public knowledge, then this does not constitute marriage and she cannot claim inheritance or anything more than her monthly salary. Both parties must desire to be married and must make this known publicly. Siang similarly defines the legal standard of marriage as a publicly expressed contract that hinges on consent of both parties. He states that when a man and a woman (or her guardians) agree to be married, and both sides express to the public that they are married, then their marriage is legitimate. However, if a man impregnates a woman but refuses to acknowledge her as his wife or the child as his, then they are not considered legally married because one party does not consent.[32]

[28] NA MR6 Yutitham 12.1 Kotmai, pramuan kotmai phaeng lae phanit, "Raingan senabodi sapha," 22 Jan. 1912.

[29] Nai Siang Netibanthit, *Kotmai phua mia* (Marriage Laws) (Bangkok, 1913).

[30] Luang Phitsalaisan Nitinethibanthit, *Laksana phua mia kap laksana moradok* (Laws on Marriage and Laws on Inheritance) (Bangkok: 1915; rev. ed.).

[31] Siang, *Kotmai phua mia,* 2–3; Luang Phitsalaisan, *Laksana phua mia,* 8–9.

[32] Siang, *Kotmai phua mia,* 4. Both manuals revive Amdaeng Muan's case from the 1860s to sup-

By the twentieth century, the law weighted heavily the subjective individual interpretation of the sexual act as well as the role of community acknowledgment in legitimating a marriage. In a court of law, heterosexual sexual intercourse no longer automatically translated into a long-term commitment but required a kind of evidentiary proof, such as consent and public recognition. By extension, a primary mode by which "wives" and "husbands" were once, in effect, produced, came under intense legal scrutiny.

While laws sought to distinguish wives from casual sexual partners, men were not subjected to a legal taxonomy or community surveillance. Their primary identity in personal law on family, inheritance, and marriage was not as husbands but as *the* prototypical legal subject endowed with rights and obligations. Women as wives and young persons as children had legal power that was derivative from the adult male subject. The context of sexual intercourse had consequences not only for determining inheritance and legitimate heirs but for the identity of women. In the absence of parental or community involvement, which was increasingly the case in Siam's burgeoning cities, sexual intercourse could constitute a woman as a prostitute or as a legitimate wife. Prostitution was not new to Siam. It had existed since at least the Ayutthaya period, when laws enabled slave owners to prostitute their female slaves and allowed fathers to sell daughters to brothels if they engaged in adultery or other displeasing behavior.[33] However, the nineteenth and early twentieth century resituated women in the urban and familial economies, such that the number of avenues to prostitution grew as did the negative estimations of it.[34]

In European colonies, governments made finite distinctions among cohabitation, concubinage, prostitution, and legally recognized (typically Christian) marriages, because citizenship and other rights accrued to members of the native population on the basis of the legality of sexual relationships with European men.[35] Within the domestic population in Siam, the boundaries

port the idea of consent, particularly the power of individual *men* (not women) to refuse their consent to marriage with the women they sexually engage.

[33] Andaya, "From Temporary Wife to Prostitute," 18; Dararat Mettarikanond, "Sopheni kap naiyobai rathaban thai pho so 2411–2503" (Prostitution and Thai Government Policy, 1868–1960), MA thesis, Chulalongkorn University, 1983. Dararat's thesis and subsequent articles provide a superb analysis of the role of the state in regulating prostitution. The earliest documentation suggests that the state was taxing sex work by at least the mid-nineteenth century. See also Dararat Mettarikanond, "Kotmai sopheni 'ti-thabian' krangraek nai prathet thai" (The First Prostitution 'Registration' Law in Thailand), *Sinlapa-Wathanatham* 5, no. 5 (Mar. 1984): 6–19.

[34] A discussion of the relationship between prostitution and mercantile capitalism in Siam compared to that in European colonies in Southeast Asia and in Europe cannot be undertaken here, but preliminary research suggests that the state regulation of morality increasingly policed women's sexuality and identities across the globe. See, for example, Stoler, *Carnal Knowledge and Imperial Power,* and Judith Walkowitz, *Prostitution and Victorian Society: Women, Class, and the State* (Cambridge: Cambridge University Press, 1980).

[35] Stoler, *Carnal Knowledge and Imperial Power,* 110. Even in Siam, where prostitution was legal, European authorities deported white sex workers when their public engagement in prostitution threatened the moral standing of all Europeans. In 1907, for example, the British consulate forcibly

between ruler and ruled was based less on the management of racial distinctions and more on the regulation of social status distinctions—distinctions that similarly depended on the meaning and context of sexual intercourse. These distinctions weighed most heavily on women. The commercialized, monetized economy combined with increased mobility from rural to urban locales and amplified demand for commercial sex to make lower-class women easy targets for prostitution/marriage scams. Despite changes in the organization of women in the economy, many women continued to think and act within a customary cultural framework in which they trusted community members, as stand-ins for their parents, to introduce them to future husbands. The existence of court cases in which women were given the promise of marriage but instead were sold into prostitution suggests that the ambiguity of the status of "wife" had increasingly dire consequences.

In one 1895 case a young woman named Tunkaeo, a twenty-one year-old servant of Chao Dararatsami, a royal consort of King Chulalongkorn, was persuaded to leave the palace when a woman she knew promised Tunkaeo she could marry a high-ranking man.[36] By agreeing to become the *mom* or consort of the prince, Tunkaeo was unwittingly recruited into a brothel that catered to elite men. It was run by Chaem and Mom Ratchawong Sanan, the son of another of King Chulalongkorn's consorts (Mom Chao Chinda), and paid a monthly tax to the state. Fearing reprisals from Tunkaeo's patron, Chaem and another recruiter brought Tunkaeo to the British consul where they hoped to find extraterritorial protection from Siamese law. The consul's housekeeper let them in but told them that the consul was not at home nor did he desire to have a Siamese wife. Again, the assumption was that any young Siamese woman being escorted around in such a fashion was being offered as a potential consort. So, they returned to the brothel where palace officials apprehended Tunkaeo, Chaem, and the woman who recruited Tunkaeo (but not Mom Ratchawong Sanan). The latter two were sentenced for the crime of abducting a woman from the Inner Palace. Tunkaeo was flogged thirty times before being sent back to her Inner Palace patron, Chao Dararatsami. The two female recruiters were tattooed, which forever barred them from entering royal compounds, and sentenced to prison. From there they were exiled to Phattalung, a city in the south, as specifically requested by King Chulalongkorn.[37] The case demonstrates the risks inherent in rely-

repatriated two British women who had established a liquor saloon and brothel because they made their living from prostitution. NA R5 Nakhonban (Capital) 8.1, file 363, box 11, "Krom kong trawen ratchakan thuapai" (Police Department, General Duties); Loos, Archival Notes, vol. 6, 147–48.

[36] She was given a choice between Prince Krommun Sapsat and a nobleman not of royal blood as potential husbands.

[37] This may have been a method to prevent them from further meddling in the Royal Palace or Bangkok. NA R5 Yutitham 13 Khadi khwam 24, "Khampruksa thot ruang amdaeng chaem raphai chakpha tunkaeo ok chak phraborommaharatchawong" (Consultations on the Case of Amdaeng Chaem and Raphai who Enticed Tunkaeo to Leave the Grand Palace); Loos, Archival Notes, vol. 10,

ing on traditional methods by which women could meet men. The promise of becoming an official's wife lured Tunkaeo (and other women whose cases are not detailed here) with the bait of securing a husband, but instead it nearly landed her in a brothel as a prostitute.[38]

Commoner women were even more susceptible to such deception. Eighteen-year-old Amdaeng Thim was a native of Chantaburi who came with her older sister to live in Bangkok in 1894.[39] Their row house neighbors, a married couple, repeatedly tried to convince Amdaeng Thim that they would find her a husband, perhaps even a Westerner, if she would agree to meet some men who could literally take a look at her (*hai farang lae phu chai du tua*). The couple escorted Amdaeng Thim to a room filled with several other men in Bangkok. Gradually everyone left the room, one by one, until only Amdaeng Thim and one man remained. As he sat speaking flirtatiously with her, the prostitution tax collector, then known as the "street tax" collector, entered the room and demanded that Amdaeng Thim pay for the price of the room, which she refused to do. Instead, the man sitting with her paid the tax collector, at which point the tax collector grabbed Amdaeng Thim, accusing her of illegal prostitution, that is, performing sex work but evading the tax. This was eventually reported up the law enforcement hierarchy until it reached King Chulalongkorn. In a letter to the king, the minister of the capital wrote that it was a common practice for street tax collectors to deceive young women by tricking them, with the help of a complicit gang, into spending time alone with a man in a room, whereupon the tax collector would barge in demanding his cut. He would then arrest the young woman, which he did not have the authority to do, and force her to sign a contract of prostitution.

By the early twentieth century, women were arguably more vulnerable than ever to such deceptive practices. The opportunities for men and women to meet socially had increased for both elites and members of the lower classes in public and gender-mixed spaces away from parental or community surveillance. The abolition of slavery by 1905 freed individuals from their former *nai* or patron-masters, allowing greater geographic mobility. Although no economic historian has analyzed the changes resulting from the monetization of the economy and the abolition of slavery for its affects on women, most agree that there was a consequent increase in the number of sex work-

---

180–90. This case is also treated by Hong Lysa, "Palace Women at the Margins of Social Change," *Journal of Southeast Asian History* 30, no. 2 (Sept. 1999): 310–24.

[38] See also NA MR5 Yutitham 13, Khadikhwam 29, mai het 38/90, "Khadi ruang amdaeng bo phayong ha wa chanwang lom kratham kankhotkhi lae bangkhap hai tham chamrao ha ngoen" (Case of Amdaeng Bo Phayong [who] Accuses Chanwang Lom of Forcing Her into Prostitution), 1895; Loos, Archival Notes, vol. 11, 48–71.

[39] NA MR5 Yutitham 13, Khadikhwam, "Khadi ruang chaophasi bamrunthanon chap amdaeng thim pai ha wa amdaeng thim pen khon ha chon" (Case of the Street Tax Collector Apprehending Amdaeng Thim and Accusing Her of Prostitution), March 1894; Loos, Archival Notes, vol. 10, 168–70.

ers.[40] It is likely that brothels absorbed many of the former slave women who had no means of subsistence.[41] In addition, the new salaried bureaucracy contributed to an increased demand for commercial sex. Barmé argues that "by the 1920s it was no exaggeration to say that, in one form or another, prostitution was one of the most ubiquitous features of the urban landscape."[42] Siam's full integration into global trading networks and the resulting monetization of the economy had helped produce circumstances in which women, with few other employment options, were channeled into sex work.

In this setting, sexual intercourse no longer so easily converted to marriage. Sex work, organized into brothels and taxed by the state, was a business that required a stricter distinction from marital unions. Not only would this clarify the collection of the street tax, and taxes collected in later years under the Law for the Prevention of Venereal Disease (Phraratchabanyat pongkan sanchonrok), but it also would distinguish as morally superior legitimate heterosexual sexual unions.[43]

Property and Wifedom

The ambiguity of a woman's position as wife is apparent in court cases dating from the late 1890s and surfaces most insistently in inheritance and property suits between men and women.[44] It is commonly assumed (but not easily proven) that most men and women refused to engage the official space of the courts except in extreme situations, preferring instead to live separately or resolve their disputes in other forums. Anecdotally this is indicated in the testimonies about abuse and attempts to resolve the marital dispute in other ways before coming to court. As a result, the divorce and inheritance cases

[40] Barmé and Dararat have come closest in showing quantifiable data. Dararat Mettarikanond, "Sopheni kap naiyobai rathaban thai." It is difficult to quantify the number of sex workers and the money they brought into economic circulation. Barmé cites a 1927 paper that estimated thirty thousand sex workers, most of whom worked illegally. Another paper claimed thirty thousand with twenty thousand in Bangkok and ten thousand in provincial centers. His conservative estimate of income generated was 3.6 million baht a year in Bangkok as the amount spent on commercial sex, which was larger than the amount devoted annually to education in the 1920s and '30s. Barmé, *Woman, Man, Bangkok,* 82.

[41] Thanh-dam Truong, *Sex, Money and Morality: Prostitution and Tourism in South-East Asia* (London: Zed Books, 1990), 153.

[42] Barmé, *Woman, Man, Bangkok,* 81.

[43] This decree required brothel keepers to make a quarterly payment of thirty baht to register their premises, maintain a list of all workers for official inspection, and display a green lantern outside the brothel. See Barmé, *Woman, Man, Bangkok,* 78; and Dararat, "Sopheni kap naiyobai rathaban thai," 84.

[44] The necessity of dissolving the ambiguity of a woman's marital or kinship position was not unique to Siam but occurred in other countries where modern courts and codes were introduced. The resolution of her position more frequently operated to her disadvantage in Siam, however. See

that surface in the court system typically involve large financial sums, extreme cases of abuse, or other complicated scenarios that propelled individuals to the court system. Kingdomwide statistics show that divorce, inheritance, and adultery cases consistently ranked as the fourth, fifth, and sixth most numerous kinds of court cases filed at the civil courts of the first instance. Arguably, a significantly larger number of cases were resolved out of court. As a consequence, even though Siamese appear nonlitigious in terms of absolute numbers of court cases per capita, they nonetheless resorted to a legal framework to resolve their disputes when other methods of dispute resolution failed.

Divorce and adultery cases are particularly relevant in a discussion about the ambiguity of wifedom and marriage. Before resolving divorce or adultery cases, judges first required proof of marriage. In both types of cases, wealth and property were often at stake. Given the comparative ease with which "marriages" could simply be dissolved by a private, personal decision to separate, few people would invite the expense of a court battle unless valuables or even lives were at stake. Divorce cases filed by women typically claimed either abuse at the hands of their husbands or desertion. Men far less frequently filed for divorce, but they often sued their "wives" for adultery, which always entailed a financial claim. In both instances, the ambiguity of the definition of wife rendered women susceptible to suits that would deprive her of material wealth. In adultery cases that perceived a woman as married to the man charging her with adultery, judges fined her the amount claimed by her "husband." In divorce cases that denied women the status of wife, judges similarly denied her the right to claim possession of "marital" property.

One of the earliest surviving court cases of this type archived involved Chin (meaning Chinese, a form of address) Tonghua, Amdaeng Thap, and Nai Lek Heng, and rose to the Dika Court in 1899.[45] Chin Tonghua accused Amdaeng Thap and Nai Lek Heng of adultery and sued for three *chang,* which was the monetary equivalent of what he had originally given to build a marital home.

Amdaeng Thap and Nai Lek Heng, who considered themselves husband and wife rather than adulterers, claimed that Amdaeng Thap had divorced Chin Tonghua over a year ago, after the death of their one child and Chin

Michael Peletz, *Islamic Modern,* and John Comaroff and Simon Roberts, *Rules and Processes: The Cultural Logic of Dispute in an African Context* (Chicago: University of Chicago Press, 1981).

[45] KSD 117 Decision 88, 12 Jan. 1899; Loos, Archival Notes, vol. 12, 35–37. Ethnic markers such as *chin* seem to apply to foreign-born Chinese and perhaps Chinese who were born in Siam but taxed as Chinese. The state only classified the ethnicity of males, not females, in their form of address, so chin and khaek never applied as an honorific to women. Also excluded from the edict were royal family members, high-ranking government officials, male and female religious, medical doctors, rulers of tributary states, and foreign-born farang, Vietnamese, Burmans, and Mon. See "Phraratchabanyat hai chai khamnam na chuchon tangtang" (Royal Act on Using Titles for Various People), approximately 1862, 6 PKPS 238–41.

Tonghua's desertion. Both sides, then, agreed that Amdaeng Thap and Chin Tonghua had not lived together for over a year. However, the courts decided that Amdaeng Thap was still considered married to Chin Tonghua in the eyes of the law because she had not made it clear to the local community that she considered herself divorced. She lost the case and had to pay three chang to her former spouse.

There are many cases in which men sued women for adultery even though they had been estranged for years. In the absence of a public announcement of divorce, a couple could be considered husband and wife despite years without contact.[46] Consequently, after a woman began a new relationship she could be sued for adultery. These cases demonstrate that the ambiguity of the definition of marriage made women vulnerable to the charge of adultery, especially when divorce was harder to prove than marriage. They also suggest that serial monogamy was not uncommon for nonelite women.

By the 1920s, court records suggest that judges had more narrowly conceived of marriage, which made it harder for men to sue their former wives. Even so, cases reveal that some men had illimitable conceptions of wifedom. Several cases attest to the all-encompassing definition of "wife." In September 1925 the Dika Court heard the case of Luang Sapsatsuphakit who sued Nai (Mr.) Chaem and Nang (Mrs.) Khluap for adultery and demanded 2,460 baht worth of valuables.[47] Luang Sapsatsuphakit claimed he had been married to Nang Khluap for fourteen years, but in 1923 she committed adultery with Nai Chaem. Nang Khluap countered that after many years of marriage to Luang Supsatsuphakit, he acquired a new wife in 1914. Not only did they argue about this but Luang Supsatsuphakit physically abused Nang Khluap. She divorced him and they divided their valuables. Nang Khluap eventually "remarried," that is, lived with Nai Bamroe Ratcha for nearly two years, then he died. Nang Khluap "married" again, this time to Nai Chaem, her codefendant in the case.

Because Luang Supsatsuphakit had made no objections to Nang Khluap's marriage to Nai Bamroe Ratcha, the civil court in Bangkok decided in favor of the defendants. Luang Supsatsuphakit appealed on the grounds that he would have sued earlier if he had known that Nang Khluap had married Nai Bamroe, but he simply was unaware of it. The Dika Court might have accepted this as plausible except that witnesses testified that they told Luang Supsatsuphakit about Nang Khluap's marriage. His case was dismissed. It appears astounding that a husband would not know for years that his "wife"

[46] KSD 119 Decision 17, Apr. 1900; Loos, Archival Notes, vol. 12, 89. KSD 123 Decision 79, 8 May 1904; Loos, Archival Notes, vol. 12, 108. KSD 123 Decision 170, 9 June 1904; Loos, Archival Notes, vol. 12, 109. KSD 2457 Decision 36, 6 June 1915; Loos, Archival Notes, vol. 13, 13. KSD 2468 Decision 1138, Mar. 1926; Loos, Archival Notes, vol. 13, 152–53. KSD 2473 Dec. 189, 14 July 1930; Loos, Archival Notes, vol. 14, 87–88. KSD 2478 Decision 563, 20 Dec. 1935; Loos, Archival Notes, vol. 14, 144–46.

[47] KSD 2468 Decision 456, 21 Sept. 1926; Loos, Archival Notes, vol. 13, 147–48.

had remarried. However, if the couple were estranged without officially filing for divorce or making it known to the community, then she would continue to be considered his wife.

Even the requirement of public demonstration was flouted by one man who attempted to sue his wife and her new partner for adultery even after he had served her divorce papers and had announced their divorce in the newspaper![48] He appealed to the highest court, claiming that he only filed divorce papers to appease his new wife, who was jealous. The Dika Court judges dismissed his case. Yet another case from 1926 involved a man who, it was eventually discovered, claimed that his wealthy widowed neighbor was his wife and then accused her of adultery and claimed her wealth worth 12,100 baht.[49] The courts surmised that they might have had some form of sexual relationship but were not legally married because the male plaintiff, who already had at least one wife, had not demonstrated that he was maintaining the defendant as a wife.

In a 1930 adultery case that originated in Samutsongkhram, the plaintiff Nai Chaem charged Nang Kep of having a lover even though Nai Chaem had never seen her with another man and had no idea who her lover might be.[50] His proof was somewhat self-incriminating. Nang Kep was six months pregnant even though the plaintiff had been "busy" for about a year and had not seen her. He claimed her prenuptial valuables as well as some of their marital possessions. Nang Kep, by contrast, argued that after the plaintiff acquired a new wife and deserted Nang Kep in 1928, she filed for divorce. This suit was in process when Nai Chaem filed the adultery case, which was ultimately dismissed by the Dika Court because witnesses testified that they saw Nai Chaem himself sneak into Nang Kep's home about seven months before. Neither Nai Chaem nor Nang Kep's cases would benefit from that revelation.

Not only do each of these cases reveal the ambiguity of marriage but they incidentally reveal the frequency of polygyny among nonelites. In every single one of these cases, original wives divorced or were deserted by their husbands after an additional wife was obtained. Although it is impossible to analyze statistically the frequency of polygyny as the ultimate cause of marital discord, these cases suggest two common themes. First, polygyny was practiced by elites and nonelites, and second, women rebelled against it by filing officially for divorce or by simply separating from their husbands and beginning a new relationship.

Inheritance cases worked in similar ways, although they are not described here. For a woman to claim inheritance from her deceased husband, she had

[48] KSD 2468 Decision 806, 7 Jan. 1926; Loos, Archival Notes, vol. 13, 149.
[49] KSD 2468 Decision 940, 3 Feb. 1926; Loos, Archival Notes, vol. 13, 150–51.
[50] KSD 2473 Decision 324, 12 Aug. 1930; Loos, Archival Notes, vol. 14, 89–90.

to first prove the validity of their marriage. Often relatives or other wives of the deceased filed cases against a woman, who understood herself to be a wife of the deceased, for illegitimately obtaining inheritance.[51] Courts scrutinized her behavior and her reputation, questioning her position as wife. Taken altogether, the issues debated in the courts centered on the interpretation of heterosexual sexual intercourse, and had at stake property ownership. The interpretation of the woman as a legitimate wife or illegitimate sexual partner was pivotal in determining the meaning of sexual intercourse and the control of property. The courts, faced with the types of cases mentioned above, required stricter guidelines for defining legitimate marriages, which ultimately depended on more precise categorizations of women in the laws on "family." Family law, however, was fraught with symbolic meaning for national identity by the early twentieth century. This indirectly affected how women could be incorporated into the nation—as wives and mothers in Siam's new family-nation.

New Taxonomy of Wives

The gendered dynamic of inclusion in the state corresponds to King Vajiravudh's conception of women's place in the nation as mothers and wives, rather than as autonomous citizens. Following on the heels of the Citizenship Law and Family Surname Act of 1913, King Vajiravudh passed several legislative acts that targeted the wives of government officials specifically, and that more generally redefined the forms of address by which official discourse referred to women. Both series of laws created a new taxonomy of wives that supplemented and gradually supplanted the former *Three Seals Laws* categories.

King Vajiravudh singled out the official classes in particular as the target of his familial moral reform. He, not Siam's busy international constellation of legal advisers, produced the 1914 Palatine Law on the families of government officials. It redefined the concept of family for officials by excluding impermanent relationships from the definition of a legitimate marriage and by branding the female partners in these illicit unions as irredeemably unfit for marriage. In this way, the king's anxiety about threats to his power from "modern" (antiabsolutist) young men was displaced onto these women. The law instructed registrars not to allow under any circumstance the registration of prostitutes (*ying nakhonsopheni*), harlots (*ying phaetsaya*), mistresses (*mialap*), women who have casual sex, or divorcées who had committed adultery, as the wives of affected royal officials. Most of these government officials worked near the palace grounds and were often referred to facetiously by Rama VI

[51] See for example, KSD 2462 Decision 686, 17 Sept. 1919; Loos, Archival Notes, vol. 14, 181–83. KSD 2478 Decision 691, 3 Feb. 1936; Loos, Archival Notes, vol. 14, 165–67.

as "modern" young men, hip to Western trends and republican political beliefs. In the law that targeted spouses of these men, registrars were required to distinguish between "genuinely proper women" and "base women" by defining "wife" in opposition to "prostitute," "harlot," and "mistress."

Because the king expected registrars to encounter difficulties determining the category into which a given woman fell, the law explicitly defined the categories of women. A woman obtained through traditional methods of marriage such as a ceremony or open, permanent cohabitation could be registered as a "wife," regardless of her class background. Any woman who engaged in sex with officials outside these traditional, acknowledged forms of union was by definition disreputable, forever barred from being registered as a wife. That included prostitutes, defined as those registered with the government as sex workers, harlots, and mistresses. Harlots constituted a new category of women who tended "to have promiscuous sex with many men" and to earn a living from sex work but were not registered with the state as prostitutes.[52] Mistresses, defined as secret wives who did not live with their misters but were housed separately in private locations, were also absolutely "not wives."[53] The law reiterated the location of mistresses outside the family even as it recognized that officials had children with their mistresses. When officials tried to legitimize their unions by registering their "mistresses" as "wives," they were consistently refused. The king eventually allowed the registration of children born to officials and their mistresses only when registrars could determine that the children's mothers had not slept with other men. In any case, the mistress-mothers could not be registered as wives.[54]

The law, which was meant to target the behavior of male officials, had intense social, moral, and sometimes legal consequences for women. It located honorable women firmly in the bourgeois family as dutiful wives and devoted mothers, subjecting these women to the surname and citizenship laws that linked them to the nation through their familial roles. By contrast, disreputable women had no place in the new ideology of family-nation (chat), but were by definition irredeemably outside its boundaries. The discourse on family in the early twentieth century was so thoroughly saturated with morality that it recast prostitution and all other extramarital sex as not simply lowly but immoral. As such, the mutually constitutive nature of the discourse on virtuous/disreputable women helped construct the boundaries of the modern family in Siam.

To abet his reconceptualization of women's roles, the king passed a series of laws that changed the forms of address used to refer to women. Forms of

[52] 27 PKPS 260.

[53] 27 PKPS 264.

[54] "Kotmonthianban waduai khropkhrua kharatchakan nai phraratchasamnak phoemtoem (khrang thi sam)" (Supplement to the Palatine Law on Families of Officials on Royal Grounds [third supplement]), 4 June 1917, 30 PKPS 64–65.

address, such as amdaeng and chin, revealed important information about individuals: their gender, class, relation if any to the royal family, and sometimes their ethnicity and religion. His 1917 decree on forms of address for nonroyal women was the most striking and detailed. No longer were women referred to as amdaeng or *ii* in official discourse—two titles that referred solely to a woman's class status—but instead their primary identification was by reference to their marital status.[55] *Nangsao,* like *miss,* referred to single women who had never been married, while *nang,* similar to *Mrs.*, referred to married women and widows.[56] After the 1917 decree, all court records accounted for these women in terms of marital status and further delineated differences among women married to high-ranking officials by including reference in their titles to their position as principle or minor wife.

In his preambles, King Vajiravudh stated that the new terms of address were meant to distinguish more clearly between royal and nonroyal women, probably because so many nonroyal women had joined high society after the rise in social status of their husbands who worked as officials. It also publicly clarified a woman's marital status for the first time.[57] What is unusual about the decree is that it was directed solely at women and that it depended on their marital and class status, which in turn was determined by their husband's rank and by their own rank vis-à-vis his other wives, if he had them. The increased coed socializing in clubs and public spaces certainly made the new system of titles useful to suitors who could quickly assess their chances with a woman by knowing her form of address, which indicated her marital status, and her husband or father's last name, which suggested her family's social position relative to his.

The focus on a nonroyal woman's marital status as her most distinguish-

[55] King Mongkut established the system of titles for nonelites used between the early 1860s and the 1910s. In that system, King Mongkut delineated the forms of address used before the names of commoners, slaves, criminals, and some women who worked for or belonged to the royal family. Amdaeng was the title for commoner women who included female phrai and women married to (and presumably daughters of) low-ranking officials with a sakdina rank of less than four hundred. Male and female slaves as well as commoners convicted of crimes or stripped of rank were referred to as *ai* (male) and *ii* (female). The social hierarchy was conflated with a moral hierarchy in which individuals at the bottom rungs of society were grouped together regardless of their differences. For example, *ai* and *ii* referred to both criminals and to all slaves including debt slaves and slaves of war, blurring the distinctions between them. "Phraratchabanyat hai chai khamnam na chuchon tangtang," (Royal Act on Using Titles for Various People), approximately 1862, 6 PKPS 238–41.

[56] Most women acquired their husband's or father's surname unless these men had standing (*bandasak*), in which case the primary wife alone could be called *nang* plus her husband's conferred title. His minor wives were referred to as nang plus their husband's last name rather than his conferred title. As the rank of the husband increased, the form of address for his primary (nonroyal) wife similarly was raised from nang, to *khunying,* to *than phuying,* plus her husband's title rather than his last name.

[57] In his preambles to the 1917 decree and its 1921 amendment, King Vajiravudh reasoned that the kingdom required clarification of the forms of address for women because the existing forms failed to distinguish between royal women and commoner women (whose husbands may have risen in the bureaucracy). "Phraratchakritsadika waduai khamnam nam satri phoemtoem" (Supplemental Royal Decree on Forms of Address for Women), 14 Sept. 1921, 34 PKPS 197–99.

ing feature also revealed the state's perception of men. Starting in 1916, all men of nonroyal blood and without conferred noble status were referred to as *nai* or *mister* regardless of their class or marital background. By 1917, King Vajiravudh had also abolished the use of ethnically distinctive identity markers, khaek and chin, before men's personal names.[58] Nai became an inclusive category that encompassed generously the male citizens of the nation without regard for their ethnicity or marital status. A second effect was more subtle, however. Nonelite men were apprehended not as Chinese, not as single, not as married, not as Muslim, but as individuals. They were the paradigm for the socially unencumbered legal subject imagined as the recipients of the modern legal codes, citizenship, and nationalist discourse. Women, by contrast, were apprehended through their relationships with male relatives—as wife, mother, daughter, and so on. Despite the flurry of activity in the development of family law, citizenship, forms of address, and other laws that identified an individual's obligations to the state, law gave male subjects alone a direct relation to the state.

The proliferation of categories of women—Mrs., Miss, major wife, minor wife, mistress, harlot, prostitute, loose woman (*ying sephle*)—were defined in relation to one another on the basis of their location inside or outside the family, which was hard to determine as long as people continued to form "temporary unions" (*taeng-ngan chua khrao*).[59] The means by which a woman became honorable or dishonorable depended on whether she associated with a man in a permanent and publicly recognized relationship. In turn, a woman's ability to dictate the terms of her sexual engagement with a male partner depended on her class background. An indigent woman had no leverage to make a man support her permanently as his minor or major wife.

Rama VI attempted to fulminate opinion against the practice of "temporary marriage" by arguing that it provided no security for women, failed to protect children from the shame of illegitimacy, made it impossible for judicial officials to arbitrate inheritance cases, and led to the prostitution of women.[60] Because the Cabinet Council could not agree to pass a monogamy law, the king decided to promulgate a law that would at minimum require people to register their marriages "to regulate the promiscuity of irregular unions."[61] Articles in the women's press similarly argued that the neglect and abandonment of wives and children resulted ultimately in an increase in pros-

[58] This is somewhat surprising given Rama VI's overwhelmingly anti-Sinitic stance in his nationalist rhetoric. Vella, *Chaiyo!,* 199. I have not found the act or decree that abolished the use of chin or khaek, but its use in court cases ceases between 1914 and 1920.

[59] A contentious 1920s divorce case between Mom Saeng Mani and Mom Chao Thongchuathammachat hinged in part on Mom Chao Thongchu's disreputable (but not illegal) relations with various *ying sephle,* or loose women. The case contains over fifteen hundred pages. NA MR6 Yutitham 8.2 Khadikhwam, "Mom Saengmoni kap Momchao Thongchuathammachat."

[60] Cited respectively in Adul and Luang Chamroon, "Some Main Features," 94; Vajiravudh, "Khlon tit lo," 108, 116–22; Vajiravudh, "Khruangmai," 8.

[61] Adul and Luang Chamroon, "Some Main Features," 92–93.

titution as abandoned daughters sought sex work as their only means of livelihood.[62] Because the family was being transformed into a badge of a strong, morally upright Siam, sex workers became symbols of the failed family and hence a threat to the positive image of the nation.

As a result of the impermanence of many sexual unions, the term "wife" failed to capture the sense of veneration and solidity that Rama VI desired. It required a concerted propaganda effort by Rama VI to reclaim the category of "wife" for his national family. In his essay "Clogs on Our Wheels," which is excerpted at the beginning of the chapter, he writes about mia or wife as a confusing category that included legally married wives, minor wives, mistresses, harlots, and prostitutes. To clarify the muddling of mia, Rama VI appealed to the nation's men: "We ought to help them [women] receive justice and equality, the honor they deserve in their status as our national mothers, and to feel pride in the name *wife* by using this term as it should be [used]!"[63] Ironically, the argument for women's justice and equality was founded on a distinction between immoral and moral women—a distinction over which women had little control.

The confusion between proper wife and prostitute discredited the term "wife," argued Rama VI. In a peculiar way, it was not far from the truth. Court cases in which women were promised they would be supported as wives but ended up being sold into prostitution suggest that lines between wife and sex worker merged on occasion.[64] Rama VI tapped into the nation's collective shame regarding the former existence of slavery to support his case against temporary marriage. "We Thai," he wrote in "The Sale of Women," "always feel proud of the fact that the monarch promulgated a law to abolish slavery," yet some men practiced a modern form of slavery in which they purchased young poor women from their parents or from agents.[65] In linking slavery to the (heterosexual) sexual excesses of self-styled modern young men, the king drew on an emotionally charged issue of national identity. The legacy of not being colonized imbued the term for slavery, *that,* with a sense of colonial subordination, while the term *thai* began to be synonymous with the concept of freedom.[66] Hence, men who indulged in the exchange of

[62] Siriphon, "Kan riakrong," 31–32; Chittima, "Kanriakrong sithi satri," 38. Both cite articles from *Satrisap* written in the early 1920s.

[63] Emphasis in original. Vajiravudh, "Khlon tit lo," 109, 111–12.

[64] NA MR5 Yutitham 13, Khadikhwam 29, mai het 38/90, "Khadi ruang amdaeng bo phayong ha wa chanwang lom kratham kankhotkhi lae bangkhap hai tham chamrao ha ngoen" (Case of Amdaeng Bo Phayong [Who] Accuses Chanwang Lom of Forcing Her into Prostitution) (1895); Loos, Archival Notes, vol. 11, 48–71. NA MR5 Yutitham 13, Khadikhwam 21, mai het 72/90, "Khadi ruang chaophasi bamrung thanon chap amdaeng thim pai hawa amdaeng thim pen khon hachon" (Case of a Street Tax Collector Apprehending Amdaeng Thim and Accusing Her of Being a Prostitute), 1894; Loos, Archival Notes, vol. 10, 168–72.

[65] Vajiravudh, "Khlon tit lo," 117.

[66] Thanet Aphornsuvan argues that slavery was "discovered" as an oppressive, un-Thai institution only after the introduction of the modern notion of freedom. Thanet Aphornsuvan, "Slavery and

women were not charged simply with being immoral and backward but with being un-Thai.

The temporary unions between "modern young Siamese men" and the women they purchased led to what Rama VI termed "irresponsible parenting."[67] Although he also blamed fathers, who usually abandoned their (temporary) families, Rama VI heaped abuse on mothers, who were the focus of his lecture. Women became "good mothers" (*manda thidi*) when they persisted in raising their children even if they received no help from their absconded husbands. A good mother devoted her life to the safekeeping of her children, raising them to be honest, polite, and good future husbands. Daughters are not mentioned. However, bad mothers abandoned their motherly duties and took no interest in their children because they focused exclusively on preventing their husbands from loving other women. Those who failed to take an interest in their children also failed to be good citizens. A bad mother's children had no ethics, were selfish, and were ultimately headed for prison.[68] The king wrote that

> we must nurture the character of the new generation of children to make them understand the significance of parental obligation to raise their children to be useful to the group and to be an upright citizen of the nation. Their sons must be able to support the monarch to do favors for their country as fitting for the name of the Thai people. Daughters should be a decoration that glorifies the nation by making herself a good wife and mother who understands her duties. (King Vajiravudh, "Khlon tit lo," 115)

The king's moral essays and laws on citizenship and family surnames facilitated the family role-specific incorporation of women into King Vajiravudh's state-building project by subordinating a woman's identity to that of her husband rather than carving out an individual space for her as an autonomous citizen of the nation. Women who fell outside these newly legitimated roles in the family found themselves denounced in the new ideology of national belonging. From the 1910s, when Rama VI first propagated his version of Siamese nationalism, discussions of national identity in Siam invariably invoked a moral discourse of the "family," which referred to heterosexual sexual practices within a long-term marital union. All sex that took place outside the moral confines of the newly defined family was pathologized as excessive, marking individuals involved as dissolute rakes and loose

---

Modernity," 161. For a similar version in Thai, see Thanet Aphornsuvan, "Sithi khon thai nai rat thai" (Rights in the Thai States), in *Chintanakan su pi 2000: Nawakam choeng krabuan that dang thai suksa* (Reflections for the Year 2000), ed. Chaiwat Satha-anan (Bangkok: Thai Research Foundation, 1996), 181–233.

[67] "Khwammai rapphitchop khong bida manda," in Vajiravudh, "Khlon tit lo," 112–16.

[68] Vajiravudh, "Khlon tit lo," 114.

women. King Vajiravudh's legal proclamations on the family demarcated women as honorable or immoral on the basis of whether they engaged in sexual intercourse inside the ideal feminine roles of dutiful wives and mothers of the future nation. Although King Vajiravudh's intentions might have been to protect potential victims of forced prostitution and an untenable life as a mistress, he relied on a good woman/bad woman distinction that stigmatized women outside the "modern" family—a conception of the family accessible to only a minority of women.

The contested nature of familial rhetoric surfaced in the cultural practices and laws that attempted to stabilize a standardized family structure. King Vajiravudh promulgated laws that privileged the concept of a stable and monogamous heterosexual union. According to his ideal family, couples stayed together rather than changed partners, and individuals in the same family adopted the same surname, giving each person a genealogy and fixed identity. Administratively, this individuated people and made it easier for the bureaucratic machinery of the state to track them down. Modernity, replete with its invasive disciplinary technologies, had arrived in Siam and was embodied in such mundane regulations as censuses, birth and death registrations, and the requirement for family surnames. Ideologically, it provided the king with a stable and identifiable family unit to anchor Thai national identity, particularly during a period when ideas about the existing social and political hierarchy were being dramatically transformed among the educated classes and urbanites. The creation of a family prototype, however, narrowed heterogeneous sexual relationships, which had previously varied in terms of length and purpose. Outside the formal settings of officialdom and the courts, women were not categorically dependent on men. However, in official contexts the creation of a standard definition of family either ossified women's formal dependence on men within the family or located them outside the boundaries of legitimacy. By contrast, the discourse of national identity defined men less in terms of their familial position as husbands or fathers than in terms of their loyalty to the monarch.

SIX

Nationalism and Male Sexuality

National identity in Siam cannot be fully understood without considering the sexing and gendering of Siam's national imaginary. Undeniable links were forged among official nationalism, domestic politics, and male heterosexuality through a discourse on the family propagated by King Vajiravudh (photograph 6). When King Vajiravudh harnessed the modern family and proper sexuality to a larger state-building project, he aimed to ensure the continued centrality of the monarchy to Siam as a nation. King Vajiravudh's discourse on family defined proper male officials and, by extension, proper male citizens, as those who engaged in stable marriages with "honorable" women, not with harlots, prostitutes, or mistresses. While the law on marriage to "honorable" women served to categorize women on the basis of sexual morality, it also helped construct ideal male citizens. The king regularly attacked male officials who agitated for a constitutional monarchy by accusing them of profligate sexual practices, conflating their libido with their "modern" political yearnings.

The vulnerability of men to such charges could not have occurred in nineteenth-century Siam, before sex, sexuality, and other subjects related to "family" were politicized as a result of imperial discourses cementing links between family law and modernity. King Vajiravudh mobilized the rhetoric of family against his domestic political enemies. He undermined his political rivals, including both the Chinese minority and the growing class of male commoner officials, by attacking their purported family values and sexuality, respectively. Rama VI also disputed the "Thai-ness" of his domestic enemies, who were glossed as Chinese or as slavish imitators of the "West," which served to eject them from Siam's national family.

Photograph 6. Crown Prince Vajiravudh in 1908.
Arnold Wright, *Twentieth Century Impressions of Siam* (London: Lloyd's Greater Britain Pub. Co., 1908), 86.

The degree of ethnic, social, and cultural proximity of these two overlapping groups (the Chinese and male nonroyal officials) to the ruling class made them a familiar, intimate threat that was easier to target than other minorities. By contrast, King Vajiravudh used inclusive language in his addresses to Muslim Malays, whose allegiance to Siam, let alone to the monarchy, was uncertain at best. In 1917, he declared himself the protector of the Muslim faith to an audience of imams and hajis in southern Siam, promising freedom for Muslims to practice Islam. He proclaimed, perhaps in hopeful anticipation, that Muslims would defend Siam with their lives because "to die in defense of one's religion is a meritorious act, and indeed they would be serving the cause of Islam when they serve the country that gives it her protection."[1] He also decreed that the derogatory designation of *khaek* before personal names would be eliminated in all government documents and invited Malay boys to join his Boy Scouts and Wild Tiger Corps, giving them permission to wear Malay-style caps instead of standard issue uniform caps.[2]

By comparison to the broad language of appeal used in addresses to Malay Muslims, King Vajiravudh's rhetoric regarding troublesome Siamese nationals required sometimes hairsplitting precision because these groups were loyal to Siam, but not necessarily to the absolute monarchy. The following close reading of King Vajiravudh's essays and laws reveals the monarch's anxiety about being replaced as the pacesetter (and gatekeeper) of Western modernity by a burgeoning middle class filled by young, educated officials. The absence of a foreign colonial overlord combined with the peculiar position of the monarch as the leading modernizer, state builder, and inventor of official nationalism had repercussions for the formation of Thai identity. As ruler of the country, the monarch was simultaneously the most radical and conservative of reformers, promulgating change and establishing the limits on how far it could go. Precisely because the monarchy from the reign of King Mongkut (Rama IV) on was regarded as an enlightened institution, it undermined demands from others for more radical political reform. This veneration empowered the king's attempts to construct a national identity that excluded groups that threatened the power of the absolute monarchy.

As Annette Hamilton has noted:

> The specific forms of nationalist ideology have largely been attributed to the fact that the constitution of the nation did not derive from nationalist anticolonialism, but rather emerged through internal struggles dominated by alternatively competing and collaborative relations between varying factions of

[1] *Bangkok Times* (4 Jan. 1916), and *Phraratchadamrat nai phrabatsomdet phra mongkutklao chaoyuhua* (Speeches of King Vajiravudh) (Bangkok: Bamrungnukunlakit, 1929), 175–76, cited in Vella, *Chaiyo!,* 198.

[2] Vella, *Chaiyo!,* 199.

> the monarchy, the aristocracy, the bureaucracy, the military and an emergent middle class.[3]

The emergent middle class, many of whom filled the administration and military, was on the whole favorably disposed toward modern reforms associated with industrialized, imperial nation-states. Some of them fiercely disputed the (slow) pace of political change set by the monarch, advocating instead a constitutional form of government. Two groups in particular posed a threat to the monarchy: the powerful and increasingly politicized Chinese minority and political radicals who demanded the end of the absolute monarchy.[4] The two groups were not mutually exclusive, but the king targeted them in different ways.

Although the scholarship on the development of nationalism in Thailand emphasizes the role of anti-Sinicism, I focus instead on a second, equally significant aspect of Thai national identity: the linkage between heterosexual sexual excess and a growing class of nonroyal officials who clamored for a representative form of government. Significantly, the state began for the first time to regulate the sexuality of male officials by linking men's antiabsolutist political beliefs to their allegedly excessive sexual practices. The linkage makes it clear that King Vajiravudh's brand of nationalism had embedded within it an inseparable discourse about gender and sexuality that has been occluded in earlier studies. It provided the king with a means to discredit those who agitated for anything less than an absolute monarchy.

The Chinese in Siam have received the lion's share of attention in scholarship on King Vajiravudh's nationalism because he was a clear proponent of anti-Sinicism.[5] For this reason, this analysis addresses them only briefly. The 1910s witnessed the rise of Chinese nationalism among members of the Chinese population in Siam and the concomitant interpretation by Rama VI of this politicization as a problem for Siam. The problem began in March 1909, when a royal decree abolished the triennial tax of 4.25 baht on Chinese men in Siam.[6] Chinese men became liable to an annual head tax of four to six baht every year, the same as the rest of the population. By 1910, when the Chinese learned that they had to pay again, secret society leaders organized and enforced a general strike in Bangkok that lasted for three days. The strike

[3] Annette Hamilton, "Rumours, Foul Calumnies and the Safety of the State," in *National Identity and Its Defenders: Thailand, 1939–1989,* ed. Craig J. Reynolds. Monash Papers on Southeast Asia 25 (Clayton, Victoria: Monash University, Centre of Southeast Asian Studies, 1991), 343.

[4] According to David Wyatt, "The best estimates indicate that the Chinese minority grew from about 230,000 in 1825 to 300,000 in 1850 and 792,000 in 1910; their proportion of the total population grew from less than 5 percent to 9.5 percent." Most of the Chinese population was located in Bangkok and its environs. Wyatt, *Thailand: A Short History,* 217–18.

[5] Skinner, *Chinese Society in Thailand,* 55–171; Benedict Anderson, *Imagined Communities,* rev. ed. (London: Verso, 1991), 100–101; Copeland, "Contested Nationalism."

[6] Skinner, *Chinese Society in Thailand,* 162.

nearly paralyzed Bangkok and succeeding in sending a clear dual message to Siam's leadership: the economic functioning of the kingdom depended on Chinese trade and business, which was not necessarily loyal to Siam. In the wake of the strike, King Vajiravudh ascended the throne.

Similarly, political events in China were observed closely, not simply by some Chinese in Siam but by the reigning Chakri dynast who must have pondered the parallels between himself and the ruling Manchu emperor. Within the first year of King Vajiravudh's rule, the Manchu dynasty in Beijing had been overthrown by the nationalists, who King Vajiravudh associated with the Chinese in Siam. According to Benedict Anderson, the Chinese revolutionaries in China and elsewhere appeared to Rama VI "as harbingers of a popular *republicanism* profoundly threatening to the dynastic principle."[7] Matthew Copeland, citing King Vajiravudh's 1915 essay "Clogs on Our Wheels" (*Khlon tit lo*), points out that King Vajiravudh chastised those who developed "'the Chinese habit' of believing the tracts of 'politicians who preached rebellion' and ignoring the public pronouncements of their own government."[8] Furthermore, by the mid-1910s, the Chinese community in Siam had become more unified than before, manifested in their support for schools that instructed students in Chinese languages; the development of horizontal, communitywide organizations such as the Chinese Chamber of Commerce (1908); and the establishment of Chinese language newspapers.[9] As a result, King Vajiravudh targeted the Chinese in many of his essays, the most infamous of which was *The Jews of the Orient.*[10]

King Vajiravudh did not restrict his vitriolic remarks to the Chinese. He also targeted a second group: new recruits in the bureaucracy and officer corps of the military. In 1912 a small group of young military officers led an abortive coup against the king. They presented a more immediate threat to the absolute monarchy, which they considered an "unprogressive and dying institution."[11] Like the eleven men in 1885 who petitioned King Chulalongkorn for a parliamentary democracy under a constitutional monarchy, this group also sought a representative form of government. Unlike the eleven men in 1885, who came from aristocratic and royal families, the 1912 group were all commoners and thus less beholden to the monarchy. Although unsuccessful, their effort made an impression on King Vajiravudh. His excoriation of the self-styled "modern" Siamese, his constant undermining of their goals, and his accusations of hypocrisy bear examining in detail.

[7] Anderson, *Imagined Communities,* 101.

[8] Translated in Copeland, "Contested Nationalism," 39. This quote comes from the section on "Excessive Belief in Written Materials" (*kanbucha nangsu chonkoenhet*). Vajiravudh, "Khlon tit lo," 83–87.

[9] Skinner, *Chinese Society in Thailand,* 169–71.

[10] Vajiravudh, *Jews of the Orient* 1985 [1914].

[11] Vella, *Chaiyo!,* 55.

From Sexual License to Sexual Limits

To understand the significance of legal reforms and essays targeting the rising bureaucratic class, three background points should be made. First, a reflexive association existed among the king, the kingdom, and the behavior of those individuals—including royal family members, women in the Inner Palace, and officials—who worked closely with the king. The second issue concerns the shifting function and meanings of polygyny for Siam's system of rule. The third point explicates the expansion and changing composition of the bureaucracy. The comportment of male officials began to reflect publicly on the monarchy, the bureaucracy, and elite classes generally in the popular press.[12] Unseemly behavior by officials also damaged the honor of king and country in the eyes of some foreigners living in Siam who were already critical of Siam's system of government.[13] The parameters of official behavior that came under the scrutiny of the press, the monarch, and foreign observers had expanded to include sexuality. Although Siam's laws had always prohibited adultery (defined as sex with the "wife" of another man) for officials and nonofficials alike, they had also granted officials privileged access to their single female constituents. For powerful officials, even adultery was often overlooked if committed with the wives of less powerful men. In addition, male homosexuality was not regulated by the state, so a male official could engage in homosexual relations without fear of prosecution.[14] By contrast, Rama VI's laws and essays effectively allowed the state to police the moral and sexual behavior of this segment of officialdom for the first time in Siam's history.

The shift in focus to a male official's sexual behavior was remarkable. Historically, the sexual comportment of male officials had been relatively free of restrictions. A reflexive connection characterized relations between an official and the king, symbolized by *sanyabat,* a writ of appointment granted by the king to an official that protected the official from lawsuits by requiring king's permission before complaints could be investigated.[15] Having sanya-

[12] Barmé, *Woman, Man, Bangkok,* chap. 4; Loos, "Gender Adjudicated."

[13] See the following rape case of a young woman by a high-ranking official: NA MR5 Yutitham 13.3 Khadikham, Chusao khomkhun 10, mai het 92/90 "Khadi nu liap chot phraya montri suriyawong chamloei chamloei tong ha wa khomkhun tham chamrao," 13 July–Oct. 1898, 5. The conflation of king and kingdom was bolstered in the 1908 Penal Code as indicated in the title for the code's first section of offenses, "Offences Against the King and the State." "Kotmai laksana aya," 22 PKPS, 44. *The Penal Code for the Kingdom of Siam (Draft Version)* (Bangkok: A. P. Mission Press, 1908), 28.

[14] The first court case in which male homosexuality surfaced occurred during the reign of Rama III (1824–51), but the perpetrator (Krommaluang Rakronnaret) was executed for traitorous acts, not for homosexuality. The fact that the case mentioned Prince Rakronnaret's sexual relations with his male actors suggests that the state frowned on such behavior. Chao Phraya Thiphakorawong, compiler, *Phraratcha phongsawadan krung ratanakosin ratchakan thi sam* (Cremation Volume for Maha Amattho Phraya Phaibun Sombat [Det Bunnak]) (Bangkok, 1934), 317–21.

[15] Although it could be interpreted as a double-edged sword because it also brought the faults of

bat operated to the advantage of officials because it deterred individuals from filing cases against powerful local officials (and their wives). David Engel, a specialist on Thailand's laws, notes that the protection clause afforded by sanyabat "emphasized the special relationship between such officials and the king, making it appear that any reproach against the officials was in some measure a reproach against the king himself."[16]

Moreover, prior to the centralization of the administration, an official exerted broadly defined authority over his constituent population in a manner that blurred the distinction between legitimate rule and abuse of power. For example, officials who received sanyabat could "eat the governed area," or *kin muang.*[17] This was the method of remuneration for officials who were not compensated by the central government but instead earned a living by procuring goods and services from the population they governed or by retaining a portion of the fines and taxes they collected.[18] Gradually, after King Chulalongkorn's 1892 administrative reforms, salary payments from the centralizing government replaced this system. As the method of remuneration shifted from one in which officials made a living directly off the population to one that forced officials to depend on the government in Bangkok, so too did the definition of appropriate official behavior. Activities that were once part of acceptable bureaucratic practice were reinterpreted as a form of corruption, bribery, or misuse of office. Previously, an official's comportment was granted license because it fell within the penumbra of the monarch's authority; by the early twentieth century an official's comportment was restricted because it might reflect negatively on the monarch's authority. It was at this point that the state began to regulate the sexual comportment of officials as well.[19]

A 1904 court case exemplifies this transitional moment. The case involved a high-ranking official in Trat who had raped one of his female constituents.[20] Sexual access to single women who were under an official's patronage counted among the privileges that some male officials believed were warranted by virtue of their office. In this 1904 case, two commoners, Nai Ket, a father, and Amdaeng Chiam, his daughter, contested such prerogatives when they accused Luang Ramarutthirong of intimidation, assault, and the rape of Amdaeng Chiam.[21] The defendant had temporarily replaced the gov-

---

the official to the king's attention, sanyabat protected officials from suits by nonofficials more often than it exposed their indecorous behavior to the king.

[16] Engel, *Law and Kingship in Thailand,* 102.

[17] Tej, *Provincial Administration of Siam,* 22; William J. Siffin, *The Thai Bureaucracy: Institutional Change and Development* (Honolulu: East-West Center Press, 1966), 31–32; Frederick Riggs, *Thailand: The Modernization of a Bureaucratic Polity* (Honolulu: East-West Center Press, 1966), 20, 140–41, 245.

[18] Tej, *Provincial Administration of Siam,* 13, 20–22.

[19] There were exceptions, including even violent rape witnessed by individuals willing to contend with a powerful official in a court of law, which sometimes failed to convict the official.

[20] Loos, "Issaraphap," 1998, 56–61.

[21] NA MR5 Yutitham 13.3, Khadikhwam, Chusao khomkhun 17, mai het 32/195, "Khadi

ernor of Trat, occupied the post of *yokkrabat,*[22] and was the supervisor of the public prosecutor's office, making him the most powerful official in Trat Province, which bordered Cambodia in eastern Siam. According to the court records, in March 1904 the defendant asked Amdaeng Chiam's mother if he could marry Amdaeng Chiam. She replied that he must make his request in the proper customary manner by appointing intermediaries to arrange a marriage. The defendant bragged pretentiously that he had never appointed intermediaries before and reminded her that he was at that time the most powerful man in the province. The implications were clear: with or without permission, the defendant understood his position as warranting access to Amdaeng Chiam. He proceeded to rape Amdaeng Chiam and later, after a second attempt, was subject to a rape suit filed by Amdaeng Chiam and her father, Nai Ket. Although the outcome of the case is not recorded, the fact that it was filed and reached the monarch indicated that constituents recognized limits to an official's power.

The need to control the behavior of officials intensified after the 1910s, when the bureaucracy had become unwieldy. A massive administrative expansion in the wake of Rama V's reforms required an enormous influx of educated young men. Prior to King Chulalongkorn's administrative reforms in 1892, the small size of the bureaucracy and the institution of polygyny made it possible to fill the most powerful positions of the administration and the military with trusted royal family members and members of elite noble families.[23] However, by the turn of the century, the scarcity of "energetic, qualified and trustworthy officials" slowed down the reform process, especially in the provinces.[24] Between 1892 and 1905, the bureaucracy quadrupled in size. The number of salaried bureaucrats in 1892, just prior to Rama V's revolutionary reforms, was about twelve thousand. By 1925 there were 86,500 officials.[25] As noted by Anderson and Mendiones in their book on Thai literature, "such a bureaucracy could not be manned exclusively by Siam's traditional nobility, and into its lower ranks flooded ambitious young commoners, some of whom studied abroad on government scholarships and returned infected with liberal, meritocratic, and egalitarian ideas."[26]

Government departments at the turn of the century were so desperate for

---

khwam kho onuyat phicharana khwam nai rawang luang ramarutthirong chamloei tong ha wa khomkhun" (Document Requesting Permission to Investigate Case of Luang Ramarutthirong, Defendant, Accused of Rape), Mar.–May 1903.

[22] Translated as *judge* by Tej, *Provincial Administration of Siam,* 21, but others prefer *royal spy.* The yokkrabat supervised provincial officials and reported back to the king if officials behaved inappropriately or misused their office. In the Muslim south, the yokkrabat was an official in the local administration alongside the governor, assistant governor, and an assistant administrator. Engel, *Law and Kingship in Thailand,* 50.

[23] Seksan, "Transformation of the Thai State," 461–63.

[24] Tej, *Provincial Administration of Siam,* 164.

[25] Batson, *End of the Absolute Monarchy,* 45, n. 40.

[26] Anderson and Mendiones, *In the Mirror,* 15.

qualified officials that they did not select among applicants but accepted practically all applicants with demonstrable qualifications, even those found guilty of crimes, who were simply transferred to a new locality. Benjamin Batson, a scholar of early twentieth-century Siam, wrote that it was only "in the 1920s, with educational opportunities expanding and economic constraints slowing, or at times even reversing, the growth of the bureaucracy, that the luxury of the selecting process could be contemplated."[27] This unrestrained expansion formed a new class of modern-educated, nonroyal bureaucrats who grew increasingly dissatisfied with the discrepancy between the oft-touted ideals of a national citizenry with obligations to the nation-state and the rather limited ways in which they could participate in the government. They vocally critiqued King Vajiravudh.[28] From them, King Vajiravudh felt a strong push for constitutionalism.

By the time Rama VI came to power in 1910, it was impossible to regulate the now massive administrative body through customary techniques. Instead, Rama VI exploited the long-standing association between the behavior of officials and the reputation of the king and country to new ends. He used it to rationalize his intervention in the sexual affairs of his officials, whose sexual practices may not have been any different than those practiced by royal and aristocratic officials, but the king's interpretation of the practices as "immoral" was new. King Vajiravudh used the discourse on sexual impropriety against certain members of his officialdom, namely those "modern Siamese men."

The Palatine Law (*kotmonthianban*) was used during the reigns of Rama IV and Rama V to regulate the sexuality of women in all royal households.[29] Regardless of whether the woman in the palace was a slave, servant, or concubine, the Palatine Law placed strict prohibitions on her sexual relations. For instance, during the reign of King Mongkut, female palace guards and royal wives were obligated by oath to prohibit any sexual contact on the palace grounds involving women in the Inner City, including sexual relations between women.[30] Many court cases from the period of Rama V detail the

[27] Batson, *End of the Absolute Monarchy,* 62, n. 6. He reminds us that a Civil Service Law that introduced civil service exams was not promulgated until 1929 because of the scarcity of qualified officials.

[28] Vella, *Chaiyo!,* 53–60.

[29] Loos, "Sex in the Inner City."

[30] NL R4, Doc. 239, "Khamsaban khangnai" (Oath of the Inner Palace); Loos, Archival Notes, vol. 2, 18–32. On *len phuan,* a reference to female same-sex sexual relations, see for examples, Loos, Archival Notes, vol. 2, 24, 26. NL R4, Doc. 380, "Phraboromaratcha-ongkan ruang chaonai lae kharatchakan khitha phuying" (Royal Order on Royalty and Government Officials in Search of [Inner Palace] Women); Loos, Archival Notes, vol. 2, 120–35. NL R4, Doc. 448, "Krapthun ruang thwai tua pen kha khangnai" (Presenting Oneself as an Inner Palace Servant); Loos, Archival Notes, vol. 2, 188–97. NL R4, Doc. 32, "Khamhaikan ruang ii sombun haikanwa nai chalaem kap sombun natnae lae rakkhrai" (Testimony of Ii Sombun Testifying that Nai Chalaem and Sombun Made an Appointment to Have an Affair), approximately 1868; Loos, Archival Notes, vol. 1, 118–20.

"protection" of palace women from sexual relations with officials and male students who worked or studied on the palace grounds.[31] Servant women, female guards, and royal daughters and granddaughters were reprimanded and imprisoned for establishing connections with men who frequented the palace. Even if these women were single, they and their paramour were found guilty of committing adultery because they "belonged" to the king.

For example, when four male students studying in the recently opened Royal Pages College (known later as the Civil Service School) were caught associating with four palace women in 1901, they were all held culpable.[32] The four women received six months in jail, while two of the young men received warnings and the other two were imprisoned for two to three months. The men received a lighter sentence because the state needed them to fill administrative posts, and because their sexual desires were deemed natural. By contrast, young women, particularly those in the royal household, were supposed to be chaste and without sexual desire, which made their involvement more shameful and worthy of a harsher penalty. Similarly, in 1906, a second lieutenant in the Household Guard Regiment and Mom Ratchawong San, a single woman who resided in the queen's palace, were caught at the early stages of a liaison, before it had been consummated.[33] Though the woman's sentence is unrecorded, the young man received one year in jail for violating the Palatine Law.

Strict prohibitions on sexual relations within the palace walls suggest that larger issues of control, masculinity, and criteria of rule for kings and princes were linked to the sexuality of women in their households. The prohibitions, then, made sense given the connections among polygyny, rule, and masculinity. The number of a ruler's wives and children symbolically reflected the prosperity of the kingdom and his own personal transcendent virtue and charisma (barami). Unlike elite female sexuality, which was always controlled, male sexuality was regulated only when it infringed on the sexual territory—

[31] See, for example, the following cases: NA MR5 Yutitham 13.3, Khadikhwam, Chusao khomkhun, "Khadi ruang nai rongphichara tonghawa kratham kankhopchu duai ying nai phraboromaharatchawong" (Case of Nai Rongphichara Accused of Committing Adultery with Royal Palace Women), Jan. 1895; Loos, Archival Notes, vol. 3, case 4. NA MR5 Yutitham 13.3, Khadikhwam, Chusao khomkhun, "Ruang momratchawong hem lopkhao pai ha momchaoying suwan nai wang phra-ongchaoto laeo thuk phuak bao thupti" (Case of Momratchawong Hem Sneaking in to Phra-ongchao To's Palace in Search of Momchaoying Suwan, Then Being Beaten by Servants), Aug. 1895; Loos, Archival Notes, vol. 3, case 6. NA MR5 Yutitham 13 Khadikhwam 71, mai het 23/195, "Momratchawong butsabong nai khwan momratchawong phong khop yingkhonchai khong phra-ongchao sriwilai" (Momratchawong Butsabong, Nai Khwan, and Momratchawong Phong Associate with the Female Servants of Prince Siwilai), 1901; Loos, Archival Notes, vol. 11, 78–91.

[32] NA MR5 Yutitham 13, Khadikhwam 71, mai het 23/195, "Momratchawong butsabong," 1901; Loos, Archival Notes, vol. 11, 78–91. On the opening of the Civil Service School, see Wyatt 1969, 259–63.

[33] NA MR5 Yutitham 13.3, Khadikhwam, Chusao khomkhun 23, mai het 79/195, "Momratchawongsan loprak kap momchaoprasopphulkasem" (Momratchawong San has a Secret Affair with Mom Chao Prasopphulkasem," 1905–1906; Loos, Archival Notes, vol. 5, 86–91.

the immense Inner City of the Royal Palace—of the king.[34] Otherwise, the sexuality of male officials appointed by the king insulated them from complaints made by individuals about their sexual excesses, which had to be quite severe (usually nothing less than violent rape or adultery with the wife of an important person) to reach the king. For example, in 1901–2, Nai Chit, a page studying to be a policeman, was sent to Nakhonratchasima to study in the Department of Gendarmerie.[35] There a quarrel arose between soldiers and the police because of an affair between Nai Chit and the wife of a soldier. An investigation revealed that Nai Chit was engaged in illicit sexual relations with the wives of soldiers, the slaves of the provincial governor, and local prostitutes. Under King Chulalongkorn's administration, Nai Chit was remanded to Bangkok and barred from working for the government, but he was not otherwise penalized.

In 1915 Nai Chit begged King Vajiravudh to be allowed to return to officialdom, but by this point a new moral regime was in place, ensuring the rejection of his appeal. In August 1914, King Vajiravudh had promulgated a new Palatine Law on the "family" of government officials that shifted the focus of the law away from palace women and onto the sexuality of men in departments that worked intimately with the king.[36] They included officials in the Ministry of the Royal Household, the Department of Fine Arts, the Department of the Royal Secretariat, and the Department of Education;[37] all royal pages and students in the Royal Pages School; all palace soldiers, police officers, and members of the royal cavalry, among others.[38] The Royal Pages School was particularly important as it was the training ground for future officials.[39] King Vajiravudh set high goals for the institution, which in 1915 he considered "a model school for the Kingdom," that was geared to churn out "manly young men, honest, truthful, clean in habits and thoughts," and to transform "a boy into a fine young man and a good citizen."[40]

[34] Loos, "Sex in the Inner City."

[35] NA MR5 Ratchalekanukan-Dika 28, Doc. 65, Petition to King Vajiravudh, Jan. 1915; Loos, Archival Notes, vol. 11, 109–12.

[36] "Kotmonthianban waduai khropkhrua haeng ratchakan nai phraratchasamnak" (Palatine Law on Families of Officials on Royal Grounds), 1 Aug. 1914, 27 PKPS 253–282.

[37] The officials in the Department of Education/Ecclesiastical Affairs were incorporated under the Palatine Law in 1920 when the department relocated within the palace grounds. "Prakat phoemtoem kotmonthianban waduai khropkhrua haeng kharatchakan nai phraratchasamnak," 2 Feb. 1920, 32 PKPS 242.

[38] 27 PKPS 259, 253.

[39] The Royal Pages School (*rongrian mahatlek luang*) was founded in 1899 for training officials to work in the Ministry of the Interior. Its student body rapidly expanded from fifty in the first class (seventeen of whom passed) to 132 in the second. Between 1899 and 1910, it had become the training ground for all civil servants. Its name was changed to the Civil Service School (*rongrian kharatchakan phonlaruan*). Tej, *Provincial Administration of Siam,* 231–34.

[40] *Bangkok Times* (21 Dec. 1915), cited in Vella, *Chaiyo!,* 161. Undated letter from King Vajiravudh to Chao Phraya Phrasadet cited in Vella, *Chaiyo!,* 163.

Legislating Official Sex

The preamble of this extraordinary law, paraphrased here, elucidates the king's motives in passing it. King Vajiravudh wrote that men who worked in close proximity to the king had to behave virtuously because their behavior reflected on and might disgrace royal prestige. Their personal conduct, contrary to what they might think, related directly to their government duties. Aside from drunkenness and *nakleng* or hoodlum-like behavior, which received only a brief mention, Rama VI focused the rest of the law on "family." Family did not refer to a nuclear unit of parents and children, or even to an extended family, but to heterosexual sexual relations between a husband and his legitimate wives. The king targeted young "modern" men who behaved dissolutely everywhere except in front of the throne, where they deceitfully acted modestly.[41] According to the king, these men rationalized their rakish comportment by maintaining that traditional marriage practices were old-fashioned and that only "stuffy old coots" (*khon phumikao khramkhra*) who did not comprehend "modern traditions" engaged in them.[42] Because they found ways to avoid following the king's lectures on proper behavior, the self-styled modern young men in the royal compound only "think themselves smart and self-important," which in turn made them grow even more daring.[43] Rama VI issued the new law for this reason and because their behavior was a source of gossip that reflected negatively on the king.

No form of misbehavior was more important, according to the preamble, than that related to having a "family." The law required government officials and personnel to register their marriages, the names of their wives and children, the names of their and their wives' parents, and their domicile. The king forbade the registrar from recording certain women as "wives." Under the guise of a law on family, then, the king concentrated on the issue of promiscuous sexual liaisons between male officials and women inappropriate for the status of wife: prostitutes (ying nakhonsopheni), harlots (ying phaetsaya), and mistresses (mialap). That gave the state authority over a man's legitimate sexual partners. For the first time in Siam's history, a moral discourse about the constitution of a proper family unrelentingly regulated the sexuality of its governmental officials. A provision covered men who remained single by not registering a wife but who continued to associate with the women of their choice. Single men, unlike their married counterparts, could be sent at any time to serve anywhere in the country regardless of their personal preferences. Furthermore, if a single man wished to stay anywhere other than his registered domicile for even a single night, he required permission from his immediate superior first.[44]

[41] 27 PKPS 256.
[42] 27 PKPS 255.
[43] 27 PKPS 256.
[44] 27 PKPS 272, clause 39, 41.

These remarkable conditions were tested in March 1915 by Khun Ratanatphithak, an appointed official caught sleeping with a prostitute in the room of Nai Pho.[45] It seems that Khun Ratanatphithak and Nai Pho became intoxicated one evening, went to a movie theater, and later gambled in a local gambling den where Khun Ratanatphithak met Amdaeng Thongsuk, a sex worker registered with the state. He brought her to Nai Pho's room, which was located on the palace grounds. The light in the room attracted the attention of a royal palace soldier, who upon investigation found Khun Ratanatphithak and Amdaeng Thongsuk in bed together.

Their act was not covered in the new Palatine Law, which forbade officials from registering prostitutes as their wives, but said nothing explicitly about conducting business with them on palace grounds. As a result, King Vajiravudh quickly issued a supplement in May 1915.[46] It stated that any man who engaged in sexual intercourse with a prostitute or harlot on palace grounds would be imprisoned for no more than one year as would the woman involved. Moreover, the law decreed that the proprietor of the room in which the act transpired would also be imprisoned for no more than a year, while others who simply knew about the transgression would be imprisoned for six months or less.

Within five months, the king issued another supplement that attempted to limit the publicity of such untoward behavior by requiring officials covered by the Palatine Law to first receive written permission from their superiors before they published the information in newspapers.[47] The king wanted to narrow the parameters of acceptable sexual behavior of officials associated most closely with him and to limit public knowledge of the existence of indecent comportment.

The preamble of the August 1914 Palatine Law suggested that the definition of sexual promiscuity included any sex outside the institution of formal marriage, whether it was polygynous or monogamous. It constructed the proper family as one headed by a husband married openly to an honorable woman through traditional marriage customs or through registration with the state. By contrast, immoral sexual liaisons with prostitutes, harlots, and mistresses were associated with those identified as "modern young Siamese men." This linkage was elucidated in the series of articles written in 1915 by King Vajiravudh called "Clogs on Our Wheels" (Khlon tit lo).[48]

[45] NA MR5–6 Ratchalekanukan-Khamphiphaksa 19, "Kho phraboromaratchawinitchai nai kanthicha wang botlongthot kae khunratanatphithak chamloei sung pha yingnakhonsopheni ma ruampraweni thi hong nai pho, thanon khuanphet" (Request for Royal Consideration Regarding the Sentencing of Khun Ratanatphithak, Defendant, Who Brought a Prostitute and Had Sexual Intercourse with Her in the Room of Nai Pho, on Khuanphet Street). Loos, photocopied Dika 79.

[46] The supplement's wording is almost identical to the king's royal remarks in the case of Khun Ratanatphithak, which reveals the process by which precedent cases establish new laws. "Kotmonthianban phoemtoem," May 1915, 28 PKPS 52.

[47] "Kotmonthianban waduai ratchakan nai phraratchasamnak phoemtoem," 4 Oct. 1915, 28 PKPS 280–81.

[48] Copeland, "Contested Nationalism," 38–39; Vajiravudh, "Khlon tit lo," 73–132.

Modernity's New Brokers

In these essays, King Vajiravudh drew an analogy between the nation and an automobile. The auto drove cautiously along the muddy, perilous road to prosperity and civilization, but collected cakes of mud on its tires along the way. The mud referred to the various disagreeable and harmful habits of Siam's educated men who posed the only real threat to Siam's progress. Rama VI fought to maintain the monarchy's monopoly on modernity by denouncing officials who were critical of the absolute monarchy as naive imitators of Western behavior and concepts. According to him, these men, unlike the monarchy, failed to consider carefully the applicability of aspects of Western modernity to Siam. He harangued modern Thais who mimicked the West in what he called a "cult of imitation" (*lathi ao yang*), which he considered the worst cake of mud on Siam's wheels of progress.[49]

Among the many disagreeable attributes they picked up was "an overinflated sense of self" (*thu kiatyot mai mi mun*), manifested when they asserted equality with those of higher social status. One way these young commoners with a modern education attempted to reveal their newly acquired status was through imitating the lifestyles of the traditional elite, namely, by accumulating women. Fully half of the king's polemic is reserved for their purported immoral sexual practices, which led to unstable "families" and ultimately to the ruin of Siam's future citizenry.

One of the practices to which he referred was "temporary marriage," a fleeting arrangement in which a man purchased a woman, cohabitated with her until he grew bored, evicted her, and then obtained another young woman. As paraphrased by historian Walter Vella, the king wrote that this sort of cohabitation without a formal marriage ceremony or without official registration "encouraged promiscuity, gave no security to women, and was subversive to morality."[50] Rama VI likened the practice of temporary marriage to animal breeding, considering it even lower than the practice of polygyny.[51] Newspaper articles about marriage a decade later remembered King Vajiravudh for his efforts to increase the social and legal significance of marriage as a ritual so that the population would take it more seriously.[52] Even though the monarch could not force his fellow ministers of state to pass a monogamy law, he pushed for increased state intervention in marital practices.

The monarch's polemic targeted a second practice engaged in by so-called progressive officials who publicly opposed polygyny: their private accumulation of mistresses (mialap).[53] The term *mialap,* which translates literally as

[49] Vajiravudh, "Khlon tit lo," 75; Vella, *Chaiyo!,* 179.
[50] Vella, *Chaiyo!,* 155.
[51] Vajiravudh, "Khlon tit lo," 110.
[52] "Marriage in Siam," *Bangkok Times Weekly Mail,* 3 Feb. 1934, 25.
[53] Vajiravudh, "Khlon tit lo," 118.

secret wife, is a puzzling neologism.[54] Mialap did not refer to a man's major or minor wives, nor did it refer to an adulteress (women married to another man). In fact, mialap made little sense in a polygynous country, where the acquisition of multiple wives was still authorized by the state and by some strains of the culture that regarded the number of wives and children possessed by a man as a reflection of his status, power, and masculinity.

Polygyny no longer served its former function of integrating the kingdom through blood ties of loyalty among monarchs and powerful families in the center and provinces. King Chulalongkorn's redefinition of the polity as a territorially administered state had put an end in theory to the system of personal loyalties. The exchange of women continued, but it no longer served to connect families to the monarch after King Vajiravudh personally disavowed polygyny and ended the practice of accepting women in the Inner Palace. Within five years after he became king, the Inner Palace population dropped from a high point of about three thousand under King Chulalongkorn to twenty-five royal wives and princesses (of King Chulalongkorn) in 1915.[55] The increasingly ambiguous cultural and political function of polygyny opened it to scrutiny, especially as it was practiced by nonelites. This nonelite form of polygyny was referred to as the accumulation of "secret wives," suggesting it was a shameful and furtive practice—unlike polygyny, in which case a man publicly acknowledged his wives. This might seem too fine a distinction—indeed, in practice the differences may have been based purely on the class of the polygynist—but it enabled King Vajiravudh to attack certain men for their accumulation of wives while sheltering polygyny as practiced by other men on whose support he relied. Pursuing "Victorian" policies on the sexual behavior of officials through family law simultaneously enabled Rama VI to refocus the moral lens on excessive, allegedly Western-inspired sexual practices (like the accumulation of mistresses) rather than on indigenous polygyny, allowing him to discredit the growing number of officials clamoring for a representative government.

In King Vajiravudh's essay, mialap referred specifically to single women who were supported financially by a man but lived separately from him and were not formally or publicly associated with him. Their "mister" was typically a man who considered himself modern and pro-monogamy yet who did not abstain from having multiple female partners. In other words, mialap referred to a woman kept by a man who practiced a certain kind of hypo-

[54] *Mialap* is not found in Pallegoix's 1856 dictionary or Dr. Bradley's 1873 Thai-Thai dictionary. It is also not found in the 1927 Thai-Thai *Pathanukrom* (dictionary). The earliest dictionary citation of *mialap* can be found in George Bradley McFarland's 1941 dictionary, where *mialap* is translated as "concubine." So Sethaputra translates *mialap* in 1965 as "mistress" or "kept woman." George B. McFarland, ed., *Thai-English Dictionary* (Stanford: Stanford University Press, 1941), 657; So Sethaputra, *New Model Thai-English Dictionary,* vol. 2. (Bangkok: Thai Watanaphanit Press, 1965), 714.

[55] Smith, *Physician at the Court of Siam,* 98.

critically progressive politics. As such, this term was deeply implicated in a contemporaneous political battle between those who supported an absolute monarchy and those who advocated representative political institutions. While Rama VI occasionally contemptuously assailed open practitioners of polygyny as laughably backward and uncivilized, he conceded that they at least tended to support their major and minor wives permanently. He placed them one level above those who acquired mialap, which was regarded as a highly unstable and impermanent arrangement. Moreover, the lack of public recognition of these relationships and the political-ethical high ground allegedly taken by the male partner made these liaisons different from polygynous ties.

The king's argument was a brilliant rhetorical strategy that functioned to discredit advocates of political reform by exposing them to charges of hypocrisy. Accusations of hypocrisy, in turn, undermined political reformers' moral claims to righteousness as advocates of individual freedom, equality, and representative government. Regardless of the actual correspondence between a man's political beliefs and his sexual practices, Rama VI consistently conflated them. Politically radical men were susceptible to the charge of being immoral hypocrites, reckless apers of all things Western, selfish womanizers, and obstacles to national "progress." The main way in which this group of men hindered national progress was through their undermining of the stability of family unions by engaging in sexual behaviors that led to irresponsible parenting, illegitimate children, and the sale of women. The king asked, "Do you think it is appropriate that Siam, a prosperous country among many, should still have such shaky family values?"[56]

Family as Microcosm for the Nation

Integral to King Vajiravudh's nationalism, then, was a stable family unit—the foundational building block of the nation. According to his ideal, love generated among family members would produce patriots loyal to the nation and its monarch. He wrote in his essay on surnames that "the governance of the family is the opposite [of that in Chinese clans]. It is a method of cultivating respect for the ruler." The king considered the family "a foundation of loyalty to the head of the family on one level and a method to induce [people to] be loyal to the ruler of the nation on another level because they understand and love that very security."[57] This notion of family involved a reconceptualization and moralization of sexuality.

Rama VI linked sexual practices to nationalism through the notion of

[56] Vajiravudh, "Khlon tit lo," 111.

[57] King Vajiravudh, "Priap namsakun kap chu sae," 53.

"family," weaving a disparaging moral discourse into a discussion of hitherto accepted sexual practices. Only those sexual connections that resulted in stable and permanent unions were virtuous, while temporary arrangements and secretive liaisons were castigated as the ruin of the nation. His discourse on sexual practice and nationalism had an impact on male heterosexual sexual practices, which began to be limited by moral interdictions rather than by financial considerations alone. Male homosexuality remained unregulated and invisible to the state. The king implored men to permanently support the women with whom they had sex rather than to abandon, divorce, or neglect partners after the men grew bored or fancied another woman.

The reign of King Vajiravudh is distinctive for his incessant public articulations about proper Siamese sexuality. While King Vajiravudh's alleged sexual preferences for men may appear to have motivated his focus on the sexuality of male officials, the two are unrelated. His perception of nonroyal middle-class men as a threat made them a target, while his moral edicts on proper sex and the family more likely reflect his upbringing in turn-of-the-century London, where sexuality was similarly regulated along class lines in bourgeois discourse. Moreover, using King Vajiravudh's alleged homosexuality as an explanatory device without interrogating the heterosexuality of his predecessors serves to reinforce heterosexuality as the implicit norm. Rama VI was arguably the most prolific royal writer. His essays and laws on family and official sexuality constitute a small but important portion of his work, which ranged broadly in theme and tone. To evaluate the impact of his alleged personal sexual preferences on his political projects, a proper study would compare it with King Vajiravudh's other work and with the sexuality of other monarchs.

As a consequence of the debates about morality, anchored to heterosexual sexual and marital practices, a new bourgeois subjectivity developed in Siam that rigorously regulated the public behavior of Siam's official class. Although he legally targeted officials, King Vajiravudh subjected the entire reading population to a legal, moral, and paradoxically "nationalistic" renegotiation of the norms of heterosexual conduct through public discourse. King Vajiravudh harnessed the modern family and proper sexuality to a larger state-building project that married the monarchy to Siam as a nation. His myriad cultural interventions and legal interdictions undermined those who advocated anything less than an absolute monarchy. Rama VI deployed this rhetoric alternately and inconsistently against Western accusations of moral depravity, the ethnic Chinese, and the excessive sexual practices of "modern" men and women.

In domestic political conflicts, the king mobilized the ideal "modern" family against those who posed internal threats as well as against Western accusations of immorality, depraved customs, and the inequality of women. Men who advocated a representative form of government were discredited by Rama VI as thoughtless imitators of Western political ideas who were, moreover, hypocritical for engaging in habits oppressive to women and sexually excessive. King Vajiravudh's perennial association between radical political thought and immoral sexual practices made it difficult to discuss one without invoking the other. Instead of targeting polygyny as an immoral practice, the monarch blamed the new middle-class men in officialdom for their ill-treatment of women, and ultimately equated the middle-class male accumulation of "secret wives" with treason. His attempt to regulate sexual practice under the guise of family law targeted men and attempted to discipline them into becoming ideal citizens. It, however inadvertently, also demarcated women as honorable or immoral on the basis of whether they engaged in sexual intercourse inside the ideal feminine roles of dutiful wives and mothers of the future nation. Identity as an honorable male citizen loyal to the absolute monarch or as a respectable mother were two powerful new subjectivities for Siam's modern citizens.

Accusations of sexual immorality outside the family and of imitating Western sexual and political practices derived their potency from Siam's position vis-à-vis the imperial powers. These charges were fundamentally informed by and strategically deployed within an asymmetrical imperial context. The language of modernity—democratic political practices and sexual morality within the nuclear family—had penetrated Siam's national boundaries. It was used both by the monarch, who favored continuation of existing domestic hierarchies, and by commoner officials, who blurred class boundaries in two ways: by advocating political and social change and by usurping sexual privileges associated with the traditional ruling class. Siam's monarch and his political opponents rivaled each other for political legitimacy through moral debates about legitimate sexual acts.

The public nature of this debate subsided after King Vajiravudh died in 1925. His successor, King Prajadhipok (Rama VII, r. 1925–35), married one woman, the daughter of publicly pro-monogamy Prince Svasti (son of King Mongkut and half-brother of King Chulalongkorn). King Prajadhipok asked the cabinet of senior statesmen to vote on monogamy, which they vetoed in favor of polygyny as Siam's enduring marital standard. The press and the monarch were relatively silent about marriage law, in contrast to the situation under King Vajiravudh. Not until after the coup of 1932, which established a constitutional monarchy and removed royal-blooded men from most official positions, did Siam's government revisit the marriage law.

SEVEN

Subjects of History

Static Revolutions

Within a three-hour period on 24 June 1932, one hundred civilians and military officers overthrew the government of King Prajadhipok (Rama VII, r. 1925–35), thereby ending absolutist rule in Siam. The Khana Ratsadon (People's Party) justified the revolutionary change in a statement that emphasized the injustice of the monarch's position above the law and the special rights given to royal family members. Legality provided a firm rationale for revolutionary change in the government. By contrast with the absolute monarchy, the new leaders would

> provide the people with equal rights (so that those of royal blood do not have more rights than the people as at present). . . . Everyone will have equal rights and freedom from being serfs [*phrai*] and slaves [*that*] of royalty. The time has ended when those of royal blood farm on the backs of the people.[1]

The People's Party that staged the bloodless coup against Rama VII received support from a wide spectrum of urban Bangkok society, including

[1] Selections are from the People's Party announcement made on 24 June 1932. The English translation comes from Pridi Bhanomyong, *Pridi by Pridi: Selected Writings on Life, Politics, and Economy*, trans. and intro. Chris Baker and Pasuk Phongpaichit (Chiang Mai: Silkworm Books, 2000), 72. For the original Thai announcement, see Charnvit Kasetsiri, *2475 Kanpatiwatsayam* (1932: Siam's Revolution) (Bangkok: Foundation for the Promotion of Social Sciences and Humanities Textbooks Project, 2000), 125–26.

business leaders, urban intellectuals, and labor organizers. Included among these supporters were four prominent Bangkok Muslims.[2] The new leaders immediately purged the government and military of high-ranking royalty and aristocrats, arresting forty members of the royal family and their assistants. The constitution drafted within the first six months of rule barred core members of the royal family from serving in the government or Assembly. King Prajadhipok's requests for veto power over legislation were repeatedly denied.

The new constitution provided for a government headed by a constitutional monarch, the People's Committee (later referred to as the cabinet), and an elected assembly or parliament. It granted universal suffrage and the right of men and women to run as members of parliament (MP) in 1932—two rights that most Western nations had not granted to their female citizens and for which no one in Siam had agitated. According to Malinee Khumsupha, who examines the issue of women's rights in the political thought of coup leader Pridi Bhanomyong, the inclusion of suffrage and women's rights to run for office made sense in the context of Western Europe where most of the coup leaders had received an education. She suggests that Pridi and others granted such rights in order to place Siam on equal political terms with European and American powers and to assure the new government of much-needed diplomatic recognition of Siam as a modern nation.[3] Given that many Western nations had not yet granted women the right to vote, Siam was one step ahead.

As a consequence, Siam joined the still relatively short list of countries worldwide (the second country in Asia) that guaranteed universal suffrage,[4] which was exercised indirectly in 1933 and directly in 1937 when people voted for half of the Assembly membership.[5] The first Assembly, which was

[2] Nakkharin Mektrairat, *Kanpatiwat sayam pho so 2475* (The Siamese Revolution of 1932) (Bangkok: Foundation for the Social Sciences and Humanities, 1992); Pasuk and Baker, *Thailand,* 267–68. Thanet, "Origins of Malay Muslim 'Separatism' in Southern Thailand," 19.

[3] Malinee Khumsupha, "Sithi satri nai khwamkhit khong pridi phanomyong" (Women's Rights in the Ideas of Pridi Phanomyong," *Warasan Thammasat* (Thammasat University Journal) 25, no. 1 (Jan.–Apr. 1999): 93–94.

[4] These included New Zealand (1893), the Cook Islands (1893), Australia (1901), Finland (1906), Norway (1907), Denmark (1915), Austria (1918), Canada (1918), Czechoslovakia (1918), Germany (1918), Hungary (1918), the United States (1920), Britain (1928), Brazil (1932), and Uruguay (1932), among others. Ceylon was the first "Asian" country to grant universal suffrage (1931), but it depends on how one defines Asia. The Cook Islands, for example, implemented universal suffrage in 1893; many people today count New Zealand as part of Asia. Mongolian women were granted the vote in 1924. See C. Daley and M. Nolan, *Suffrage and Beyond: International Feminist Perspectives* (New York: New York University Press, 1994), 349–52. See also Tamara Loos, "The Politics of Women's Suffrage in Thailand," in *Women's Suffrage in Asia: Gender, Nationalism and Democracy,* ed. Mina Roces and Louise Edwards (London: RoutledgeCurzon, 2004), 170–94.

[5] Men and women voted for a village representative, who then elected a *tambon* (a commune or group of villages) representative, who then voted for the parliament member. Pridi, *Pridi by Pridi,* 74–75.

fully appointed by the coup group, found the issue of family law a high enough priority that they immediately initiated a discussion of a law on monogamy that would apply everywhere except the Muslim provinces of Pattani, Yala, Narathiwat, and Satun. Luang Wichitwathakan, later a renowned nationalist propagandist and historian, astutely pointed out that Assembly members would be criticized regardless of how they decided on the issue of marriage because it involved custom, honor, and politics.[6] He personally felt that one wife was already too many. Joking aside, he advocated monogamy as a policy but expressed a concern that one law be applied to the entire nation, including the Muslim provinces. From the first instance, these two issues—a monogamy law and Muslim exceptionalism—were discussed in tandem. Before his comments were redressed, Siam's premier, Colonel Phraya Phahon, following the suggestion of several of the members, postponed further debate until after (indirect) elections were held so that Assembly members elected by the people would also be present to weigh in on the matter.[7] This occurred on 18 and 22 January 1934, when the Assembly argued at length about the law on marital registration, the resolution of which was necessary before the government could promulgate Books V (family) and VI (inheritance) of the Civil and Commercial Code.[8] The first general election elected Thai Buddhist MPs in Yala, Narathiwat, and Pattani, and a single Muslim MP in Satun.[9] Very few Muslims weighed in on these key parliamentary debates regarding polygyny.

Chao Phraya Srithammathibet, the head of the commission in charge of drafting the law, presented arguments in defense of monogamy. The proposed law allowed for the legal registration of one wife for each male citizen except for Muslims residing in the four southern provinces. The law soft-pedaled on polygyny, which was not criminalized. However, in instances where a man had multiple wives, only the registered wife had legal standing or could receive an inheritance or marital property in divorce proceedings.[10] Anticipating a defense of polygyny based on the potential for a monogamy law to create a large class of illegitimate children, the head of the commission reported that *all* children acknowledged by their father and regardless of the legal status of their mother would receive the same legal rights and inheritance provided to children of the registered wife. He also allayed other unspoken

[6] Meeting 14/1933 (Regular Session) on 17 Aug. 1933, *Rai-ngan kan prachum sapha phuthaen ratsadon* (Bangkok: Akson-niti, 1933), 404–5.

[7] Ibid., 406. "The Assembly: That Big Family Problem," *Bangkok Times Weekly Mail* (19 Jan. 1934), 21.

[8] One of the coup leaders and member of the People's Committee, a civilian commoner named Pridi Phanomyong, joined the codification committee in September 1932. For a list of the members added to the committee, see Pakdi, "Kanchatrang," 103–4.

[9] Thanet, "Origins of Malay Muslim 'Separatism' in Southern Thailand," 19–20.

[10] In stark contrast to custom, the law would not recognize any couple as married even if they cohabited and had children unless they formally registered their marriage.

anxieties by pointing out that women could not force men to register them as a wife, but that men had control over this process. The commission chair justified the shift to monogamy by consciously comparing Siam to other formerly polygynous "Eastern" countries, especially Muslim Turkey, which had all adopted monogamy. Siam, he argued, would appear stagnant by contrast unless it too adopted monogamy. By so doing, Siam would not only prove to the world its progressive stance but would domestically enhance the status of women, increase family harmony, and protect all children.[11]

The all-male Assembly then debated (ad nauseam, according to some members) the rationale for allowing the legal registration of one wife as opposed to more than one wife.[12] The arguments in favor of polygyny ranged widely, and provoked righteous condemnation and likely some laughter. Polygyny's defenders argued that it protected men from undue hardship if their first wife was insane, barren, or diseased. Much of the discussion debated the ability of polygyny to increase the population, with members clinging to population statistics as irrefutable scientific proof of the power of polygyny to augment Siam's population. Others approached this argument from a different tack by blaming women for the persistence of polygyny because they had not demanded its dissolution, or alternately, because they dressed immodestly. Two MPs contended that the upshot of a monogamy law would be an increase in prostitution, apparently because unmarried women had few other options.[13] Finally, one member facetiously argued that because polygyny was the source of irresolvable debate, decisions about it should be postponed for ten years, during which the population might soar and women might agitate for change.

More compelling and relevant in retrospect were arguments by Assembly members that questioned the ultimate motives for restricting the registration of more than one wife and interrogated the constitutionality of the exemption of the Muslim areas in the south. According to Assembly records, the MP from Nongkhai demanded to know why "must we imitate the West? It is unclear why, aside from the fact that they practice monogamy and therefore we should practice monogamy. This is an insufficient reason to make any decision."[14] Another MP argued that civilized folks the world over have ended the custom of polygyny because it is barbaric. However, he contin-

[11] Session 7/1934 (18 Jan.), *Rai-ngan kan prachum sapha phu thaen ratsadon,* Samai thi 2, Saman (Second Special Session) (Bangkok: Akson-niti, 1934), 242.

[12] All of the arguments come from Session 7/1934 (18 Jan.), and Session 8/1934 (22 Jan.), *Rai-ngan kan prachum sapha phu thaen ratsadon,* Samai thi 2, Saman (Second Special Session) (Bangkok: Akson-niti, 1934), 234–79, 300–339. See also "The Assembly: That Big Family Problem," *Bangkok Times Weekly Mail* (19 Jan. 1934), 20–22, and "The Assembly: The Wife Again," *Bangkok Times Weekly Mail* (23 Jan. 1934), 7.

[13] Session 7/1934 (18 Jan.), *Rai-ngan kan prachum sapha phu thaen ratsadon,* Samai thi 2, Saman (Second Special Session) (Bangkok: Akson-niti, 1934), 252, 261.

[14] Ibid., 247.

ued, even though Siam's system of government is now democratic like that of civilized countries, it still legally allows polygyny.[15] In other words, this MP made the case that Siam's modernity could include Western-style democracy but not necessarily Western marital standards.

In response to the committee chairperson's arguments about equality, by which he meant equality between men and women, the MP from Nongkhai demanded to know what was unequal about the current situation. He shifted the discussion away from gender to ethnicity and religion: "If Muslims [*khaek*] are allowed to have many wives but Thais can have only one—how can [the committee chair] talk about equality? If we are to make Thais civilized like them [Westerners], then we should make Muslims civilized as well. Why distinguish between them? The Turkish Muslims did it [adopted a monogamy law], so too can the Muslims in the south."[16]

Significantly, a majority of the MPs who debated the monogamy law discussed it in relation to the southern Muslim provinces, even though this is not reflected in the scholarship about the passage of the monogamy law or in government discourses under the absolute monarchy. In particular, MPs questioned the constitutionality of the exemption of the southern Muslim provinces. Most members felt strongly that Siam's laws on family should apply to the entire country. Treating the south separately suggested that Siam was a divided nation rather than a uniform whole.[17] They also maintained that the Quran *allowed* four wives but in no way *compelled* a man to take four wives and that in fact the holy book advocated one wife. Luang Wichitwathakan resorted to anecdotes about the Muslims he knew who had only one wife, preferred monogamy, and felt misunderstood by non-Muslims.[18] His views are important because he worked closely with the wartime government of Field Marshall Phibun Songkhram, which issued a "cultural mandate" in the early 1940s that abolished the Islamic courts and revoked the use of Islamic law. In their place, the government enforced Siam's national laws on family and inheritance in the south. However, because of the consternation this caused Muslims, the postwar government reestablished Islamic law and courts in 1946.[19] The MP from Satun foreshadowed this when he argued that it would be impossible to change the traditions of the Pattani pop-

[15] Session 8/1934 (22 Jan.), *Rai-ngan kan prachum sapha phu thaen ratsadon,* Samai thi 2, Saman (Second Special Session) (Bangkok: Akson-niti, 1934), 309.

[16] Another MP requested that the Assembly adopt the term *khon itsalam* (Muslims) rather than use the derogatory word *khaek.* Session 7/1934 (18 Jan.), *Rai-ngan kan prachum sapha phu thaen ratsadon,* Samai thi 2, Saman (Second Special Session) (Bangkok: Akson-niti, 1934), 247. See also "The Assembly: That Big Family Problem," *Bangkok Times Weekly Mail* (19 Jan. 1934), 22.

[17] Session 7/1934 (18 Jan.), *Rai-ngan kan prachum sapha phu thaen ratsadon,* Samai thi 2, Saman (Second Special Session) (Bangkok: Akson-niti, 1934), 247–56.

[18] Ibid., 252.

[19] Narong, *Khwampenma,* 9.

ulation.[20] The chair of the commission finally clarified that "local law" (stated in English) applied to the south in order to safeguard freedom of religion there, but that the south was nonetheless an integral part of the nation.[21]

In any case, polygyny could not become the basis of unity between Buddhists and Muslims because of the radical divide institutionalized and maintained since the turn of the century between the two groups culturally, politically, and legally. Asserting sameness through a shared practice would imply equality when Siam's Buddhist leadership saw themselves as dominant.

Buddhist Siam was caught between the two—polygyny for Muslims and monogamy for the West. Assembly members, eschewing a Buddhist defense of polygyny as an authentic national practice, ultimately voted to adopt monogamy as the marital standard. It was promulgated as law in October 1935.[22] This set in motion a series of changes in international treaties. The equivocation of Siam's leaders and legal reformers regarding a decision on a marital standard in Siam had delayed the completion of the civil code, which in turn delayed the abolition of unequal treaties between Siam and a dozen foreign nations. Francis B. Sayre, Siam's adviser of foreign affairs in the mid-1920s, and Prince Traidos, Siam's foreign minister, had renegotiated each treaty with foreign powers in the mid-1920s.[23] As a result, all foreign powers agreed to relinquish their remaining extraterritoriality and commercial privileges within five years *after* Siam promulgated the last of its modern laws. The 1935 decision about marriage enabled the Assembly to promulgate the final two books (on family and inheritance) of Siam's modern law codes and consequently to eradicate the remaining foreign privileges.

It would appear that Western modernity *did* compel Siam to adopt a monogamous family structure. However, despite the passage of a single-wife law and public disavowal of polygyny, the law's gendered double standard and loopholes regarding acknowledging out-of-wedlock children created an alternative form of monogamous marriage in Siam. This was a conscious part of the monogamy law decision that even the chair of the commission that drafted the law acknowledged. He assured MPs in 1934 that the monogamy law did not limit the number of one's minor wives in practice but merely limited the number that a man could register.

Unsurprisingly, contemporaries noted that the new marriage law ultimately made little difference and that it failed at the level of implementation. In December 1935, the *Bangkok Times Weekly Mail* revealed the no one but

[20] Session 7/1934 (18 Jan.), *Rai-ngan kan prachum sapha phu thaen ratsadon,* Samai thi 2, Saman (Second Special Session) (Bangkok: Akson-niti, 1934), 255.

[21] Ibid., 266.

[22] "Phraratchabanyat chot thabian khropkhrua" (Royal Act on Registering Families), Sept. 1935, 48 part I PKPS 354–93. Clause 1451 of the new monogamy law states that if an individual has already registered a marriage, that individual cannot register another marriage unless the first marriage has ended by death, divorce, or cancellation by the court.

[23] Prince Traidos was the son of Prince Devawongse, the former foreign minister.

the educated and rich registered their marriages.[24] The majority preferred the customary methods of marriage and sought to avoid at any cost police stations and government offices, where they had to register marriages. One contemporary American observer, Kenneth Landon, notes that by the end of 1936 officials had registered only fifteen marriages in a district in Bangkok with a population of 58,400 people.[25]

In addition to the relative insignificance of the monogamy law, except at a symbolic level, to most people in Siam, none of the former laws on family associated with the absolutist regime were revoked. All of Rama VI's patriarchal legal provisions regarding the modern family, citizenship, and forms of address (based on marital status for women but not for men) survived the 1932 coup without modification. Indeed, the national rhetoric about family introduced by Rama VI resurfaced, in modified form, in the cultural mandates of the 1940s government led by one of the original coup leaders (Field Marshall Phibun Songkhram). The monarch's vision of the national family ideal had persevered. This raises vital questions about the degree to which the 1932 "revolution" and the 1935 passage of a monogamy law made a difference for women, male political culture, the concept of the family, Muslims in the south, and ultimately for the subjects and structure of Thai historiography as a whole.

Subjects of History

The overthrow of the monarchy makes 1932 a moment ripe with potential for the birth of a revisionist history of Siam that could recast the monarchy as oppressive, autocratic, and crushingly elitist. The People's Party's revolutionary statement quoted at the beginning of this chapter indicates that class differences between the ruling (mostly royal) elite and lower classes served as the impetus for the coup group's revolutionary change in leadership and in political institutions of rule. As a result of the tensions between the monarch and Siam's new leaders, King Prajadhipok permanently removed himself from Siamese politics by abdicating in 1935 and moving to Switzerland. Siam had no resident king between 1935 and 1951, when King Bhumibol Adulyadej returned to live in Bangkok.[26]

[24] *Bangkok Times Weekly Mail* (20 Dec. 1935), 18.

[25] *The Nation* (10 Apr. 1937), cited in Kenneth Perry Landon, *Thailand in Transition: A Brief Survey of Cultural Trends in the Five Years since the Revolution of 1932* (Chicago: University of Chicago Press, 1939), 193.

[26] The government chose as King Prajadhipok's successor his nephew (and grandson of King Chulalongkorn), Prince Ananda Mahidol, who was then in school in Switzerland. After King Ananda Mahidol's (Rama VIII, r. 1935–1946) mysterious death by gunshot in Bangkok in 1946, his younger brother, Prince Bhumibol Adulyadej, assumed the crown. King Bhumibol grew up in Boston and Switzerland, received a thoroughly foreign education, and yet was thrust into the position of sym-

Despite this, there was no birth of an alternative narrative of Siam's history. Within two days of the coup, the leaders of the People's Party repudiated their antiroyalist statements and invited senior nonroyal figures back into the administration.[27] The initial antimonarchical impulse of 1932 has been silenced or suppressed as an anomaly, blamed on one particular leader (Pridi Bhanomyong) rather than tainting the entire event, which itself has been recuperated in the dynastic-as-nationalist historical narrative. What made this possible? Siam's noncolonization. It sutured the gap between dynastic and post-1932 national histories. The perceived role of the monarchy in protecting Siam from invasion by imperial powers made it antithetical for the new government to be both antimonarchical and nationalist.

The requirement to come to terms with the "fact" of Siam's independence is as productive *today* in its effects: it perpetually recenters the institution of monarchy, which maintains a stranglehold on the imagination of Thailand's past, present, and future. The king stands in for Siam, used interchangeably, such that a critique of one necessarily implies a critique of the other. The compulsive structuring of Thai history began during the reign of King Chulalongkorn, when every major policy was justified through recourse to the potential threat of Siam's extinction as an independent entity. Only by revisiting this crucial period in the formation of Siam as a nation can historians offer alternative accounts that displace the privileged royal subject of history.

The previous chapters recast events during this crucial period by placing at the center of the narrative legal modernity and family law, both of which are transnational projects that offer new vantage points on the role of the monarchy and Western forms of modernity. This book pivots on the fulcrums of family law and legal modernity, using them as a base from which to reconsider three questions that preoccupy scholars of Thailand: How can one end the isolation of Siamese history as exceptional because Siam alone in the region remained independent from control by a European colonizing power? How can one avoid crediting the monarchy as responsible for Siam's independence? How can one write about Siam's strategies of modernization, which helped the country endure and in some ways thrive during the colonial period, in ways that reveal Siam's distinction from European modernity?

The questions themselves set up an intractable set of provocative contrasts. The focus on Siam's independence sets up two and only two alternative political tracks for Siam as either a colonized or an independent state. It se-

---

bolizing all that was sacred and traditional about Thailand when he moved back to Thailand in late 1951 as king. Francis B. Sayre, former adviser of foreign affairs to Siam's government and professor at Harvard, enjoyed a close friendship with the father of Thailand's present king, Bhumibol, when he lived in Boston. Francis B. Sayre, Oral History Project at Columbia, "The Reminiscences of Francis B. Sayre" (New York: Columbia University, Oral History Research Office, 1957). The interview with Sayre was conducted in 1951.

[27] Pasuk and Baker, *Thailand,* 269.

ductively obfuscates a third trajectory: Siam as an imperial power. Siam simultaneously traveled along all three paths, which suggests these were not mutually exclusive modes by which states modernized.

The focus on Siam's endangered sovereignty is a red herring that ineluctably compels pursuers to follow the trail blazed by the monarch who heroically saved Siam rather than the furtive path simultaneously taken by Siam's leaders who institutionalized an imperial juridical hierarchy in Pattani, Yala, Narathiwat, and Satun. Individuals including Prince Damrong, Chao Phraya Yomarat, and others—not Siam's kings alone—followed the British lead in developing separate courts for Islamic family law disputes in the south. The existence of a sizable Malay Muslim population next door to British Malay territories made Bangkok officials sensitive about offending Muslims, who might then prefer British over Siamese rule. Rather than deal with their genuine grievances about autonomy and power, Bangkok's officials consciously modeled local judicial structures after those in British territories, not because Muslims desired this but because British authorities would be hard pressed to criticize Bangkok's policy. The British on the Malay Peninsula and in the Straits Settlements could hardly justify intervention if Siam made similar reforms. As a result, separate Islamic courts were created to apply "religious" laws in inheritance and marital disputes among a population ethnically, culturally, and religiously distinct from that of the ruling class.

From this perspective, Siam's history is most directly comparable to the British colonial government in the Federated and Unfederated Malay States, but would also benefit from a broader comparative analysis with other colonial states that introduced a hierarchical, plural legal system for local populations in contradistinction to European populations. In British Burma, for example, a series of acts made Buddhist law isomorphic with family law, as encapsulated in the Burma Laws Act of 1898. The Burma Laws Act determined that Buddhist law would be applied only in cases relating to succession, inheritance, marriage, or any religious usage or institution.[28] A legal scholar, Dr. Maung Maung, quotes from a case recorded in the postcolonial period in which customary law gradually was confined to family law, with some reference to religious institutions: "Because the British administrators identified it as having force among the Burmese who professed the Buddhist faith they called it 'Burmese Buddhist Law' and this name has passed into common use."[29] Law texts written after independence in 1948 and after the army seized power in 1962 suggest how successful the British were in narrowing

[28] Dr. Maung Maung, *Law and Custom in Burma and the Burmese Family* (The Hague: Martinus Nijhoff, 1963), 32–33, 35.

[29] J. Ba U in *Daw Thike vs. Cyong Ah Lin,* 1951, BLR 133 S.C., quoted in Dr. Maung Maung, *Law and Custom,* 32. Portions of the Burma Laws Act are still theoretically in force in Burma today because they have not been formally repealed.

the scope of Buddhist ethics to secular, substantive family law regardless of the form of government.[30] Sometimes books on Buddhist law cease to encompass even a discussion of lay and ecclesiastical regulations for Buddhists.[31]

Siam's situation is paradoxically parallel to both that of European colonial governments and the colonized position of its subjects. Because Siam *did* experience forms of political, economic, and legal infringements on its sovereignty by imperial powers, its history also has much in common with colonized countries. Within the broader international imperial context, Siamese and foreigners alike considered Siam's traditional inheritance and marital laws to be sources of Siamese "native" identity as Thai Buddhists. The battles waged within Siam over the meanings of polygyny as Buddhist, traditional, backward, or as authentic occurred because family law was equated with local, customary, or religious "traditions." Looking at Siam's political trajectory from the perspective of family law demonstrates that Siam was independent at the same time it was colonized and colonizing.

The second question raised above asked how scholars could avoid crediting the monarchy as being solely responsible for Siam's independence. The idea that there exists *anywhere* at any historical moment a nationally delimited, individual font of agency is problematic. The transformation to modernity, exemplified herein through law, was a deeply and resolutely transnational process in terms of the context of the reforms, the subjectivities of legal reformers, the corpus of codes, and the languages mediating Siam's domestic laws. Most studies of Siam's legal transformation fail to analyze their subject within an international context, focusing instead on exclusively domestic rationales, events, and individuals. However, the international context of imperialism is vital to analyses of Siam's legal reform throughout the nineteenth and twentieth centuries.

The imperial value-laden ideology of civilization that treated monogamous marriage as the benchmark of modernity dictated which of Siam's "traditions" would become lightning rods for debate. Polygyny became a multivocal symbol that, depending on one's beliefs about it, could signify one's loyalty to authentic national identity, to Buddhism as opposed to (imperial) Christianity, to a debauched and invalidated tradition, or to an antimonarchical and modern political stance. Polygyny's multivocality meant that

[30] For example, in 1937 Dr. E Maung, a Burmese Supreme Court justice in the late 1940s and early 1950s, first published a book entitled *Burmese Buddhist Law* that covered exclusively matters of marriage, divorce, and inheritance. See also Dr. E Maung, *Burmese Buddhist Law* (Rangoon: 1970); Myint Zan, "Of Consummation, Matrimonial Promises, Fault, and Parallel Wives: The Role of Original Texts, Interpretation, Ideology, and Policy in Pre- and Post-1962 Burmese Case Law," *Columbia Journal of Asian Law* 14, no. 1 (Spring 2000): 156 n. 5; Sisir Chandra Lahiri, *Principles of Modern Burmese Buddhist Law* (Calcutta: Eastern Law House, 5th ed., 1951).

[31] The fact that so-called Buddhist law dealt exclusively with family matters was addressed in a 1969 Supreme Court case, which determined that it would be called Burmese customary law from then on. For a discussion of this, see Zan, "Of Consummation," 155–56.

it obtained different meanings for individuals depending on their position in the social hierarchy. For Muslims, polygyny was reified as a symbol of their distinctiveness and as the legal institutionalization of their subordinate status within Buddhist Siam. For royal and aristocratic elites, it remained a privilege of their class and a mode for making political and economic alliances. For commoner officials, it was a practice associated with political power and thus might have indicated to them that they had "arrived." For women, the reactions varied by class, if the court cases and public press is any indication. They were anything but unified in their responses, nor is there much evidence that this process empowered women. Polygyny indexed Siam's asymmetrical place in the international imperial context and as a result became a potent weapon to deploy domestically. Transnational hegemonies collided and colluded with national ones, as King Vajiravudh's castigation of politically suspect officials through their accumulation of "secret wives" demonstrated.

Transformations in law were a cumulative process negotiated among various hierarchically positioned subjects within a transnational context rather than dictated by a single monarch within the confines of a single nation. For example, legal reformers working in Siam embodied a transnational subjectivity. They arrived from around the world, from colonized states, imperial metropoles, and Siam. They migrated within colonial circuits of legal exchange that dotted the globe. Modern international law and personal experience in colonized settings informed their understanding of Siam and their application of legal reforms. This was as true of foreigners hired to work in Siam's administration as it was for Siamese legal experts. Siamese officials made pilgrimages to European centers of empire in the nineteenth century, which made them participants, alongside foreign legal advisers, in a global circulation of ideas about jurisprudence that paid little attention to national boundaries. In fact, no simple dichotomy exists between Siamese and foreign legal reformers, who shared many of the same experiences and spoke the same (non-Thai) languages. Siamese elite who spent their formative years in England before returning to Siam could place Siam in global perspective. This cosmopolitan viewpoint characterized their approach to reform rather than a narrowly nationalistic or monarch-centric one. More often than not, their values had more in common with other foreign-born and foreign-educated officials than with their own fellow nationals.

Views advocated by Siam's foreign advisers often were more conservative than those of Siamese individuals educated abroad. King Prajadhipok asked former legal adviser Francis B. Sayre in 1926 for advice on whether the king should introduce representative institutions.[32] Sayre, in an interview in 1951, reminisces on his meeting with the young king. Sayre approached the issue by describing the effect of a foreign education on commoner officials:

[32] Batson, *End of the Absolute Monarchy*, 37–38.

> When those students returned home it was hard for them. They came back to Siam filled with Western ideas and Western forms of culture which would not fit into this Far Eastern life. You begin to see seeds of discontent and troubled minds and disorder. I remember certain individual students who as youngsters had returned from France feeling that the old Siamese culture was outdated. Their minds were seething with modern Western ideas, and some of these were half-baked and misunderstood. It was the juxtaposition of the ultra modern West and the ancient East that made for trouble. Returned students, for instance, wanted a Western legislature, for they were filled with Western parliamentary ideas. . . . I pointed out to the King that the setting up of a legislature and clothing it with power before the development of an intelligent, educated electorate might be a source of danger and possible corruption. (Sayre, "Reminiscences of Francis B. Sayre," 103)

Sayre's subtle form of racialized elitism and historicist denial of modernity to Siam's educated classes dovetailed with the political conservatism of Siam's king.

In addition to the personalities who reformed and directed Siam's legal modernity, the procedures by which the law was reformed were also remarkably cosmopolitan. The bulk of the reforms were drafted in English rather than Siamese by dozens of foreign legal experts. The examples from which they prepared Siam's national code of law came from European law and colonial law rather than from Siam's *Three Seals Laws*. The transnationality of law—who labored on it, the language within which it was drafted, and the context within which reform was demanded—could not be more profound than in Siam. To praise Siam's monarchs for affecting this process simply obscures a complicated process of linguistic and cultural exchange.

Although a study of Siam's legal modernity cannot ignore its monarchs, particularly the prolific King Vajiravudh, neither can it pretend that the monarchy was driving the reform process. Siam's kings were one among many powerful voices advocating an agenda in Siam. The lack of consensus among Siam's ruling elite blocked Siam's allegedly absolute monarchs from promoting certain legal reforms (such as abolishing polygyny) unless they could muster adequate support among Siam's high-ranking ministers. In addition, "the king" more often than not operated as shorthand for a much more complex and contingent decision-making process, whether it concerned legal codes (drafted by foreigners under Siamese supervision) or policy in the Malay areas (where Prince Damrong and Chao Phraya Yomarat led the reform process). Deploying "the king" this way produces a history of omnipotence that supports the monarchy as an institution. By refusing to credit the monarch unless he was specifically involved, this book denies the primacy of the monarchy and credits instead judicial reformers who negotiated Siam's modernity through the discourse of law. Although other authors have eschewed an examination of the monarchy and monarchical writings altogether, I show that Siam's kings cannot be ignored—that would produce a spurious account of Siam's political history—but they can be deemphasized through careful examination of the limited roles they often played.[33]

The final question raised in the introduction can now be broached. It asked how one can write about Siam's strategies of modernization in ways that reveal Siam's distinction from European forms of modernity. My emphasis on the transnational impetus driving the legal reform detracts from the agency of Siam's monarch only to risk empowering an equally pernicious narrative centered on European modernity. It claims that modernity in countries across the world replicated European forms of political, legal, and cultural modernity.

There is some truth to this, given the military dominance and cultural capital supporting Western imperialist governments in nineteenth-century Asia. Siam's leaders *did* consciously imitate British models of colonial modernity when they created separate religious courts for Muslims in southern Siam. However, even there the motivations for imposing Islamic courts did not derive from a desire to secularize official power. Instead, Bangkok officials made little effort to separate the Buddhist sangha and state. Siam's alternative modernity exists in its promotion of Buddhism as a feature of national identity and state power.

In the process of categorizing and institutionalizing the Malay Muslim population as a minority, Siam's officials nationalized reformed Theravada Buddhism as the state religion in all but name. For example, in the early twentieth century, the state authorized Buddhist ceremonies—involving monks, chanting, and alms—to bless the opening of provincial courthouses.[34] The accumulation of sacred Buddhist objects from Java and India and the appointment of one of Siam's most credentialed Buddhist intellectuals, Chao Phraya Yomarat, to head reforms in the Muslim south reflect the conflation of state power and reformed Buddhism. Siam's alternative modernity can be found in its advocacy of Buddhism not simply as part of national identity but as a core practice of state rule.

Even today the Dika Court of Appeals in Bangkok houses Buddhist statuary that some Dika Court justices propitiate in an annual ritual. The democratic 1997 Constitution of Thailand dubs its monarch a "professed Buddhist and preeminent defender of the faith," who, moreover, must uphold the con-

[33] Scot Barmé most convincingly articulates a rationale for deemphasizing monarchical writings. Barmé, *Woman, Man, Bangkok*, 254.

[34] NA MR6, Yutitham 4 Huamuang, maihet 1/62, Letter from Chao Phraya Aphairatcha to Kromaluang Prachinkitibodi, Royal Secretariat, 7 Jan. 1914. The file discusses seven monks chanting at the opening of a muang-level court in monthon Roi-Et. It includes a detailed list of food, beverages, and gifts of furniture to the court by a high-ranking government official and local merchants, many of whom were Chinese.

stitution, which equally protects all Thai people "regardless of their race, sex, or *religion*."[35] This may seem a contradictory task: for a devout Buddhist king to defend his faith but to equally protect the approximately three million Malay Muslims who are nonetheless citizens of his realm. It is not considered inconsistent to regard the Buddhist monarch as the patron of all religions, however. He has helped finance the translation of the Quran into Thai, the construction of mosques, and related tasks. Despite the constitutional promise of equal religious treatment to all citizens, some have demanded that the state formally proclaim Buddhism as Thailand's official religion. In September 2002 conservative Buddhist monks and their supporters in Bangkok demanded the renaming of the Ministry of Religion as the Ministry of Buddhism and Thai Culture.[36] These calls have been unsuccessful but have lent credence to the view that many elements in Thailand do not embrace the Muslim Malay population as full citizens.

The promotion of Buddhism in government institutions in the southern Malay provinces has been a source of contention for Muslims since the turn of the century when King Chulalongkorn funded the reconstruction of a Buddhist temple in Pattani so that it could also be used as a government training center. Most government school teachers, officials, and police officers in the south historically and today are Thai Buddhists, typically originating from outside the Muslim provinces. The intimate connection between Thai Buddhism and state security forces was made unforgettably clear in July 2002, when the national police chief, Sant Sarutanond, and a revered Buddhist monk, Luang Pho Khun, assembled police officers in Narathiwat to dispense morale, bullet-proof vests, and protective Buddhist amulets blessed by the monk.[37] Unsurprisingly, police officers, school teachers, and monks have been the targets of assassination attempts by radical groups in the south for decades. The declaration of martial law in Pattani, Yala, and Narathiwat in January 2004 is intertwined with local and global events since September 11, 2001, but the precedents for the tension are historical and can be traced back to the turn of the century. The Thai government's policies with regard to its Muslim population remain, as they were in the era of high colonialism, impossibly entangled with international power politics.

A second example of Siam's alternative form of modernity is found in the perpetuation of polygyny, which is also associated with Buddhism. Because Buddhism historically signified Siam's difference from Western imperial powers, it was often used to justify other kinds of national distinctions, such as polygyny. This occurred even though doctrinal Buddhism does not priv-

[35] Emphasis added. *1997 Constitution of the Kingdom of Thailand* (Bangkok: Office of the Council of State, 1997), articles 9 and 5 respectively.

[36] "Bid to End Religious Discord: Senate Vote in Favour of 'Culture Ministry,'" *Bangkok Post* (21 Sept. 2002).

[37] Don Pathan, "Violence in the South," *The Nation* (17 July 2002).

ilege polygyny as a specifically Buddhist form of marriage. However, in mid-nineteenth century Siam, Chao Phraya Thiphakorawong articulated a Buddhist defense of polygyny that helped cement an association between Buddhism and polygyny. In the imperial era this connection and the notion that "family" structures were the source of cultural authenticity legitimated polygyny as a national practice at the same time that it undermined Siam's claims to civilizational equality. Siam's "family law," meaning primarily polygynous marriage, served to index Siam's relative barbarity compared to Western monogamous nations until 1935. Although the global context of imperialism made the family the litmus test for morality and political ethics, Siam's specific domestic context provided the monarch an opportunity to target rival male officials for their (hetero)sexual practices.

Women in particular were vulnerable to inequities embedded in modern laws on citizenship and surnames, which were patronymic and depended on state-authorized forms of marriage. Male officials also found their politics and libidos regulated by "family" laws because of the ambiguity over what constituted legitimate heterosexual sexual practices in the wake of Siam's transformation to modernity.

The formal legal support of polygyny up to 1935 and its unofficial support after 1935 offers evidence that Siam's reformers and population pursued an alternative marital modernity despite continued condemnation of it abroad and domestically. Some Assembly members debating a monogamy law in 1933 and 1934 supported polygyny in law and openly practiced it. Seventy years later, the law and the ability to practice it openly have changed, but polygyny continues. In December 2003, Prime Minister Thaksin Shinawatra contemplated prohibiting any politician from joining the ruling Thai Rak Thai (Thais Love Thais) party if they cheated on their wives by taking minor wives (*mia noi*) or by visiting sex workers. A Member of Parliament from Nonthaburi responded by claiming that "it's a man [*sic*] personal right to visit massage parlours or have more than one wife. I'm afraid that if they really implement this kind of rule, they will find no man suitable to be the party's candidate."[38] In other words, if the ruling party banned from membership men who had minor wives, it ran the risk of depleting itself of eligible bodies.

The operation of the modern discourse of rights as articulated by the MP—it's a man's right to have more than one wife—now shields polygyny, as opposed to reliance on a Buddhist defense. The fact that the exercise of "rights" by wronged first wives sparked this public display went relatively unnoticed. Both the Buddhist defense and the discourse of individual rights overlay a historically profound set of gender practices that continue to ex-

[38] MP Suchart Bandasak is quoted in Kesinee Jaikawang, Sukanya Lim, and Naparisa Kaewthoraket, "Thai Rak Thai Plan: No to Philanderers," *The Nation* (1 Dec. 2003).

press the masculinity of political culture through polygynous relations. The proposed Thai Rak Thai ban, in itself a minor blip on the screen of Thailand's political radar, is important because it indicates the persistent ambivalence and profound ruptures that continue to divide Thailand's body politic on the issue of polygyny.

Two images close the photo album of Thailand's national present: the declaration of martial law in the southern Malay provinces and the indignation of male politicians at the hint of state regulation of their extramarital affairs. These two incendiary issues burn through the modern history of Siam and continue to seethe and roil below the surface calm of Thailand today. Though seemingly unrelated, they share a common past and trajectory. They both grew out of the Thai state's ambiguity about how to manage domestic priorities and cultural difference within the context of European transnational hegemony.

Glossary of Frequently Used Thai and Malay Terms

Adat—tradition, custom, customary law
Amdaeng—title for commoner women
Anuphanraya—formal term for minor wife
Barami—transcendent virtue, charisma, merit
Chang—a unit of weight and money
Chao—royalty
Chaochom—consort of the monarch who has not (yet) given birth to royal children
Chaomuang—governor of a muang or province
Chao Phraya—the second highest nonhereditary title and rank for officials in Siam's former civil administration (Somdet Chao Phraya is the highest)
Chat—nation, birth, lineage
Chu—adulterer; tham chu is to commit adultery
Chin—title for Chinese men
Dato—Malay term for "elder" that is used as an honorific for a nonroyal official
Dato Yutitham—Islamic family court judge in Siam's reformed administration
Farang—white westerner
Hadith—a secondary body of Islamic scripture attributed to the Prophet Muhammad that provides religious guidance and describes law and customs
Haji—a Muslim man who has made the pilgrimage to Mecca
Imam—leader of a mosque or *surau* congregation
Issaraphap—liberty
Kadi—judge or magistrate in an Islamic court
Khaek—literally "guest"; a derogatory reference to Muslims, Malays, South Asians, Middle Easterners, and North Africans; Khaek Malayu refers to Malay Muslims
Khun—the lowest nonhereditary title and rank for officials in Siam's former civil administration, below the rank of Phra
Khunnang—aristocrats, noble officials
Khwaeng—district, a territorially defined administrative unit in Siam's administration
Kinmuang—literally "to eat the governed area," refers to the system in Siam by which officials were remunerated by their constituents rather than the central government

Kitab—commentaries on the Quran and Hadith
Kotmonthianban—Palatine law
Luang—second lowest nonhereditary title and rank for officials in Siam's former civil administration, above the rank of Khun but below Phra
Mia—colloquial term for wife
Mia klang muang—major wife
Mia klang nok—minor wife
Mia lap—literally "secret wife," mistress
Mia noi—minor wife
Mia that—slave wife
Mom—title for the commoner wife of a prince; a nonhereditary title conferred on lower ranking royalty
Mom chao—grandchild of the king
Monthon—largest administrative unit in Siam's provincial government composed of several provinces
Muang—province, can also mean community, town, city, and country
Nai—title for commoner men until the 1910s after which it became the general title used for all men, equivalent to Mr.
Nang—title for a married woman equivalent to Mrs.
Nangsao—title for an unmarried woman equivalent to Miss
Penghulu—headman of a parish
Phanraya—formal term for wife
Phrai—commoner
Phra—a nonhereditary title and rank for officials in Siam's former civil administration, above the rank of Luang but below Phraya
Phraya—a nonhereditary title and rank for officials in Siam's former civil administration, above the rank of Phra but below Chao Phraya
Raja—pre-installation title for rulers in the Malay Muslim principalities
Sakdina system—a social hierarchy that functioned during the Ayutthayan and early Chakri period that ordered individuals according to their birth, position, rank, and size of their client and territorial base
Sae—clan
San—court of law
San Borisapha—magistrate courts
San Dika—Royal or Supreme Court of Appeals
Shari'a Court—an Islamic court with jurisdiction over Islamic matrimonial, personal law, property law, and violations of Islamic moral law
Sultan—ruler of an Islamic state
Surao—Muslim prayer house
Tengku—Malay term for prince
That—slave
To-Kali—Islamic judge in Malay principalities under Siamese authority prior to their formal incorporation into Siam
To Khwaeng—district headmen in Malay principalities under Siamese authority prior to their formal incorporation into Siam
Ying nakhon sopheni—prostitute, early twentieth-century reference to a prostitute who was formally registered with the state
Ying phaetsaya—harlot, early twentieth-century reference to a woman who occasionally engaged in commercial sex but was not registered with the state
Yokkrabat—a rank in the provincial department of public prosecution

Bibliography

Archival Materials

Most of the material cited from Thailand's National Library, National Archives, and Dika Court Library was transcribed by the author in one of fifteen volumes referred to as Archival Notebooks, which follows the citation of the original source. For example, a reference that is followed by "Loos, Archival Notebooks, vol. 10, 121–43" means that a transcribed version of the source can also be found in volume 10, pages 121–43, of the notes on file with the author. In addition, several Dika Court cases have been printed from the microfilm, in which case they are listed as "Photocopied Dika," followed by the number by which they are filed in the author's collection.

National Library of Thailand

Each citation of sources from Thailand's National Library is prefaced with the initials NL. The National Library houses microfilmed and accordion-style folded black books from the reigns of Kings Mongkut and Chulalongkorn. They are listed according to the bundle (*mat*) number, file number within the bundle, and the document number and year, if it is listed. NL R4, 107/3, No. 239 refers to the National Library, the reign of Rama IV (King Mongkut), bundle 107, file number 3, and document number 239. Similarly, NL MR 4 C.S. 1228 (~1866), No. 103 refers to document number 103 in the National Library microfilm collection on Rama IV (King Mongkut) from the regnal year 1228, which corresponds roughly to 1866. I have tried to include a title for the source when it is given.

National Archives of Thailand

Each citation of sources from Thailand's National Archives is prefaced with the initials NA. Sources at the National Archives are documented as follows. For microfilmed sources, "NA" is followed by an "M" for microfilm, the reign from which a document comes, the ministry, and a number indicating a ministerial administrative division (and subdivision, if applicable). This may be followed by another number that refers to the document in that administrative division, the title of the case, and date. For instance, this citation—NA MR5 Yutitham 13.3,

Khadikhwam, Chusao khomkhun, "Ruang momratchawong hem lopkhao pai ha momchaoying suwan nai wang phra-ongchaoto laeo thuk phuak bao thupti" (Case of Momratchawong Hem sneaking into Phra-ongchao To's palace in search of Momchaoying Suwan, then being beaten by servants), Aug. 1895; Loos, Archival Notebooks, vol. 3, case 6— refers to a document in the National Archives (NA), it is on microfilm (M), and comes from the reign of Rama V (R5; King Chulalongkorn). The document is filed in the Ministry of Justice (Yutitham), division of Court Cases and subdivision of Adultery and Rape (13.3 Khadikhwam, Chusao khomkhun). In this reference, only a title is given, which is translated, dated, and followed by a reference to the author's transcribed notes.

National Archive sources that have not been microfilmed are cited as NA, followed by the reign, the ministry from which the source comes, and numbers that refer to a division and subdivision in the ministry. For example, NA R5 Nakhonban 6.2 refers to the National Archives, reign of Rama V, and the Ministry of the Capital (Nakhonban). The 6 refers to the Penitentiary Division under the Ministry of the Capital, which is further broken down into a division (.2) of prisoners. These numbers are typically followed by a fraction, such as 75/klong 40, which indicates the file number (75) and the box (40) in which the file is located.

Listed below are the abbreviations used by the ministries and the categories of documents within each ministry that have been consulted in this work. They are divided by reign, following the system at the National Archives.

Rama V Documents

- N Ministry of the Capital (Nakhonban). Not on microfilm
  - Division 8.1 Police
  - Division 16 Special Patrol Division
- Y Ministry of Justice (Yutitham). On microfilm
  - Division 1 Miscellaneous Documents
  - Division 13 Court Cases
  - Division 13.3 Court Cases. Adultery and Rape
  - Division 13.4 Court Cases. Assault and Murder
  - Division 13.5 Court Cases. Quarrels
  - Division 14.1 Verdicts. Imprisonment
  - Division 23 Penal Code
  - Division 99 (1) Miscellaneous
- RL Ministry of the Royal Secretariat (Ratchalekanukan). On microfilm
- D Royal Petitions (Dika)
  - Division 99 Miscellaneous

Combined Rama V and VI Documents

- RL Ministry of the Royal Secretariat (Ratchalekanukan). On microfilm
- KPh Court Verdicts (Khamphiphaksa)

Rama VI Documents

- Y Ministry of Justice (Yutitham). On microfilm
  - Division 4 Provincial Courts (Sanhuamuang)
  - Division 8.2 Court Cases. Mom saengmoni kap mom chao thongchuathammachat
  - Division 12.1 Laws. Civil and Commercial Code

Dika Court Library of Thailand

All sources from the Dika Court Library are cited as follows. They begin with the initials KSD, which refers to a multivolume source book, *Dika Court Verdicts* (*Khamphiphaksa san dika*), in which summaries of all Dika Court cases are bound. This is followed by the Buddhist calendar year of the decision, the decision number, the Western date of the decision, and its location in the author's collection. For example, KSD 2457 Decision 36, June 1914; Loos, Archival Notebooks, vol. 13, 13, refers to Decision 36 in the *Dika Court Verdicts* volume from Buddhist Era 2457, which corresponds to 1914.

Prachum Kotmai Pracham Sok (PKPS)

Another legal source that deserves a special explanation is the *Prachum kotmai pracham sok* (Collected Laws), a sixty-nine volume collection of Siam's laws and decrees, compiled by Sathian Laiyalak et al. in Bangkok in 1935. Citations from it begin with the volume number, followed by PKPS, followed by the page references. For example, 6 PKPS 30–60 refers to a proclamation printed in the sixth volume of the PKPS on pages 30 through 60. Specific information including the title of the proclamation and years has been included when available.

Harvard University Law School, Modern Manuscript Collection

Papers of Jens Iverson Westengard
  Box 1, Correspondence: Wife. Folders 4, 5, 6, 7, 8, 9, and 11.
  Box 2, Official Siam. Folders 6, 9, and 10.
  Box 3, Biographical Sketches. Folder 1.
Papers of Harold Hazeltine
  Box 4, Folders 21 and 25.

Harvard University Archives

Biographical Folder for Edward Henry Strobel, HUG 300.
Biographical Folder for Francis B. Sayre, HUG 300.
Biographical Folder for Jens I. Westengard, HUG 300.

Newspapers

Bangkok Calendar, 1863.
Bangkok Times Weekly Mail, Bangkok, 1934–35.

Bibliography

Adul Wichiencharoen and *Luang* Chamroon Netisastra. 1968. "Some Main Features of Modernization of Ancient Family Law in Thailand." In *Family Law and Customary Law in Asia: A Contemporary Legal Perspective,* edited by David C. Buxbaum, 89–106. The Hague: Martinus Nijhoff.
Ahmed, Leila. 1992. *Women and Gender in Islam: Historical Roots of a Modern Debate.* New Haven: Yale University Press.
Akin Rabibhadana. 1969. *The Organization of Thai Society in the Early Bangkok Period, 1782–1873.* Data Paper 74. Ithaca: Cornell University, Southeast Asia Program.
Andaya, Barbara. 1998. "From Temporary Wife to Prostitute." *Journal of Women's History* 9, no. 4 (Winter): 11–34.
Andaya, Barbara Watson, and Leonard Y. Andaya. 2001. *A History of Malaysia.* 2nd ed. Honolulu: University of Hawai'i Press.
Anderson, Benedict. 1998. "Withdrawal Symptoms." In his *The Spectre of Comparisons: Nationalism, Southeast Asia and the World.* New York: Verso, 139–73.
——. 1991. *Imagined Communities.* Rev. ed. London: Verso.
——. 1978. "Studies of the Thai State: The State of Thai Studies." In *The Study of Thailand: Analyses of Knowledge, Approaches, and Prospects in Anthropology, Art History, Economics, History, and Political Science,* edited by Eliezer B. Ayal, 193–247. Papers in International Studies, Southeast Asia Series, 54. Athens: Ohio University, Center for International Studies.

Anderson, Benedict, and Ruchira Mendiones, eds. and trans. 1985. *In the Mirror: Literature and Politics in Siam in the American Era.* Bangkok: Duang Kamol Editions.

Anuson nganphraratchathan phloengsop nai somsak chanthanasiri (Cremation Volume for Nai Somsak Chanthanasiri). 2000. Bangkok.

Ashcroft, Bill, Gareth Griffiths, and Helen Tiffen. 1998. *Key Concepts in Post-Colonial Studies.* London: Routledge.

Bachofen, Johann. 1861. *Das Mutterrecht.* Stuttgart: Krais and Hoffman.

Backus, Mary, ed. 1884. *Siam and Laos: As Seen by Our American Missionaries.* Philadelphia: Presbyterian Board of Publication.

Bangkok Post. 2002. "Bid to End Religious Discord: Senate Vote in Favour of 'Culture Ministry.'" (21 Sept.).

Barang, Marcel. 1995. Preface to *The Circus of Life,* by Akatdamkeung Rabibhadana. Bangkok: Thai Modern Classics.

Barlow, Tani. 1997. "Introduction: On 'Colonial Modernity.'" In *Formations of Colonial Modernity in East Asia,* edited by Tani Barlow, 1–20. Durham: Duke University Press.

Barmé, Scot. 2002. *Woman, Man, Bangkok.* Lanham, Md.: Rowman and Littlefield.

——. 1999. "Protofeminist Discourses in Early Twentieth-Century Siam." In *Genders and Sexualities in Modern Thailand,* edited by Peter A. Jackson and Nerida M. Cook, 134–53. Chiang Mai: Silkworm Books.

Batson, Benjamin A. 1984. *The End of the Absolute Monarchy in Siam.* Singapore: Oxford University Press.

Bowring, Sir John. 1857. *The Kingdom and People of Siam.* Vols. 1–2. London: John W. Parker and Son.

Bradley, Dan Beach. 1874. *Dictionary of the Siamese Language.* Bangkok.

Bradley, William L. 1981. *Siam Then: The Foreign Colony in Bangkok before and after Anna.* Pasadena, Calif.: William Carey Library.

Bristowe, W. S. 1976. *Louis and the King of Siam.* New York: Thai-American Publishers.

Buls, Charles. 1994 [1901]. *Siamese Sketches.* Bangkok: White Lotus.

The Burney Papers. 1910. 4 vols. Bangkok: Committee of the Vajiranana National Library.

Burns, Peter. 1988. "The Netherlands East Indies." In *Laws of South-East Asia,* vol. 2, edited by M. B. Hooker. Singapore: Butterworth and Co. (Asia).

Caddy, Florence. 1889. *To Siam and Malay in the Duke of Sutherland's Yacht, 'Sans Peur.'* London: Hurst and Blackett.

Cain, P. J., and A. G. Hopkins. 1993. *British Imperialism: Innovation and Expansion, 1688–1914.* London: Longman.

Chaiwat Satha-Anand. 1986. "Islam and Violence: A Case Study of Violent Events in the Four Southern Provinces, Thailand, 1976–1981." Monographs in Religion and Public Policy 2. Tampa: University of South Florida.

Chali Iamkrasin. 1991. "Sao phu su phua sithi satri samai ro si" (A Young Woman Who Fought for Women's Rights during the Reign of Rama IV). In *Muang thai samai kon* (Thailand in the Past). Bangkok.

Chakrabarty, Dipesh. 2000. *Provincializing Europe.* Princeton: Princeton University Press.

——. 2002. *Habitations of Modernity: Essays in the Wake of Subaltern Studies.* Chicago: University of Chicago Press.

Chalk, Peter. 2001. "Militant Islamic Separatism in Southern Thailand." In *Islam in Asia: Changing Political Realities,* edited by Jason F. Isaacson and Colin Rubenstein, 165–86. New Brunswick, N.J.: Transaction Publishers.

Chanock, Martin. 2001. *The Making of South African Legal Culture, 1902–1936: Fear, Favour and Prejudice.* Cambridge: Cambridge University Press.

——. 1998. *Law, Custom and Social Order: The Colonial Experience of Malawi and Zambia.* Portsmouth, N.H.: Heinemann.

Charnvit Kasetsiri. 2000. *2475 Kanpatiwatsayam* (1932: Siam's Revolution). Bangkok: Foundation for the Promotion of Social Sciences and Humanities Textbooks Project.

——. 1976. *The Rise of Ayudhya*. Kuala Lumpur: Oxford University Press.

Charnvit Kasetsiri and Wikal Phongphanitan. 1983. "Khamnam" (introduction) to *Prawatisat kotmai thai* (Thai Legal History), by Robert Lingat. Bangkok: Foundation for Sociological and Anthropological Texts.

Chatterjee, Partha. 1993. *The Nation and Its Fragments: Colonial and Postcolonial Histories*. Princeton: Princeton University Press.

Chatthip Nartsupha and Suthy Prasartset, eds. 1981. *Socio-Economic Institutions and Cultural Change in Siam, 1851–1910*. Bangkok: Social Science Association of Thailand.

Chit Phumisak [Somsamai Sisuttharaphan]. 1957. "Chomna khong sakdinathai nai patchuban" (The Real Face of Thai Sakdina Today). In *Nitisat 2500 chabap rap sattawatmai* (The Faculty of Law Yearbook 2500 to Greet the New Century). Bangkok: Thammasat University, Faculty of Law.

Chittima Pornarun. 1995. "Kanriakrong sithi satri nai sangkhom thai pho so 2489–2519" (Demands for Women's Rights in Thai Society, 1946–1976). MA thesis, Chulalongkorn University.

Chulalongkorn, King. 1993. *Itineraire d'un Voyage à Java en 1896*. Translated and introduced by Chanatip Kesavadhana. Paris: Cahier d'Archipel 20.

——. 1927. Phraratchadamrat nai phrabatsomdet phrachulachomklao chaoyuhua. *Songthalaeng phraboromaratchathibai kaekhai kanpokkhrong phaendin* (Speech Explaining the Governmental Reforms). Bangkok: Sophonphiphanthanakon.

Comaroff, Jean, and John L. Comaroff. 1997. *Of Revelation and Revolution*. Vol. 2, *The Dialectics of Modernity on a South African Frontier*. Chicago: University of Chicago Press.

——. 1991. *Of Revelation and Revolution*. Vol. 1, *Christianity, Colonialism, and Consciousness in South Africa*. Chicago: University of Chicago Press.

Comaroff, John, and Simon Roberts. 1981. *Rules and Processes: The Cultural Logic of Dispute in an African Context*. Chicago: University of Chicago Press.

Copeland, Matthew P. 1993. *Contested Nationalism and the 1932 Overthrow of the Absolute Monarchy in Siam*. PhD diss., Australian National University.

Cort, Mary Lovina. 1886. *Siam: Or, The Heart of Farther India*. New York: Anson D. F. Randolph and Co.

Daley, Caroline, and Melanie Nolan, eds. 1994. *Suffrage and Beyond: International Feminist Perspectives*. New York: New York University Press.

Damrong Rajanubhap, Prince. 1988. *Prawat bukkhon samkhan* (Histories of Important People). Bangkok: Bannakit.

——. 1972. "Praphaeni taengngan baosao" (Tradition of Marrying Young Men and Women). In *Latthi thamniam tang tang* (Miscellaneous Traditional Practices), compiled by Phraya Ratchawaranukun [Ouam]. Vol. 1. 5th ed. Bangkok: Department of Fine Arts.

——. 1933. *Laksana kanpokkhrong prathet siam tae boran* (The Administration of Siam from Ancient Times). Bangkok.

Dararat Mettarikanond. 1984. "Kotmai sopheni 'ti-thabian' krangraek nai prathet thai" (The First Prostitution 'Registration' Law in Thailand). *Sinlapa-Wathanatham* 5, no. 5 (Mar.): 6–19.

——. 1983. "Sopheni kap naiyobai rathaban thai pho so 2411–2503" (Prostitution and Thai Government Policy, 1868–1960). MA thesis, Chulalongkorn University, Bangkok.

Day, Tony. 2002. *Fluid Iron*. Honolulu: University of Hawai'i Press.

——. 1996. "Ties That (Un)Bind: Families and States in Premodern Southeast Asia." *Journal of Asian Studies* 55, no. 2 (May): 384–409.

Department of Fine Arts. 1993. *Ratchasakunwong* (Royal Lineage). Bangkok.

Dhiravat na Pombejra. 1993. "Ayutthaya at the End of the Seventeenth Century." In *Southeast Asia in the Early Modern Era*, edited by Anthony Reid, 250–72. Ithaca: Cornell University Press.

Don Pathan. 2002. "Violence in the South." *The Nation*. Bangkok (17 July).

Duplatre, Louis. 1922. "Essai sur la condition de la femme au Siam." PhD diss., University of Grenoble.

——. 1990. *Sathana khong ying mi sami nai prathet sayam* (Status of Married Women in Siam), translated by Phairot Kamphusiri. Bangkok: Thammasat University Press.

"Editor's Comment on Querying Alternativity." 1999. *Public Culture* 11, no. 1.

Engel, David. 1978. *Code and Custom in a Thai Provincial Court.* Association for Asian Studies Monograph No. 34. Tucson: University of Arizona Press.

——. 1975. *Law and Kingship in Thailand during the Reign of King Chulalongkorn.* Michigan Papers on South and Southeast Asia No. 9. Ann Arbor: University of Michigan, Center for South and Southeast Asian Studies.

Engels, Friedrich. 1972 [1884]. *The Origin of the Family, Private Property, and the State.* New York: International Publishers.

Foucault, Michel. 1979. *Discipline and Punish: The Birth of the Prison.* New York: Vintage.

Fustel de Coulanges, Numa Denis. 1956 [1864]. *The Ancient City.* Garden City, N.Y.: Doubleday.

Gallagher, John, and Ronald Robinson. 1953. "The Imperialism of Free Trade." *Economic History Review* 6, no. 1: 1–15.

Gaonkar, Dilip Parameshwar. 1999. "On Alternative Modernities," *Public Culture* 11, no. 1: 1–18.

Geertz, Clifford. 1983. "Centers, Kings, and Charisma: Reflections on the Symbolics of Power." In his *Local Knowledge,* 121–46. New York: Basic Books.

Gerini, G. E. 1895. "Trial by Ordeal in Siam and the Siamese Law of Ordeals." *Asiatic Quarterly Review.*

Göle, Nilufer. 1996. *The Forbidden Modern.* Ann Arbor: University of Michigan Press.

Graham, W. A. 1908. *Kelantan, A State of the Malay Peninsula: A Handbook of Information.* Glasgow: James Maclehose and Sons.

Greene, Stephen. 1999. *Absolute Dreams: Thai Government under Rama VI, 1910–1925.* Bangkok: White Lotus.

Grindrod, Katharine. 1982 [1892]. *Siam.* Personal diary, vols. 1–2. Hong Kong: University of Hong Kong.

Guyon, René. 1949 [1939]. *Sexual Freedom,* translated by Eden and Cedar Paul. London: John Land and the Bodley Head.

Hall, Stuart, et al., eds. 1996. *Modernity: An Introduction to Modern Societies.* London: Blackwell.

Hamilton, Annette. 1991. "Rumours, Foul Calumnies and the Safety of the State." In *National Identity and Its Defenders: Thailand, 1939–1989,* edited by Craig J. Reynolds, 341–79. Monash Papers on Southeast Asia 25. Clayton, Victoria: Monash University, Centre of Southeast Asian Studies.

Harris, Townsend. 1959. *The Complete Journal of Townsend Harris.* Introduction by Mario Emilio Cosenza, preface by Douglas MacArthur II. Rev. ed. Rutland, Vt.: Charles E. Tuttle.

Hobsbawm, Eric, and Terence Ranger, eds. 1983. *The Invention of Tradition.* Cambridge: Cambridge University Press.

Hong Lysa. 2004. "'Stranger within the Gates': Knowing Semi-colonial Siam as Extraterritorials." *Modern Asian Studies* 38, no. 2: 327–54.

——. 2003. "Extraterritoriality in Bangkok in the Reign of Chulalongkorn, 1868–1910: The Cacophony of Semi-colonial Cosmopolitanism." *Itinerario: European Journal of Overseas History* 27, no. 2: 25–46.

——. 1999. "Palace Women at the Margins of Social Change: An Aspect of the Politics of Social History in the Reign of King Chulalongkorn." *Journal of Southeast Asian Studies* 30, no. 20 (Sept.): 310–24.

——. 1998. "Of Consorts and Harlots in Thai Popular History." *Journal of Asian Studies* 57, no. 2 (May): 333–53.

Hooker, M. B. 1986. "The 'Europeanization' of Siam's Law, 1855–1908." In *Laws of South-East Asia,* edited by M. B. Hooker. Singapore: Butterworth and Co. (Asia).

——. 1984. *Islamic Law in South-East Asia.* Singapore: Oxford University Press.

Howard, E. C. 1914. "Prefatory Note." In Mahiudin Abu Zakaria Yahya ibn Sharif en Nawawi,

Minhaj et Talibin: A Manual of Muhammadan Law according to the School of Shafii, translated by E. C. Howard. London: W. Thacker and Co.

Ingram, James C. 1971. *Economic Change in Thailand, 1850–1970.* Stanford: Stanford University Press.

Ishii, Yoneo. 1994. "Thai Muslims and the Royal Patronage of Religion." *Law & Society Review* 28, no. 3: 453–60.

——. 1986. "The Thai Thammasat (with a Note on the Lao Thammasat)." In *Laws of South-East Asia,* vol. 1, *The Pre-Modern Texts,* edited by M. B. Hooker. Singapore: Butterworth and Co. (Asia).

Jackson, Peter. 2004. "Semicoloniality and Duality in Siam's Relations with the West." Paper presented at "The Ambiguous Allure of the West" conference at Cornell University, Ithaca, New York, November.

Jones, Robert B. 1971. *Thai Titles and Ranks: Including a Translation of Traditions of Royal Lineage in Siam by King Chulalongkorn.* Data Paper 81. Ithaca: Cornell University, Southeast Asia Program.

Jottrand, Mr. and Mrs. Émile. 1996 [1905]. *In Siam: The Diary of a Legal Adviser of King Chulalongkorn's Government.* Translated by Walter E. J. Tips. Bangkok: White Lotus.

Kamala Tiyavanich. 2003. *The Buddha in the Jungle.* Seattle: University of Washington Press.

——. 1997. *Forest Recollections: Wandering Monks in Twentieth-Century Thailand.* Honolulu: University of Hawai'i Press.

Kannika Sattraprung. 2004. *A True Hero: King Chulalongkorn of Siam's Visit to Singapore and Java in 1871.* Bangkok: Tana Press and Graphic Co.

Kesinee Jaikawang, Sukanya Lim, and Naparisa Kaewthoraket. 2003. "Thai Rak Thai Plan: No to Philanderers." *The Nation* (1 Dec.).

Kessler, Clive S. 1978. *Islam and Politics in a Malay State: Kelantan, 1838–1969.* Ithaca: Cornell University Press.

Khukhrit Pramoj. 1973. *Farang sakdina* (European Feudalism). Bangkok: Kaona Publishers.

Kitiyakara, Prince, comp. 1970. *Pathanukrom bali thai angkrit sansakrit* (Pali-English-Thai-Sanskrit Dictionary). Bangkok.

Kobkua Suwannathat-Pian. 1988. *Thai-Malay Relations: Traditional Intraregional Relations from the Seventeenth to the Early Twentieth Centuries.* Singapore: Oxford University Press.

Koizumi, Junko. 2000. "From a Water Buffalo to a Human Being: Women and the Family in Siamese History." In *Other Pasts: Women, Gender, and History in Early Modern Southeast Asia.* Honolulu: University of Hawai'i at Manoa, Center for Southeast Asian Studies.

Kotmai tra sam duang (Three Seals Laws) [KTSD]. 1938. Bangkok: Thammasat University Press.

Krom Silpakon. 1969 [1917]. *Chotmaihet sadet praphat tang prathet nai ratchakan thi 5 sadet muang singkhapo lae muang betawia khrang raek lae sadet praphat india kap chotmaihet khong mo brad-le* (Documents concerning Rama V's First Trips Abroad to Singapore, Batavia, and His Trip to India with Documents by Dr. Bradley). Bangkok.

Kullada Kesboonchoo Mead. 2004. *The Rise and Decline of Thai Absolutism.* London: Taylor and Francis.

Lahiri, Sisir Chandra. 1951. *Principles of Modern Burmese Buddhist Law.* Calcutta: Eastern Law House.

Lamphan Nuambunlu. 1976. "Sithi lae nathi khong satri tam kotmai thai nai samai krung ratanokosin" (The Rights and Duties of Women according to Thai Laws during the Bangkok Period). MA thesis, Chulalongkorn University.

Landon, Kenneth Perry. 1939. *Thailand in Transition: A Brief Survey of Cultural Trends in the Five Years since the Revolution of 1932.* Chicago: University of Chicago Press.

Lariviere, Richard W. 1989. "Justices and *Panditas:* Some Ironies in Contemporary Readings of the Hindu Legal Past." *Journal of Asian Studies* 48: 757–69.

Lazarus-Black, Mindie, and Susan Hirsch, eds. 1994. *Contested States: Law, Hegemony, and Resistance.* New York: Routledge.

Lenin, V. I. 1939. *Imperialism: The Highest Stage of Capitalism.* New York: International Publishers.

Leonowens, Anna. 1988 [1870]. *The English Governess at the Siamese Court.* Singapore: Oxford University Press.

——. 1953. [1873] *Siamese Harem Life.* New York: E. P. Dutton.

Lev, Daniel. 1972. "Judicial Institutions and Legal Culture in Indonesia." In *Culture and Politics in Indonesia,* edited by Claire Holt. Ithaca: Cornell University Press.

——. 1985. "Colonial Law and the Genesis of the Indonesian State." *Indonesia* 40 (Oct.): 57–74.

Lingat, Robert. 1983. *Prawatisat kotmai thai* (Thai Legal History). Bangkok: Foundation for Sociological and Anthropological Texts.

——. 1973. *The Classical Law of India.* Berkeley: University of California Press.

——. 1937. *L'influence Indoue dans l'ancien droit siamois.* Paris: Domat-Monchretien.

Liu, Lydia, 1999. "Legislating the Universal: The Circulation of International Law in the Nineteenth Century." In *Tokens of Exchange: The Problem of Translation in Global Circulations,* edited by Lydia Liu, 127–64. Durham: Duke University Press.

Loos, Tamara. 2005. "Sex in the Inner City: The Fidelity between Sex and Politics in Siam." *Journal of Asian Studies* 64, no. 4 (Nov.).

——. 2004. "The Politics of Women's Suffrage in Thailand." In *Women's Suffrage in Asia: Gender, Nationalism and Democracy,* edited by Mina Roces and Louise Edwards, 170–94. London: RoutledgeCurzon.

——. 1999. "Gender Adjudicated: Translating Modern Legal Subjects in Siam." PhD diss., Cornell University.

——. 1998. "Issaraphap: The Limits of Individual Liberty in Thai Jurisprudence." *Crossroads: An Interdisciplinary Journal of Southeast Asian Studies* 12, no. 1: 35–75.

——. Archival Notes. Vols. 1–15. Transcriptions of documents from the National Archives, National Library, and Dika Court, Bangkok.

Maine, Henry S. 1861. "Primitive Society and Ancient Law." In his *Ancient Law,* chap. 5. New York: Charles Scribner.

Malinee Khumsupha. 1999. "Sithi satri nai khwamkhit khong pridi phanomyong" (Women's Rights in the Ideas of Pridi Phanomyong). *Warasan Thammasat* (Thammasat University Journal) 25, no. 1 (Jan.–Apr.): 91–104.

Maluleem, Jaran. 1998. "The Coming of Islam to Thailand." Occasional Paper 15. Taipai: Academia Sinica Program for Southeast Asian Area Studies.

Mani, Lata. 1987. "Contentious Traditions: The Debate on SATI in Colonial India." *Cultural Critique* (Fall): 119–56.

Marx, Karl. 1974. *The Ethnological Notebooks of Karl Marx (Studies of Morgan, Phear, Maine, Lubbock).* Transcribed, edited, and introduced by Lawrence Krader. Assen: Van Gorcum.

Masao Tokichi. 1908. "The New Penal Code of Siam." *Yale Law Journal* (Dec.): 85–100.

——. 1905. "The Sources of Ancient Siamese Law." *Yale Law Journal* (Nov.): 28–32.

Mattani Mojdara Rutnin. 1988. *Modern Thai Literature.* Bangkok: Thammasat University Press.

Maung, Dr. E. 1970. *Burmese Buddhist Law.* Rangoon.

Maung Maung, Dr. 1963. *Law and Custom in Burma and the Burmese Family.* The Hague: Martinus Nijhoff.

McClintock, Anne. 1995. *Imperial Leather: Race, Gender and Sexuality in the Colonial Contest.* London: Routledge.

McFarland, George B., ed. 1941. *Thai-English Dictionary.* Stanford: Stanford University Press.

McLennan, John F. 1865. *Primitive Marriage.* Edinburgh: Black.

Merry, Sally Engle. 2003. "From Law and Colonialism to Law and Globalization: A Review Essay on Martin Chanock, *Law, Custom, and Social Order: The Colonial Experience in Malawi and Zambia.*" *Law and Social Inquiry* 28, no. 2: 269–90.

——. 2000. *Colonizing Hawai'i: The Cultural Power of Law.* Princeton: Princeton University Press.

Ming, Hanneke. 1983. "Barracks-Concubinage in the Indies, 1887–1920." *Indonesia* 35 (Apr.): 65–93.

Ministry of Education, Textbook Department. 1927. *Pathanukrom* (Dictionary). 2nd ed. Bangkok: Krom-tamra krasuang thamakan.

Ministry of Foreign Affairs, Thailand. 1969. *Sonthisanya lae khwamtoklong thawiphaki rawang prathet thai kap tang prathet lae ongkan rawang prathet* (Bilateral Treaties and Agreements between Thailand and Foreign Countries and International Organizations). Vol. 2 (1870–1919). Bangkok: Ministry of Foreign Affairs, Treaty and Legal Department.

Moffat, Abbot Low. 1961. *Mongkut, King of Siam*. Ithaca: Cornell University Press.

Mommsen, Wolfgang. 1986. "The End of Empire and the Continuity of Imperialism." In *Imperialism and After: Continuities and Discontinuities,* edited by Wolfgang J. Mommsen and Jurgen Osterhammel, 333–58. London: German Historical Institute, Allen and Unwin.

Morgan, Lewis H. 1877. *Ancient Society, or Researches in the lines of human progress from savagery, through barbarism to civilization*. Calcutta: Bharati Library.

——. 1871. *Systems of Consanguinity and Affinity of the Human Family*. Washington, D.C.: Smithsonian Institution.

Morgan, Susan. 1996. *Place Matters: Gendered Geography in Victorian Women's Travel Books about Southeast Asia*. New Brunswick, N.J.: Rutgers University Press.

Murashima, Eiji. 1988. "The Origin of Modern Official State Ideology in Thailand." *Journal of Southeast Asian Studies* 19, no. 1 (Mar.): 80–96.

Nakkharin Mektrairat. 1992. *Kanpatiwat sayam pho so 2475* (The Siamese Revolution of 1932). Bangkok: Foundation for the Social Sciences and Humanities.

Narong Siripachana. 1975. *Khwampenma khong kotmai itsalam lae dato yutitham* (The Origins of Islamic Law and Judges). Bangkok: Khana kamakan klang itsalam haeng prathet thai (National Central Committee of Islam).

Niranjana, Tejaswini. 1992. *Siting Translation: History, Post-Structuralism, and the Colonial Context*. Berkeley: University of California Press.

Nishii, Ryoko. 2002. "Social Memory as It Emerges: A Consideration of the Death of a Young Convert on the West Coast in Southern Thailand." In *Cultural Crisis and Social Memory,* edited by Shigeharu Tanabe and Charles F. Keyes, 180–200. London: RoutledgeCurzon.

Nitisat Phaisan, Phra [Wan Chamaraman]. 1923–24. *Thammasat Lectures*. Bangkok: Daily Mail.

Office of the Council of State. 1997. *Constitution of the Kingdom of Thailand*. Bangkok.

Ortner, Sherry. 1996. "The Virgin and the State." In her *Making Gender: The Politics and Erotics of Culture,* 43–58. Boston: Beacon Press.

——. 1995. "Resistance and the Problem of Ethnographic Refusal." *Comparative Studies in Society and History* 37, no. 1 (Jan.): 173–93.

Padoux, Georges. 1986 [1906]. "Report on the Proposed Penal Code for the Kingdom of Siam." Bangkok: American Presbyterian Mission Press, 1906. Reprinted in *Laws of South-East Asia,* vol. 2, *European Laws in South-East Asia,* edited by M. B. Hooker. Singapore: Butterworth and Co. (Asia).

Pakdi Phakakrong. 1994. "Kanchatrang pramuan kotmai phaeng lae phanit haeng sayam: p. s. 2451–2478" (The Drafting of the Siamese Civil and Commercial Code, 1908–1935). MA thesis, Silpakorn University.

Pallegoix, D. J. B. 1972 [1854]. *Sapha, Phachana, Phasa Thai: Dictionarium Linguæ Thai*. Paris: Gregg International.

Pasuk Phongpaichit and Chris Baker. 2002. *Thailand: Economy and Politics*. 2nd ed. Oxford: Oxford University Press.

Peirce, Leslie. 1993. *The Imperial Harem: Women and Sovereignty in the Ottoman Empire*. New York: Oxford University Press.

Peleggi, Maurizio. 2002. *Lords of Things: The Fashioning of the Siamese Monarchy's Modern Image*. Honolulu: University of Hawai'i Press.

Peletz, Michael. 2002. *Islamic Modern: Religious Courts and Cultural Politics in Malaysia*. Princeton: Princeton University Press.

——. 2002. "Judicial Process and Dilemmas of Legitimacy and Sovereignty: The Malaysian Case in Comparative Perspective." In *Sovereignty under Challenge: How Governments Respond,* edited by John Montgomery and Nathan Glazer, 221–58. New Brunswick, N.J.: Transaction Publishers.

The Penal Code for the Kingdom of Siam (Draft Version). 1908. Bangkok: A. P. Mission Press.

Phitsalaisan Nitinethibanthit, Luang. 1915. *Laksana phua mia kap laksana moradok* (Laws on Marriage and Laws on Inheritance). Rev. ed. Bangkok.

Phlai-noi, S. 1995. *Chao tang chat nai prawatisat thai* (Foreigners in Thai History). 4th ed. Bangkok: Ruamsan Co.

Phonsiri Bunranakhet. 1997. *Nangnai: Chiwit thang sangkhom lae botbat nai sangkhom thai samai ratchakan thi 5* (Inner Palace Women: Social Lives and Roles in Thai Society during the Reign of Rama V). MA thesis, Thammasat University.

Prakai Nonthawasi. 1992. "Siao nung khong mo chik" (One Aspect of Dr. Cheek). *Sinlapa Wathanatham* 5 (Mar.): 120–25.

Pranee Javangkun. 1985. "The Case of Phra Preechakonlakan (1879–1880) and Thai Internal Politics." MA thesis, Silpakorn University.

Prasong Sukhum. 2000. *Chak yomarat thung sukhumwit* (From Yomarat to Sukhumwit). Bangkok: Chulalongkorn University Press.

Pratt, Mary Louise. 1992. *Imperial Eyes: Travel Writing and Transculturation.* London: Routledge.

Pridi Bhanomyong. 2000. *Pridi by Pridi: Selected Writings on Life, Politics, and Economy.* Translated and introduced by Chris Baker and Pasuk Phongpaichit. Chiang Mai: Silkworm Books.

Ragataf, Iqbal. 2000. "Thailand: Hunting Muslims to Death." *Islam Online* (13 Feb.). www.islamonline.net (accessed 3 Apr. 2003).

Rai-ngan kan prachum sapha phuthaen ratsadon (Parliament Reports). Aug. 1933–Jan. 1934. Bangkok: Akson-niti.

Ratburi, Prince. 1910. *Khot aya: Chabap luang kap chabap thiap* (Penal Code: Official and Comparative Editions). Vol. 1. Bangkok: Kong Lahuthot.

Reynolds, Craig J. 1999. "On the Gendering of Nationalist and Postnationalist Selves in Twentieth Century Thailand." In *Genders and Sexualities in Modern Thailand,* edited by Peter Jackson and Nerida Cook, 261–74. Chiang Mai: Silkworm Books.

——. 1987. "Feudalism in the Thai Past." In *Thai Radical Discourse: The Real Face of Thai Feudalism Today,* edited and translated by Craig Reynolds. Ithaca: Cornell University, Southeast Asia Program.

——. 1985. "Feudalism as a Trope or Discourse for the Asian Past with Special Reference to Thailand." In *Feudalism: Comparative Studies,* edited by Edmund Leach et al. Sydney: Sydney Studies in Society and Culture No. 2: 136–54.

——. 1977. "A Nineteenth Century Thai Buddhist Defense of Polygamy and Some Remarks on the Social History of Women in Thailand." Paper presented for the Seventh Conference of the International Association of Historians of Asia. Chulalongkorn University, Bangkok, August.

——. 1976. "Buddhist Cosmography in Thai History, with Special Reference to Nineteenth-Century Culture Change." *Journal of Asian Studies,* 35, no. 2 (Feb.): 203–20.

——. 1973. "The Case of K. S. R. Kulap: A Challenge to Royal Historical Writing in Late Nineteenth Century Thailand." *Journal of the Siam Society* 61, no. 2 (July): 63–90.

——. 1972. "The Buddhist Monkhood in Nineteenth Century Thailand." PhD diss., Cornell University.

Reynolds, Craig J., ed. 1991. *National Identity and Its Defenders: Thailand, 1939–1989.* Monash Papers on Southeast Asia 25. Clayton, Victoria: Monash University, Centre of Southeast Asian Studies.

Reynolds, Craig, and Hong Lysa. 1983. "Marxism in Thai Historical Studies." *Journal of Asian Studies* 43, no. 1: 77–104.

Riggs, Fred W. 1966. *Thailand: The Modernization of a Bureaucratic Polity.* Honolulu: East-West Center Press.

Rofel, Lisa. 1999. *Other Modernities: Gendered Yearnings in China after Socialism.* Berkeley: University of California Press.

Roff, William. 1974. "The Origin and Early Years of the Majlis Ugama." In *Kelantan: Religion, Society and Politics in a Malay State,* edited by William Roff, 101–52. Kuala Lumpur: Oxford University Press.

Rungsaeng Kittayapong. 1990. "The Origins of Thailand's Modern Ministry of Justice and Its Early Development." PhD diss., University of Bristol.

Saint-Hubert, Christian de. 1965. "Rolin-Jaequemyns (Chao Phya Aphay Raja) and the Belgian Legal Advisors in Siam at the Turn of the Century." *Journal of the Siam Society* 53, no. 2 (July): 180–90.

Saipin Kaewngamprasoet. 1995. *Kanmuang nai anusawari thao suranari* (The Politics of Thao Suranari's Monument). Bangkok: Sinlapa Wathanatham.

Salleh, Mohamed B. Nik Mohd. 1974. "Kelantan in Transition: 1891–1900." In *Kelantan: Religion, Society and Politics in a Malay State,* edited by William Roff, 22–61. Kuala Lumpur: Oxford University Press.

Sarit Thanarat. 1963. "Khamnam" (introduction) to *Phichan anuson* (Cremation Volume for Phichan Bunyong [René Guyon]). Bangkok.

Sawaeng Bunchaloemwiphat. 2000. *Prawatisat kotmai thai* (Thai Legal History). Bangkok: Winyuchon Publication House.

Sayre, Francis B. 1957. *Glad Adventure.* New York: Macmillan.

——. 1957. "The Reminiscences of Francis B. Sayre." New York: Columbia University, Oral History Project, Oral History Research Office.

——. 1928. "The Passing of Extraterritoriality in Siam." *American Journal of International Law* 22 (Jan.):70–88.

——. 1927. "Siam's Fight for Sovereignty." *Atlantic Monthly* (Nov.): 674–89.

——. 1926. "Siam." *Atlantic Monthly* (June): 841–51.

Scott, Joan Wallach. 1996. *Only Paradoxes to Offer: French Feminists and the Rights of Man.* Cambridge: Harvard University Press.

Seksan, Prasertkul. 1989. "The Transformation of the Thai State and Economic Change (1855–1945)." PhD diss., Cornell University.

Service, Elman R. 1985. *A Century of Controversy: Ethnological Issues from 1860 to 1960.* Orlando: Academic Press.

Siang Netibanthit. 1913. *Kotmai phua mia* (Marriage Laws). Bangkok.

Siffin, William J. 1966. *The Thai Bureaucracy: Institutional Change and Development.* Honolulu: East-West Center Press.

Siriphon Skrobanek. 1983. "Kan riakrong sithi satri khong ying thai (2398–2475)," (Thai Women's Feminist Movement [1855–1932]). *Satrithat* (Friends of Women magazine) 1, no. 3 (Aug.–Oct.): 28–35.

Skinner, G. William. 1957. *Chinese Society in Thailand.* Ithaca: Cornell University Press.

Smith, Malcolm. 1982 [1947]. *A Physician at the Court of Siam.* Kuala Lumpur: Oxford University Press.

So Sethaputra, comp. 1991. *New Model Thai-English Dictionary.* Bangkok: Thai Watanaphanit.

——. 1965. *New Model Thai-English Dictionary.* Vols. 1–2. Bangkok: Thai Watanaphanit Press.

Somchot Ongsakun. 1978. *Kan-patirup kanpok-khrong monthon pattani (p. s. 2449–2474)* (The Administrative Reform of Monthon Pattani [1906–1931]). MA thesis, Sri Nakharinwirot University, Bangkok.

Sommot Ammoraphan, Prince. 1920. *Raya thang sadet praphat laem malayu nai ratchakan thi 5 ruam 3 khrao* (Itineraries of Three Royal Trips to the Malay Peninsula by Rama V). Bangkok: Sophanaphiphanthanathon.

Stoler, Ann. 2002. *Carnal Knowledge and Imperial Power.* Berkeley: University of California Press.

——. 1992. "Sexual Affronts and Racial Frontiers." *Comparative Studies in Society and History* 34, no. 3 (July): 514–51.

Sukit Nimmanhemin. 1971. "Khamnam" (introduction) to *Nangsu sadaeng kitchanukit* (A Book Explaining Various Things) by Chao Phraya Thiphakorawong. Bangkok: Khuru Sapha.

Sumalee Bumroongsook. 1995. *Love and Marriage: Mate Selection in Twentieth-Century Central Thailand.* Bangkok: Chulalongkorn University Press.

Sunait Chutintaranond. 1982. "Political Kinship Relations in Early Thai History." MA thesis, Cornell University.

Suphatra Singloka, Khunying, ed. 1992. *Khruangmai haeng khwamrunkruang khu saphap haeng satri* (A Symbol of Civilization: The Status of Women). Bangkok: Samakhom banthit satri thang kotmai haeng prathet thai.

Syukri, Ibrahim. 1985. *The History of the Malay Kingdom of Patani,* translated by Conner Bailey and John Miksic. Monographs in International Studies, Southeast Asia Series, No. 68. Athens: Ohio University

Tej Bunnag. 1977. *The Provincial Administration of Siam, 1892–1915.* Kuala Lumpur: Oxford University Press.

Thailand Official Yearbook. 1968. Bangkok: Government Printing Office.

Thanet Aphornsuvan. 2004. "Origins of Malay Muslim 'Separatism' in Southern Thailand." Working Paper Series No. 32. Singapore: National University of Singapore, Asia Research Institute.

——. 1998. "Slavery and Modernity: Freedom in the Making of Modern Siam." In *Asian Freedoms: The Idea of Freedom in East and Southeast Asia,* edited by David Kelly and Anthony Reid, 161–86. Cambridge: Cambridge University Press.

——. 1996. "Sithi khon thai nai rat thai" (Rights in the Thai States). In *Chintanakan su pi 2000: Nawakam choeng krabuan that dang thai suksa* (Reflections for the Year 2000), edited by Chaiwat Satha-anan, 181–233. Bangkok: Thai Research Foundation.

Thiphakorawong, Chao Phraya. 1971 (1867). *Nangsu sadaeng kitchanukit* (A Book Explaining Various Things). Bangkok: Khuru Sapha.

——, comp. 1934. *Phraratcha phongsawadan krung ratanakosin ratchakan thi sam* (Royal Chronicle of Rama III's Reign), Cremation Volume for Maha Amat-tho Phraya Phaibun Sombat (Det Bunnak). Bangkok.

Thongchai Winichakul. 2000. "The Others Within: Travel and Ethno-Spatial Differentiation of Siamese Subjects, 1885–1910." In *Civility and Savagery: Social Identity in Thai States,* edited by Andrew Turton. Richmond, Surrey: Curzon Press.

——. 1995. "The Changing Landscape of the Past: New Histories in Thailand since 1973." *Journal of Southeast Asian Studies* 26, no. 1: 99–120.

——. 1994. *Siam Mapped: A History of the Geo-Body of a Nation.* Honolulu: University of Hawai'i Press.

Thornely, P. W. 1923. *The History of a Transition.* Bangkok: Siam Observer Press.

Tilleke, W. A. G. 1908. "The Administration of Justice." In *Twentieth Century Impressions of Siam,* edited by Arnold Wright, 94–99. London: Lloyd's Greater Britain Pub. Co.

Tips, Walter E. J. 1996. *Gustave Rolin-Jaequemyns and the Making of Modern Siam.* Bangkok: White Lotus.

——. 1992. *Gustave Rolin-Jaequemyns (Chao Phraya Aphai Raja) and the Belgian Advisers in Siam (1892–1902).* Bangkok: White Lotus.

Truong, Thanh-dam. 1990. *Sex, Money and Morality: Prostitution and Tourism in South-East Asia.* London: Zed Press.

Trautmann, Thomas. 1987. *Lewis Henry Morgan and the Invention of Kinship.* Berkeley: University of California Press.

Turton, Andrew. 1980. "Thai Institutions of Slavery." In *Asian and African Systems of Slavery,* edited by James L. Watson, 251–92. Berkeley: University of California Press.

Udom Srisuwan [Aran Phrommachomphu]. 1979. *Sen-thang sangkhom thai.* Bangkok: Akson. Rpt. of *Thai kung-muang-khun* (Thailand, a Semicolony). Bangkok: Mahachon, 1950.

Vajiravudh, King. 1961. "Priap nam sakun kap chu sae" (A Comparison of Surnames with Clan Names). In *Pramuan bot phraratchaniphon (phak pakinnaka suan thi 2) nai phrabatsomdet phra mongkutklao chaoyuhua* (Compilation of the Writings of King Vajiravudh [Miscellaneous Pieces, Part 2]). Bangkok: Sirisan.

——. 1951 [1915]. "Khlon tit lo" (Clogs on Our Wheels). In *Plukchai suapa lae khlon tit lo* (Instilling the Wild Tiger Spirit and Clogs on Our Wheels). Bangkok.

——. 1985 [1914]. *Phuak yiu haeng buraphathit* (Jews of the East). Bangkok: Krom Sinlapakon.

—— [Asvahabu]. Nd. *The Jews of the Orient*. Bangkok: Siam Observer Press. Originally serialized in the *Siam Observer*, July 1914.

Van der Veer, Peter. 2001. *Imperial Encounters: Religion and Modernity in India and Britain*. Princeton: Princeton University Press.

Vella, Walter. 1978. *Chaiyo! King Vajiravudh and the Development of Thai Nationalism*. Honolulu: University of Hawai'i Press.

——. 1957. *Siam under Rama III*. Locust Valley, N.Y.: J.J. Augustin.

Wales, H. Q. Quaritch. 1965. *Ancient Siamese Government and Administration*. New York: Paragon Book Reprint.

Walkowitz, Judith. 1980. *Prostitution and Victorian Society: Women, Class, and the State*. Cambridge: Cambridge University Press.

Warren, James F. 1993. *Ah Ku and Karayuki-san: Prostitution in Singapore, 1870–1940*. Singapore: Oxford University Press.

Woraphong Chirawuti. 1973. *Raphiphatonsak ramluk* (Recalling Prince Ratburi). Bangkok.

——. 1973. "Phraprawat yo krom luang ratburi direkrit" (An Abridged Royal History of Prince Ratburi Direkrit). *Wan raphi* 33 (7 Aug.).

Wyatt, David. 1994. "Family Politics in Seventeenth and Eighteenth Century Siam." In *Studies in Thai History*, 98–106. Chiang Mai: Silkworm Books.

——. 1984. *Thailand: A Short History*. New Haven: Yale University Press.

——. 1969. *The Politics of Reform in Thailand: Education in the Reign of King Chulalongkorn*. New Haven: Yale University Press.

Zan, Myint. 2000. "Of Consummation, Matrimonial Promises, Fault, and Parallel Wives: The Role of Original Texts, Interpretation, Ideology, and Policy in Pre- and Post-1962 Burmese Case Law." *Columbia Journal of Asian Law* 14, no. 1 (Spring): 153–212.

Index

Abdul Kadir, Tengku (also Raja), 1–2, 83–86
adat ("customary law"), 79, 90
address, forms of, 149–51
adultery, 5, 114, 165
  definition of, 160
  divorce and, 10, 145–47
  marital status and, 37, 102
  Palatine law on, 164
  penalties for, 9, 38n25, 86, 91–92
  Vajiravudh on, 122
  wife's status and, 7, 138–40
  See also fornication; polygyny
advisers to Siamese government
  British, 17, 30–31, 36, 38, 47–48, 84–85
  colonial experience of, 64–65
  foreign affairs, 52, 178
  French, 62, 66n131, 108
  general, 52–59, 107
  Harvard connection of, 53–59
  hiring of, 47
  legal, 4, 34, 43, 46n53, 47–48, 52–53, 59–66, 69, 103, 106–9, 120, 122, 183
  nonlegal, 17, 30–31, 36, 38, 47–48, 84–85
  numbers of, 3n6, 53n69, 65n126
  photographs of, 50, 58, 61
  publications by, 63–64
Ahmed, Leila, 119
Akin Rabibhadana, 37n23
Ananda Mahidol (Rama VIII), 180n26
Anderson, Benedict, 14–15, 159, 162
Anglo-French Convention, 80
Anglo-Siamese Secret Convention (1897), 83
Anglo-Siamese Treaty (1902), 85
Anglo-Siamese Treaty (1909), 56, 58
animism, 90
anti-Sinicism, 134–35, 151n58, 158–59, 171
Appeals Court, 8–9, 45–46, 52
Archives, Thailand National, 6–7, 23n49, 26, 74n7
Asiatic protégés, 4, 18, 43, 44
  See also extraterritoriality
Austria-Hungary, 43

Bachofen, Johann, 105
Bagan Rubber Company, 60
Baker, Chris, 41n38
Bangkok Calendar (newspaper), 114–15, 118
Bangkok Times Weekly Mail (newspaper), 178–79
barami, 114–15, 128, 164
Barmé, Scot, 110n21, 125–27, 144
Batson, Benjamin, 163
Battambang, 34
Baudour, A., 61
Belgium, 4, 43, 47, 48, 54–55, 61–64, 108
Bhumibol Adulyadej (Rama IX), 15, 94, 179
borisapha courts, 45–46, 52
boriwen. See monthon courts
Bowring, John, 41
Bowring Treaty, 32, 39–43, 117, 121
Bradley, Dan Beach, 39, 104, 118, 119, 169n54

Buddhism
Burmese, 181–82
chat and, 133
Christianity versus, 11, 120, 182–83
Chulalongkorn's reforms of, 76, 94, 95
"holy man" rebellions and, 23, 95
Islam and, 73, 87, 95, 185–86
kingship in, 35–36, 185–86
modernity and, 20–21, 94–99, 120, 185–87
polygyny and, 10, 89, 101, 116, 119–23, 128, 186–87
relics of, 97
Sangha Law of, 22–23, 27, 75–76, 185
Thammayut, 22–23, 75–76, 95
Theravada, 10, 22–24, 33, 76, 95, 97, 185
wedding ceremony in, 137
Burma, 4, 43, 49, 87, 90, 95, 98, 181
Burma Laws Act (1898), 181–82
Burney Treaty, 40–42
Burns, Peter, 101

Cambodia, 43, 79, 90
Cattier, Félicien, 61, 64
Ceylon, 4, 48, 59–60
Chakrabarty, Dipesh, 20, 21n44
Chakrabongse, Prince, 116
Chamnong Wongkhaluang, 125–26
Chanock, Martin, 31
Chantaburi, 1, 56
chaomuang, 87, 90
salaries of, 86n42
Charnvit Kasetsiri, 111
chat, 132–36, 149
See also nationalism
Chatterjee, Partha, 67, 106n12
Chatthip Nartsupha, 14
Chawalit, Princess, 116
Chiang Mail, 79
Chile, 66
China, 43, 159
monogamy in, 101
Siam trade with, 41
Chinese in Siam, 4, 25, 96, 145, 151
discrimination against, 134–35, 151n58, 158–59, 171
marriages of, 105
religious affiliations of, 36
taxation of, 145n45, 158–59
Chit Phumisak, 14, 37n23
Christianity, 5n8, 20, 95
Buddhism versus, 11, 120, 182–83
monogamy and, 7, 11, 101, 109–10, 141
Chulalongkorn (Rama V), 1–2, 15–16, 22–23, 180–81
Buddhist reforms of, 76, 94, 95
education of, 48–49
foreign advisors of, 47–48, 54, 57–58, 62
gifting of women and, 111–13, 115
Inner Palace of, 111–13, 117, 119, 121, 164–65
legal reforms of, 44–47, 88, 108, 115–16, 121–22
Malay principalities and, 1–2, 81–88, 92–99, 186
Palatine Law and, 163
progeny of, 113–14
Three Seals Laws and, 33
travels of, 57, 97
citizenship law (1913), 133–34
Civil and Commercial Code (CCC), 63, 65–66, 103, 123–24, 175
clan *(sai),* 135
cohabitation. *See* concubinage
colonialism, 1–4, 5n8, 14–15, 17, 31
competitive, 80–88
legal reforms and, 3–6, 48
modernity and, 2–4, 20–21
monogamy and, 103–10
translation and, 67–68
See also imperialism
Comaroff, Jean, 31
Comaroff, John, 31
concubinage, 104, 138, 141–42, 168, 169n54
Congo, Belgian, 54, 64
conscription, 87
Copeland, Matthew, 125, 159
corvée, 35
court cases
adultery, 7–8, 86, 145–47, 164, 165
definition of marriage and, 9–10
divorce, 10–11, 145–47, 151n59
as historical sources, 25–27
homosexuality, 160n14, 163n30
inheritance, 148n51
liberty (*issaraphap*), 69–70
magic spells, 8, 23–24
murder, 86
poison, 8
prostitution, 141n35, 142–43, 152n64, 165, 167
rape, 160n13, 161–62
treason, 23–24, 160n14
Crocker, Courtney, 53n70

Damrong Rajanubhab, Prince, 48–49, 67, 78, 97
foreign advisors of, 54, 58
Malay principalities and, 81–88, 94–99
photographs of, 50, 58
reforms of, 181, 184
Vajiravudh and, 116
Damrong Thammasan, Luang, 60

dato yutitham, 29–30, 72, 91, 93–94, 132
Dauge, Auguste, 61
Day, Tony, 110–11
De Busscher, L., 61
Denmark, 43, 47, 56
Devawongse, Prince, 48–50, 57, 59, 67, 104, 116
Dika Court, 26, 45–46, 51–52, 60–65, 185
divorce, 5, 107–8
  adultery and, 10–11, 145–47
  inheritance and, 102, 124n69, 138–40
  Shari'a laws on, 90, 93
  of Thongchua and Saengmoni, 10–11
Dolbeare, Frederick, 53n70
Duplatre, Louis, 62, 64

East Timor, 98n77
Egypt, 54
Eliot, Charles, 57
elopement (*lakpha*), 137, 138
Engel, David, 45n50, 161
Engels, Friedrich, 105
English. *See* translating
ethnographies, kinship, 105–6
extraterritoriality, 2–9, 18, 38, 40n33, 41–45, 58–59, 74, 85, 92, 101–3, 119, 124, 142, 178

family law, 4–6, 25–26
  Chulalongkorn's reforms of, 88, 108, 115–16, 121–22
  Islamic, 2, 6–7, 29–30, 72–75, 88–94
  monogamy and, 24, 100–129, 175–79, 187
  Vajiravudh's reforms of, 108–11, 116–17, 120, 130–40, 148–72, 179
  See also jurisprudence; marriage
Federated Malay States (FMS), 30, 80, 82, 83n27, 85, 181
  See also Malaya
feudalism, 24, 35
forms of address, 149–51
fornication
  definition of, 104
  legislation of, 165–67, 170–72
  marriage and, 139–44
  penalties for, 38n25
  See also adultery
Foucault, Michel, 20, 28
France
  advisors from, 4, 47, 48, 62–66, 107–8
  gunboat diplomacy of, 1, 55–56, 62n107, 85
  Indochina and, 1, 4, 65, 105
  Siam treaties with, 43, 44, 55–56, 62
Furnivall, John Sydenham, 38
Fustel de Coulanges, Numa Denis, 105

gambling, 42, 90
Geertz, Clifford, 96
Gerini, G. E., 40n33
Germany, 43, 47, 49, 66
gifting of women, 111–15, 119–21
globalization, 15
Government Gazette (Ratchakitchanubeksa), 39–40
Graham, William A., 30–31, 85, 89, 90, 92, 93
Great Britain
  advisors from, 4, 47, 48, 53–54, 65
  Asian subjects of, 4, 44, 85
  Islamic law and, 2, 72–75, 82, 88–90, 94
  Malay territories and, 2, 6, 8, 41, 72–89, 97, 181
  Opium War and, 33, 41
  Pangkor Treaty and, 82
  Siam treaties with, 17, 39–44, 56, 58, 80, 83, 85, 117, 121
  Singapore and, 2, 49, 76, 87, 97
Grindrod, Katherine, 104
Guyon, René, 62, 63, 107, 108

hadith, 30, 92
Haji Sulong, 94
Hamilton, Annette, 157–59
harlots, 130, 148–49, 166
  See also prostitution
Harris, Townsend, 118–19
Harvard Law School, 54–56, 58–59
Hay, John, 55n78
hegemony, 43n44, 103–10, 183
Henvaux, A., 61
Hinduism, 96
historiography, 13–18, 21, 77–80, 179–82
"holy man" *(phumibun)* rebellions, 23, 95
homosexuality, 104, 110n21, 114, 116, 160, 160n30, 171
Hong Lysa, 43
Howard, E. C., 29

imperialism, 32, 40–46
  colonialism and, 2–4, 17
  family and, 103–10
  monogamy and, 7, 100–129
  See also colonialism
India, 5, 21, 40n35, 41, 49, 66, 85, 97, 98, 105, 128
Indochina, 1, 4, 65, 105
Indonesia, 30, 98n77, 101, 105
  See also Java
Ingram, James, 41n38
inheritance laws, 5, 30, 102, 107–8, 124, 138–40, 144–48, 175
Inner Palace (or Inner City), 111–13, 117, 119, 121, 164–65

Ishii, Yoneo, 39
Islam
British legal reforms and, 2, 72–75, 82, 88–90, 94
Buddhism and, 73, 87, 95, 185–86
demographics of, 73
family law of, 2, 6–7, 29–30, 72–77, 88–94, 175
Kelantan and, 88–91, 93
polygyny and, 89, 175, 177
Thai legal reforms and, 2, 6–7, 79–80, 88–94, 131–32, 157, 177–78
issaraphap ("liberty"), 68–70
Italy, 43, 66

James, Eldon, 53n70
Japan, 43, 66, 101
advisors from, 4, 48, 60–64, 108
legal reforms in, 47
monogamy in, 60, 101
Siam treaties with, 43, 104, 107
Java, 4, 43, 49, 97, 185
See also Indonesia
Jottrand, Émile, 61, 62, 64, 108
jurisprudence
imperialism and, 40–46
religious versus civil, 92
translating of, 4, 62–71
See also law

kadi courts, 89, 91
Kannika Sattraprung, 49n61
Kedah, 41, 78, 79, 85
Kelantan, 30, 41, 60, 78, 79, 83–93
khaek, 36, 86, 157
kha luang phiset, 46
Kham Bunnag. *See* Thiphakorawong, Chao Phraya
Khana Ratsadon (People's Party), 173–74, 179–80
khanmak, 137n20
Khuna-dilok. *See* Tilleke, William Alfred
khwaeng courts, 46, 52, 92
kin muang, 161
kinship ethnographies, 105–6
Kirkpatrick, Emile, 61
kitab, 30, 92, 93
Kitchanukit (A Book Explaining Various Things), 121
Kotmai Tra Sam Duang (KTSD). *See Three Seals Laws*
kotmonthianban. See Palatine Law
Kraisi (Pleng Wephara), Khun Luang Phraya, 51n65, 52n67
Kulap, K. S. R., 127

lakpha ("elopement"), 137, 138
Landon, Kenneth, 179
Laos, 43, 79, 85, 95
law, 40–46
customary, 79, 90
inheritance, 5, 30, 102, 107–8, 124, 138–40, 144–48, 175
judges of, 51–52, 59
lèse-majesté, 15–16, 23–24
Palatine, 163–65, 167
plural, 5–6, 31, 38, 42, 74–75
property, 90, 102, 144–48
public health, 144
Quranic, 30, 79, 90–93
reach of, 33–34, 39, 42, 45
reform of, 32, 44–46
Roman, 66
Sangha of, 22–23, 27, 75–76, 185
Siamese school of, 51, 52, 65–66, 140
"traditional," 32–34, 37–40
value of, 32–40
See also family law; Islam
law school
Harvard, 54–56, 58–59
Oxford, 49, 65
Siam's, 51, 52, 65–66, 140
legitimacy, 104
of children, 102, 124
of wives, 10, 128, 136–41, 144–48, 152
Leonowens, Anna, 48, 104, 118–19
lèse-majesté, 15–16, 23–24
Lev, Dan, 31
L'Evesque, Charles, 62
liberty. *See issaraphap*
Lingat, Robert, 40n33
literacy, 40n31
Luang Pho Khun, 186

magic, 23–24, 75–76, 90
Mahithon (La-o Krairoet), Chao Phraya, 51n65, 52n67
Maine, Henry S., 105
Malaya, British, 2, 6, 8, 41, 72–88, 97, 181
Malay principalities of Siam, 41, 72–81, 175–78, 181
Chulalongkorn and, 1–2, 81–88, 92, 94–99, 186
historiography of, 77–80
Islamic law in, 88–94, 98–99
map of, 78
modernity and, 87–88, 98–99, 177–79
religious freedom in, 42, 157, 185–86
Vajiravudh and, 131–32, 157
Malinee Khumsupha, 174
Mani, Lata, 67, 119

Maoists, 14, 101
marriage, 5, 37, 127–28, 136–44, 183
ceremonies for, 137
Christianity and, 7, 11, 101, 109–10, 141
definitions of, 9, 11, 122, 131, 140
inheritance law and, 102, 124, 137–40, 146–48
Islamic law on, 30, 90, 93
kinship ethnographies and, 105–6
parents' permission for, 137–38
See also family law; monogamy
Masao, Tokichi, 60–62, 64, 67n132, 108
masculinity, 7, 10, 115–17, 187–88
barami and, 114–15, 128, 164
nationalism and, 120, 155–72
Maung Maung, 181
McClintock, Anne, 103–4
McFarland, George Bradley, 169n54
McLennan, John F., 105
Mendiones, Ruchira, 162
Merry, Sally, 31
mialap. See mistresses
mia that ("slave wives"), 136–39, 152
military conscription, 87
Minhaj et Talibin, 29–30, 72
mistresses, 12, 104, 115, 148–49, 166, 168–70
See also polygyny
modernity, 17, 76–77, 168–70, 179–88
Buddhist, 20–21, 94–99, 120, 185–87
colonialism and, 2–4, 20–21
definitions of, 19–21
Malay principalities and, 87–88, 98–99, 177–79
Mongkut (Rama IV), 2, 25, 39, 42, 157
ailments of, 115
Bowring Treaty and, 41–42, 117, 121
Buddhist reforms of, 75–76, 94, 95
death of, 48
foreign advisors of, 47
forms of address of, 150n55
gifting of women and, 111–13, 121
Ingram on, 41n38
monogamy law and, 102, 119
Palatine Law and, 163–64
wives of, 114–15, 118
monogamy, 11–13, 19, 60, 63
Christianity and, 7, 11, 101, 109–10, 141
colonialism and, 103–10
family law and, 24, 100–129, 175–79, 187
See also marriage; polygyny
monthon courts, 46, 52, 92, 98
Morgan, Lewis Henry, 105
muang courts, 46, 52, 92
Murashima, Eiji, 133n4

Nai Mot Amatayakul, 39
Nakhonchaisri, Phraya, 23
names. *See* Surname Act
Narathiwat, 72–74, 175, 181, 186
Naret, Prince, 67
Narongwangsa, Phra, 86
National Archives of Thailand, 6–7, 23n49, 26, 74n7
nationalism, 12–13, 170–72
chat and, 132–36, 149
ethos of, 70–71
masculinity and, 120, 155–72
religion and, 75–76, 94, 185–88
naturalization law (1912), 133–34
Nawawi, Mahiudin Abu Zakaria Yahya ibn Sharif en, 29
Negri Sembilan, 82
Netherlands, 43, 72–75
See also Java
Niel, C. R. A., 61, 62
Niranjana, Tejaswini, 67–68
Nong Chik Principality, 77, 78
Norway, 43

opium, sale of, 42
Opium War, 33, 41
Ortner, Sherry, 70n143
Orts, Pierre, 61, 64
Oxford Law School, 49, 65

Padoux, Georges, 62–65, 66n131, 107–9, 122, 123
Pahang, 82
Paknam incident (1893), 1, 55–56, 62n107, 85
Palatine Law, 163–65, 167
Pan Sukhum. *See* Yomarat, Chao Phraya
Pasuk Phongpaichit, 41n38
Patani (Pattani), 22, 41, 74, 76–81, 175, 181
Chulalongkorn and, 1–2, 81–88, 92, 94–99, 186
Islamic law in, 2, 6, 72–75, 88–94, 98–99
map of, 78
martial law in, 186
mosque of, 73
Vajiravudh and, 131–32, 157
Patton, Kenneth, 53n70
Peirce, Leslie, 119
Peletz, Michael, 31, 89
Penal Code (1908), 37, 47, 62, 66, 67
People's Party (Khana Ratsadon), 173–74, 179–80
Perak, 78, 82
Perlis, 78, 79, 85
Phahon, Colonel Phraya, 175
Phakdi, Luang Raya, 86

Phibun Songkhram, Field Marshall, 25, 94, 177, 179
Phichan Bunyong. *See* Guyon, René
Phicharana Pruchamat, Phraya, 52n67
Phichit Prichakon, Prince, 49n62
Philippines, 5n8
Phisalaisan, Luang, 140
Phonsiri Bunranakhaet, 111
Phraphiphaksa Stayathipatai, 52n67
phumibun ("holy man") rebellions, 23, 95
phuphiphaksa (judge in Siamese government), 131
Phya Vides Dharmamontri. *See* Sheridan, René
Pin Klao, Phra, 114–15
Pitkin, Wolcott, 53n70
polyandry, 121
polygyny, 7n12, 11–13, 19, 182–88
  Buddhism and, 10, 89, 101, 116, 119–23, 128, 186–87
  concubinage and, 104, 138, 141–42, 168, 169n54
  domestic politics of, 24, 120–29
  foreign perceptions of, 7, 60, 63, 104–9, 118–20
  Islam and, 89, 175, 177
  mistresses and, 12, 104, 115, 148–49, 166, 168–70
  prostitution and, 12, 126, 127
  as slavery, 118–19, 136–39, 152
  state politics of, 89, 110–20, 175–77
  Thai phrase for, 106
  See also adultery; monogamy
Portugal, 43, 66
Prajadhipok (Rama VII), 108, 123–24, 172
  abdication of, 179
  coup against, 22, 173–75, 179–80
  legislative reforms of, 183–84
Pridi Bhanomyong, 174, 180
property laws, 90, 102, 144–48
prostitution, 104, 139–44, 151–53, 166
  definition of, 148–49
  demographics of, 144
  harlotry versus, 130
  polygyny and, 12, 126, 127
  race and, 141n35
  taxation of, 143–44
protégés, Asiatic, 4, 18, 43, 44
  See also extraterritoriality
provincial courts, 45–46, 88–94

Qing dynasty, 134n11
Quran, 30, 79, 90–93, 177, 186
  See also Islam

Rakronnaret, Prince, 160n14
Rama I, 33, 77n14
Rama II, 77
Rama III, 39, 160n14
Rama IV. *See* Mongkut
Rama V. *See* Chulalongkorn
Rama VI. *See* Vajiravudh
Rama VII. *See* Prajadhipok
Rama VIII, 179n26
Rama IX. *See* Bhumibol Adulyadej
Raman Principality, 77, 78, 84, 86, 92
Ra-ngae Principality, 77, 78, 84, 86, 92
rape, 7, 70, 121, 138–39, 161–62, 165
Ratburi, Prince, 22, 31, 48–51, 67, 97, 116
Ratchakitchanubeksa (Government Gazette), 39–40
religion
  freedom of, 42, 157, 185–86
  magic and, 23–24, 75–76, 90
  nationalism and, 75–76, 94, 185–88
Revue de Droit International et de Législation Comparée, 64
rice exports, 42
Robijns, Charles, 61
Rolin-Jaequemyns, Gustave, 53–55, 60–64
Russia, 43, 49

Saiburi Principality, 77, 78, 84, 92
sai ("clan"), 135, 170
sakdina system, 34–37, 69, 149–51
Sangha Law, 22–23, 27, 75–76, 185
Sant Sarutanond, 186
sanyabat, 160–61
Sapsat, Prince, 142n36
Sarit Thanarat, 63n114
sasana ("religion"), 76
Satun, 72–74, 131–32, 175, 181
Sayre, Francis B., 53n70, 58–59, 64, 107, 178, 180n26, 183–84
Schlesser, Corneille, 61–62
Scott, Joan Wallach, 68n139
secret wives, 125–29, 149, 168–70, 172, 183
Selangor, 82
Senoi peoples, 81
September 11 attacks, 74, 186
sexual intercourse. *See* fornication
sexually transmitted diseases (STDs), 144
sex workers. *See* prostitution
Shafii law, 29–30, 92
Sheridan, René, 61, 64
Siang Netibanthit, 140
Singapore, 2, 49, 76, 87, 97
sinsot, 137n20
slavery, 19, 35
  forms of address and, 150n55
  polygyny as, 118–19, 136–39, 152
"slave wives" *(mia that),* 136–39, 152

Somchot Ongsakum, 74n7
Songkhla, 78, 86, 96, 98
Spain, 43, 66
Sri Suriyawong, Chao Phraya, 48–49
Srithammathibet, Chao Phraya, 175–76
Stevens, Raymond, 53n70
Stoler, Ann, 5, 20, 103–4
Stowe, Harriet Beecher, 118
Straits Settlements, 84, 181
Strobel, Edward Henry, 53, 55–56
Suchart Bandasak, 187n38
suffrage, 174
Sunait Chutintaranond, 111
Surname Act (1913), 134, 135, 187
Svasti Sobhon, Prince, 49n62, 116–17
Sweden, 43, 66
Swettenham, Frank, 82, 84, 85, 89
Symon, Charles, 61

Taiping Rebellion, 41
taxation, 41, 42, 91
  of Chinese, 145n45, 158–59
  of prostitution, 143–44
"temporary unions," 12, 151–53, 168
Thai Rak Thai party, 187
Thai thai (newspaper), 125–26
Thaksin Shinawatra, 187
Thammayut Buddhism, 22–23, 75–76, 95
Thanet Aphornsuvan, 152n66
Theravada Buddhism, 10, 22–24, 33, 76, 95, 97, 185
  See also Buddhism
Thianwan (T. W. S. Wannapho), 125, 127
Thiphakorawong (Kham Bunnag), Chao Phraya, 121, 187
Thomson, H. W., 85
Thongchai Winichakul, 15, 79, 81
Thornely, P. W., 38
Three Seals Laws, 33–40, 47, 184
  marriage laws in, 132, 134, 136–40
  translating of, 65, 68–69
Tilleke, A. F. G., 60
Tilleke, William Alfred, 59–61
Tilmont, R., 61
to-kali, 39, 91–93
to khwaeng, 91
Tooth, Lawrence, 61
Traidos, Prince, 59, 178
translating, 4, 25, 62–71
  of legal reforms, 48, 62–63, 66, 67, 93, 99, 121
  of *Minhaj et Talibin,* 29–30
  of Quran, 186
  of Three Seals Laws, 65, 68–69
Trat, 1
treason, 15–16, 23–24
Trengganu, 41, 79, 83–85
Turkey, 101, 126, 176, 177
Turner, Skinner, 62, 65

Udom Srisuwan, 14
"unions, temporary," 12, 151–53, 168
United Kingdom. *See* Great Britain
United States
  advisors from, 4, 48
  Siam treaties with, 43, 59n92, 107, 119

Vajiravudh (Rama VI), 12, 70, 116–17
  anti-Sinicism of, 134–35, 151n58, 158–59, 171
  Buddhist reforms of, 76, 94
  coup against, 159
  foreign advisors of, 57
  forms of address and, 149–51
  legal reforms of, 108–11, 116–17, 120, 130–40, 148–72, 179, 184
  Malay principalities and, 131–32, 157
  Palatine Law of, 165, 167
  photograph of, 156
  polygyny and, 117, 120, 122–23, 126–29, 170
  sexuality of, 110n21, 116, 171
  Westengard and, 57–58
van den Berg, L. W. C., 29
van der Veer, Peter, 20
Vella, Walter, 40–41, 168
venereal diseases, 144
voting rights, 174

Wannapho, T. W. S. (Thianwan), 125, 127
Watson, C. L., 61
Westengard, Jens Iverson, 34, 53n70, 55–58
Wichitwathakan, Luang, 175, 177
Wichit Worasat, Phra. *See* Yomarat, Chao Phraya
Williamson, W. J. F., 58
Wilson, Woodrow, 59n92
wives
  categories of, 137–39, 148–54
  "legitimate," 10, 128, 136–41, 144–48, 152
  property laws and, 144–48
  "secret," 125–29, 149, 168–70, 172, 183
  "slave," 136–39, 152
  See also marriage
women
  equality of, 128–29, 152, 171–72
  gifting of, 111–15, 119–21
  status of, 12, 64, 130, 183
  suffrage for, 174
  surnames of, 134, 135, 187
Wyatt, David, 111, 158n4

Yala Principality, 72–74, 77, 78, 86, 92, 175, 181, 186
Yale Law Journal, 64
Yaring Principality, 77, 78, 86
yokkrabat ("judge"), 162
Yomarat (Pan Sukhum), Chao Phraya
  Buddhism of, 97–98
  Malay principalities and, 80–84, 86–87, 90–93
  photograph of, 50
  reforms of, 181, 184, 185
Yot, Phra, 60